PELICAN BOOKS

THE IMMIGRANT EXPERIENCE

Thomas C. Wheeler was born in Stamford, Connecticut. After earning his B.A. and M.A. degrees at Harvard in 1951 and 1952, he embarked on a career that has included political speech-writing, journalism, book reviewing, and teaching. In 1964, he edited *A Vanishing America: The Life and Times of the Small Town,* a book of essays by contemporary writers on old American towns. Mr. Wheeler currently teaches English in the SEEK program at York College, The City University of New York. He is married and the father of one child.

The Immigrant Experience

The Anguish of Becoming American

JACK AGUEROS

WILLIAM ALFRED

EUGENE BOE

CZESLAW MILOSZ

ALAN PRYCE-JONES

MARIO PUZO

HARRY ROSKOLENKO

JOHN A. WILLIAMS

JADE SNOW WONG

Edited with an Introduction by
THOMAS C. WHEELER

PENGUIN BOOKS

Penguin Books Ltd, Harmondsworth,
Middlesex, England
Penguin Books, 625 Madison Avenue,
New York, New York 10022, U.S.A.
Penguin Books Australia Ltd, Ringwood,
Victoria, Australia
Penguin Books Canada Limited, 2801 John Street,
Markham, Ontario, Canada L3R 1B4
Penguin Books (N.Z.) Ltd, 182–190 Wairau Road,
Auckland 10, New Zealand

First published in the United States of America
by The Dial Press 1971
Published in Pelican Books 1972
Reprinted 1973, 1975, 1976, 1977

Printed in the United States of America by
Kingsport Press, Inc., Kingsport, Tennessee
Set in Century Schoolbook

English translation of "Biblical Heirs and
Modern Evils" copyright © Czeslaw Milosz, 1971.
Originally published in Polish in Kultura, Paris,
France, 1969. "America, the Thief" first appeared in
The Time That Was Then, published by The Dial Press,
copyright © Harry Roskolenko, 1971. "Pride and
Poverty" by William Alfred first appeared in
the Atlantic Monthly. "Choosing a Dream"
by Mario Puzo first appeared in McCall's.

Contents

The Immigrant
Experience

Introduction

Thomas C. Wheeler

The Immigrant Experience has required from its contributors an extraordinary self-revelation; each in his way has had to face pain. For the America of freedom has been an America of sacrifice, and the cost of becoming American has been high. For every freedom won, a tradition lost. For every second generation assimilated, a first generation in one way or another spurned. For the gains of goods and services, an identity lost, an uncertainty found. The colonial settlement of America perhaps wrought more physical than emotional hardship, but the great immigration created a scarred American soul. As Oscar Handlin has written in the classic study of immigration, *The Uprooted,* "the history of immigration is the history of alienation and its consequences." From the great surge of immigration in the late nineteenth and early twentieth centuries the scars as well as the strengths are still here to see.

The vitality the great immigration brought into American life is nowhere more conspicuous than in American writing. Much of contemporary fiction and nonfiction springs from the conflict of the immigrant and America. And that vitality is apparent in these essays. In this book American writers, closely descended from immigrants, tell the tale of those before them who came to America and of their own transition into American life. Many of them novelists or poets, the writers tell in personal narratives the story of the human heart in conflict over America, of old ways desperately persevering, of new ways transforming a people. The time is apt, for in another generation the intimate story of the immigrant transition will have passed from American writing.

The writers, of various ethnic backgrounds, have no sociology to tell, but rather the stories of life lived and felt by particular people in particular places. None pretend to give a typical picture of an ethnic group. Rather, by describing human experience as each has seen it, the writers are able to say something about the human condition of America. Common denominators of ethnic life—northern and southern European, white and black—speak louder than tribal differences. Written especially for this book, the essays perhaps get as close as we can to the nervous system of Americanization. Though rich in ethnic feeling, the pieces are often interchangeable in crises faced. For in spite of the antagonism between ethnic groups, in spite of the particular customs that gave identity to each, all had the challenge of earning a livelihood by means they didn't know. All had the strain, not only of loss, but of living in a land that said their ways were not good enough.

The writers report from an Irish, Norwegian, Jewish, Chinese, and Italian origin. Another is black and another is Puerto Rican. Two are recent arrivals to America, one Polish and the other English. Though blacks are among the oldest Americans and Puerto Ricans have been citizens since 1917, both still suffer an immigrant disadvantage and both endure what one writer calls an immigrant state of mind. The two recent immigrants not only represent a continuing, though curtailed, immigration, but speak for "an immigration of talents" as old as the Republic itself.

When Franklin Roosevelt reminded the Daughters of the American Revolution in 1938 that "all of us . . . are descended from immigrants," the truth was arresting, but how close the conditions of immigration still bear on American life is less obvious. As Handlin has pointed out in his vastly human history, "the immigrants were American history." From the turn-of-the-century immigration comes a substantial part of the current population; if to foreign-born and second-generation Americans are added the present nonwhite population, approximately a third of America has been vulnerable to the immigrant condition—a condition of poverty and prejudice, of uprooting and cultural conflict. Add to this those less recently descended from immigration and we know something more about the tensions, as well as the vitality, of American society. The immigrant easily stands for American experience. The industrial changes that uprooted him at the same time uprooted native Americans, and the immigrant's uprooting merged with the uprooting by the industrial age of the whole of American society. In the deep difficulty of his transition, the immigrant speaks for America's transformation. He was not merely one of its founders, but the first to feel the difficulty of the American dream. In him and in his sons, America has played out its tensions and hopes.

The Anglo-Saxon founders—sons of the Enlightenment, wise witnesses to the political tyrannies of Renaissance Europe—foresaw a multiracial America. And in the Declaration of Independence, they gave us an ethical force with which to meet our eventual urgency—of making one nation out of a world. However unfit they may have been for the American future, they did not bend to human limitation, the capacity of all people to suspect people who are "different." While they compromised with slavery, for what they thought was the greater good of unity, they gave life to a creed of human rights, which is slowly undoing the tragic error of allowing bondage. The abolition of primogeniture in aristocratic Virginia, assuring the equality of sons, foretold our concern with equal opportunity. The paradox of America—an offer of brotherhood and a reality of racial tension—is greatly preferable to the alternative, the tension alone. The contradiction, born in immigration as well as in slavery, has been resolved more easily for some ethnic groups than others, and hasn't been resolved for blacks. But the final test of the American idea of freedom and fulfillment may not be the color line, crucial as the solution to race is. The final difficulty, with which we have been battling since the inception of the country, is of truly making a nation out of an uprooted people. The social problems of the first half of the century will be merely superficial if freedom and fulfillment mean, finally, acquisition and glut. Because we do not have a nation yet, but a series of subnations, we have not produced a culture able to solve fundamental problems. And we do not have such a culture because America has demanded of all its settlers—new and old—that they discard the past. We have a literature, arisen from the ferment of change in the last century, and we may be gaining a literature of our period out of ethnic conflict. But we do not have, in amorphous, polyglot, materialistic America, the life of a people which can be called a culture. And that of course is a life which gives people identity, a sense of custom and tradition, a sense of place and grace. Our founders—Anglo-Saxon and European immigrants—had that, and their triumphs, national and personal, could not have occurred without a scale of values fortifying them in the face of difficulty. Freedom finally depends on culture. Without a culture of life, political freedom can turn into tyranny. Without a culture of life, the machine grinds down the human being and pollutes and destroys the environment. Without a culture of life, wars are miscalculated in the name of patriotism. The immigrant nature of American life, creating a rootless people, explains much about the menace of materialism, the onslaught of the ugly, the victories of the machine in America today.

In these essays we see an old order yielding only to the grave, leaving little behind. In life America makes of the immigrant parent, of his ways and concerns, anachronisms. Whether for the young the promise of America is for freedom—for a man to have a sense of himself—or for riches, for comfort, for goods and services—is never clear. It is confused, it is for both, and in the terrible poverty of immigrant life the lure of money is immense. While parents try to keep peasant customs and rural religions intact, they are saving, in some cases, coins for their sons to open businesses The American-born break away toward a dream they fear but cannot resist. The fathers and mothers are victims of the sweatshop or the prairie blizzard, of low wages or unyielding soil. Most immigration was urban, and the uprooting from the land, from which most immigrants came and from which most of their values were derived, was cruel in the crowded, treeless cities. The one rural story, of Norwegians on the prairie, has the most prosperous ending. As often as not, the first generation dies in as much poverty and despair as it came. But it survives and persists, by dint of religion, by dint of values no longer applicable to the new life. The common tragedy is in the family. Fathers who in the old world had respected their fathers are often humiliated by failure before their sons. Mothers who have saved, scrubbed, and prayed see their sons reject the prayers that saved them. The cultural conflict is often centered in religion, but religion was the symbol of a way of life. The immigrants brought more than America let them keep. And what they could keep was insufficient for them, impossible for their sons. What America substituted looks thin compared to what was lost. *We'll never see their like again* is not only a theme of one piece but a refrain of many. Often the third generation sees valor in immigrant grandparents where the second saw only difficulty; and the second sees valor in hindsight.

The first generation immigrants here are spirited people, come back to life with the force of actors. Nineteenth-century Irish forebears, "deliberately" living in decay, have no difficulty calling Queen Victoria "a goddamned old water dog" and defy poverty by denying America any existence at all. The young Norwegian who walks four hundred miles to stake his homestead claim, who begins in a sod hut and becomes a well-to-do farmer, assembles his progeny in his last years and presents them, not with the inheritance they hope for, but with a new book on religion. A God-fearing Jewish-Ukrainian mother, losing the strength of her husband to the sweatshop, the life of a daughter to a truck accident, the religion of her son to the streets, cries out, "America, the thief." A Chinese Christian father first blesses his daughter only after she has published a book; she first experiences physical affection when an American schoolteacher takes her in her arms after an injury. A formidable Italian peasant picks up a cobblestone and demolishes the fender of her son's tin lizzie because he is driving girls around, rather than driving her to market. Her boy at her side in an African Methodist Episcopal Church, a black mother waits eternally for him to go forward and renounce his sins, ceasing only when home from World War II he again resists the pleadings of preacher and choir. Scolding his college-educated son for mocking the poor and illiterate, a Puerto Rican father veers back to affection by telling him how he was rudely attacked by his own father.

Thrift and poverty characterize the households entered. All the mothers keep the households, tenement or farm, scrubbed free of sin. In a hostile world, pride becomes the means of survival. Pride proving insufficient, the immigrant often discovers fanaticism, religious fervor. More than ethnic characteristics, more than characteristics brought by the immigrants, the essays suggest characteristics brought out by America. Because America could not welcome them, they became exaggerations of themselves. As those early dissenters who settled in New England became intolerant, so often did the urban immigrants. When their ways were put to severe test, challenged by an offspring, they could eject a son from the family. Bearing unforeseen burdens, courageous by necessity, sure of their God, thrifty and self-reliant, the immigrants are Puritans—Irish, Scandinavian, Chinese, Jewish, Italian, black Puritans. The Puritan spirit is probably less a cultural inheritance than it is a conditioned response of the human species to America. How else in a strange and difficult land can a man of any nationality prove his worth before God or to himself but by his own purity, his own endeavor? To the America of dreams and difficulty, Calvinism is a natural immigrant.

Pride when precarious can turn to prejudice, but pride when denied turns to self-hate. Emotional illnesses of poverty—apparent in today's ghetto—have white immigrant precedents here. Alcoholism and suicides occur. Family instability—characteristic of the black poor today—is a part of the immigrant possibility. In three cases—Irish, Italian, and black families—the father leaves home or disappears. In some of the white immigrant homes, a matriarchy is evident, if not an open necessity, so necessary that it is tacit. It is the mother who often manages and saves the money, who disciplines and controls the children. The fathers are too beaten by slave wages or steam presses to lead. Yet, in the Puerto Rican account, we see the ghetto of today—of dropouts, drugs, and violence—leap into life after World War II, an abrupt change from a "clean and open world" the writer had previously known. For the black poor, poverty is undoubtedly more intense and dense than it was for white immigrants. Racism born in slavery, hounding the male in the South or simply keeping him in the fields, giving the woman better work opportunities in the North, has never allowed blacks the family coherence many white immigrants kept. A larger society no longer needs the unskilled labor which kept the white immigrant alive. In drugs, social disorder has been commercialized with criminal ingenuity.

Here there is no charitable, benevolent America at work—much less in the early years any public aid—to help the new arrivals, only the nationality benefit societies to give back savings at death or in need. Help from the outside world was for children. For the immigrant parents, any suggestion of help was an offense to dignity and self-respect. William Alfred's forebears "would sooner die than cry out for mercy or relief." So felt their immigrant successors. When public relief became inevitable during the Depression, the taking of it became a nightmare of humiliation. Here a black and a Puerto Rican family seek any work possible to escape the relief roll, and when relief comes, endure it as "wounds" the sleeve of hard work would later cover. During the Depression Italian, Irish, Polish immigrant families were often accused of shiftlessness; now their sons sometimes accuse blacks and Puerto Ricans of the same. The suspicion that the "poor" are lazy and milk the public purse for all its juice meets here the rebuttal of self-respect common to men of all race and color. Instead of enjoying public assistance, the poor—since they are Puritans, too— often punish themselves for taking it.

Difficult as life was, it was not all dismal. Harry Roskolenko recalls steaming samovars, huge stews, the merriment of a clan at Russian-Jewish gatherings. "During the great Depression of the 1930s, though we were the poorest of the poor, I never remember not dining well," Mario Puzo writes of his Italian-American home. "Many years later as a guest of a millionaire's club, I realized that our poor family on home relief ate better than some of the richest people in America." John A. Williams, writing of black lives in Syracuse, speaks of a joy coexisting with the grief apparent in these essays. "Oh, they worked the most menial jobs, performed the toughest labor, but I remember laughter and parties and singing and dancing; remember picnics and loud voices; suits and dresses carrying the odor of just coming out of the cleaners that afternoon. All was not totally grim; life bubbled, or forever sought to, beneath the hard grind of everyday life." In some of the writers, nostalgia emerges for the definable place, for customs willingly abandoned, for the wooden building and the soft-down comforter. Nostalgia, as much as anything, attests to the cost in human qualities of Americanization. Only in America could the uprooted be nostalgic for the uprooted.

The conflict between the old culture and the new America

pulls the second generation in opposite directions. The resolution, on the side of the new, a rejection of the old, argues acts of strength over a legacy of suffering. As Harry Roskolenko writes, the second generation lived "between bits and pieces of two countries, the mixture serving to fuse and confuse us all the more." The change America required meant loving many of the customs and the people spurned. In many ways, these essays, close to the bone of every writer, are confessions of love, propitiations for guilt felt and remaining. "None of the grown-ups I knew were charming or loving or understanding. Rather they seemed coarse, vulgar, and insulting," Mario Puzo writes. "They wore lumpy work clothes and handlebar mustaches, they blew their noses on their fingers and they were so short that their high-school children towered over them. They spoke a laughable broken English and the furthest limit to their horizon was their daily bread. Brave men, brave women, they fought to live their lives without dreams. Bent on survival they narrowed their lives to the thinnest line of existence.

"It is no wonder that in my youth I found them contemptible. And yet they had left Italy and sailed the ocean to come to a new land and leave their sweated bones in America. Illiterate Columbos, they dared to seek the promised land. And so they, too, dreamed a dream."

The American-born had homemade compasses, but the needle pointed into a mist. More than the public school, the settlement house and public library became beacons to the young. Parents insisted on school, as a proof of worth, but too serious an interest in books was sometimes taken, rightly, as a further break from the old. The parents often couldn't read or write, and the boy who first read and then set out to be a writer set out to be a stranger. The ambition was suitable only to an aristocrat, the desire would go away like a bad cold, the son had a "foolish head." Further, whether the slum was Italian or Puerto Rican, the boy who hauled home books from the public library had to defend himself from neighborhood taunts of "sissie" and prove his toughness on the street. To some, writing seemed the only avenue of individuality open. In the imagination of one boy, crime seemed the only alternative.

The settlement house, the gesture of the settled America toward the new Americans, brought the offspring in touch with prototype Americans, often gave them models to emulate. Football teams and Boy Scout expeditions, summer vacation camps and debating clubs gave the young their first sense of being American. Mario Puzo, leaving Hell's Kitchen every summer for two weeks in the New Hampshire village home of a strict Baptist couple, found not antagonists, but an American opening. "They disapproved of dancing, they were no doubt political reactionaries; they were everything that I came later to fight against.

"And yet they gave me those magical times children never forget. . . . The man was good with tools and built me a little playground with swings, sliding ponds, seesaws. The woman had a beautiful flower and vegetable garden and let me pick from it. A cucumber or a strawberry in the earth was a miracle." Such goodwill from white America has not touched many young blacks, and unless some spirit akin to it does, the delicate balance of America will further collapse. For John A. Williams, growing up in Syracuse, white gestures proved merely condescending. Giving a plaque to a marching band of black youngsters, the white patrons misnamed the band, and this casual error remains for him, and was, a symbol of white indifference. The discovery of racial prejudice came as a shock to Jack Agueros in New York, is still the shock with which he contends. "When, as a group of Puerto Rican kids, we decided to go swimming to Jefferson Park Pool, we knew we risked a fight and a beating from the Italians. And when we went to La Milagrosa Church in Harlem, we knew we risked a fight and a beating from the blacks. But when we went over Cooney's Hill, we risked dirty looks, disapproving looks, and questions from the police, like, 'What are you doing in this neighborhood?' and 'Why don't you kids go back where you belong?' Where we belonged! Man, I had written compositions about America." White immigrants may have met similar rebuffs, but nonwhite Americans still do, daily.

Some immigrants to America, uprooted from family, land, customs, expectations in the Old World, literally died from the uprooting, unable finally to stir from the stifling tenement in which they were set down. But the emotional suffering of the second generation, the American-born, may have been as intense.

For, in rejecting those who bore them, they could take on a feeling of betrayal and a burden of guilt. The sore sacrifice America has asked of its immigrant sons has been a denial of origin, and the consequences of that denial, though often invisible, are real. Changed names, altered faces, dropped religions are but the conspicuous signs of the identity crisis America provoked. Blacks today, in demanding that they be accepted for themselves, are building a personal strength America hasn't allowed many ethnic groups. Is it any wonder that Freud—along with Calvin—settled in the America of cultural conflict, of lost identity, of inevitable guilt? If not the leading nation in neurosis, we lay claim to being the most open, and the soul splitting of Americanization, breeding sexual and emotional confusion, is a social fact become psychological. The wound becomes the anxiety filling psychiatrists' offices, the nervousness and tension agitating American life.

Old American life, as well as the life of peasant Europeans, had been centered in a home in which the father was visible and strong. His work, if not agricultural and joined by the family, was still there to see and emulate. Industrialism destroyed all that, not only for peasants but for Yankees, buried it in gold rushes and railroad building, sweatshops and slaughterhouses, finally in assembly lines and offices, in city jobs distant from suburban homes. The immigrant uprooting became the American loss, the condition, though varying, of Anglo-Saxon and European, of white and black, sundered from the land, vulnerable to incoherence. Immigrant labor was cruel, but modern work is often a vacuum designated only by salary. Today the young are accused of defying their elders, but in truth they may not really see in their elders people at all. Energies which traditionally had gone into the family, an economic as well as social entity, in America went into the competitive market. It may not be affluence as much as the family insufficiency immigration began that boils beneath the rage of the young revolutionary. With the black revolutionary, of course, the father may have been destroyed by the system. It has not been until now that much of a generation has needed a "high" and some are willing to kill themselves in order to get it. Drugs perhaps are not like drink, but the need may be like the need for getting drunk. Both needs show an emotional insufficiency. Yet we also know that loss, even guilt, if faced, can produce gentleness and striving—traits apparent in much of American youth. It is the health of the young that places high value on personal relationships, that uses the word "family" the way families used to speak of God.

The requirement of America's settlement, from early to late, has been the demolition of culture, and from that demolition comes much of our trouble. The irony of American opportunity is that it has required rootlessness, and opportunity will grow more and more hollow until values are struck. The industrial system, not merely fragmenting the family but now poisoning the environment, has not failed; it is America's use of it that has failed. Shorn of tradition, we have been extremists in materialism. Without a past to preserve, we have lacked that Greek wisdom of restraint. We have celebrated the gross national product, while much of the world has quietly held onto life. Until recently, America prodded and pitied Western Europe for antiquated methods, low production rates. Perhaps now we can see that restraint on industrialism has been an advantage to civilization. In Europe and Asia, in democracies and totalitarian states, tradition has held industrialism back. Stubborn peasants, holding back technology in Russia and China, contented bourgeois, big and small, in Western Europe, insisting on siestas, month-long vacations, long lunches, and small businesses, may have preserved not only the beauty of their countries but the heart of themselves. Young Americans, returning from Europe today, sigh more deeply over the cleanliness and grace of its cities and suburbs than did their predecessors. America's demand for a new life for everyone has made us suckers for the new, and our innocence has meant commercialism and glut, tall buildings and vacant lives, decaying cities and destroyed countryside. Instead of tradition, America asked for mass production and has gotten mass pollution.

The second generation writers are more in doubt than in certainty about our—and their—transformation. Harry Roskolenko, fleeing the strict Judaism of his parents, returns to New York's lower East Side to note "the high-rises making a more anonymous world of the new tenements. . . . All our words were God-graced, and we were humble as we prayed and sang about the glories of the Lord on Cherry Street.

"That has changed, of course. America, as an image, has changed the edifice, the manner, if not all the tokens of faith. The American way, for all of us, from Jews to Gentiles, has given us the vulgar interludes of added attractions to a fading faith. The dollar's green sign hangs seen and unseen from churches and synagogues."

No one, least of all these writers, is able to resolve the national paradox of attainment and malaise, running deeper than the Vietnam War, but surfacing and struggling within that terrible issue. "What has happened here has never happened in any other country in any other time," Mario Puzo writes. "The poor who had been poor for centuries—hell, since the beginning of Christ—whose children had inherited their poverty, their illiteracy, they hopelessness, achieved some economic dignity and freedom. You didn't get it for nothing, you had to pay a price in tears, in suffering, but why not?" But he wonders. "All the Italians I knew and grew up with have escaped, have made their success. We are all Americans now, we are all successes now. And yet the most successful Italian man I know admits that though the one human act he never could understand was suicide, he understood it when he became a success. Not that he ever would do such a thing; no man with Italian blood ever commits suicide or becomes a homosexual in his belief. But suicide has crossed his mind. And so to what avail the finding of the dream? He went back to Italy and tried to live like a peasant again."

The American drive for success produces neurosis—perhaps because so much of the natural self must be denied. But if we have a dominant culture, it is a culture of success. And success has come increasingly to mean submission to mass organization, to which identity is further sacrificed. Unlike Europeans, Americans ask each other, "What do you do?" as a way of identifying a person; and people come more and more to see themselves in terms of an organization or profession. It has been fashionable to say that the melting pot never worked. Not only for blacks, but for some ethnic groups—Oriental and often Eastern European—America is still a foreign land. Many Eastern Europeans remain segregated from the mainstream of life due to little more than long, unpronounceable names, and from the neglect they have suffered is coming an ethnic unity similar to black power. The interesting sociological book, *Beyond the Melting Pot,* by Nathan Glazer and Daniel P. Moynihan, surely shows that in residential pattern and marriage Americans, to any large extent, have yet to fuse. But fusion is not only increasing, in suburban housing development and in ethnic intermarriage, but it took place a long time ago and takes place daily in the mind. America has brought second and third generations, whether of Western or Eastern European origin, Asian or Negro, to live noticeably alike; taste in clothes and furnishings is determined by class rather than ethnicity, and by television rather than grandparents. The middle class standards —of worldly possession to show success or perhaps Calvinistic worth—has brought a disparate nation so much together it falters at change. The old conflict in American life—between equality and diversity, first seen in Tocqueville's stunning fear that the individual would get "lost in the crowd"—is still with us after the greatest immigration from the greatest variety of sources a nation has ever known.

The cultural problem today—in art and architecture and life —is to discover forms that suit the country's inherent originality. That originality, as it was in the beginning of the country, derives from a delicate balance between old and new. The tipping of the scale one way or another, in culture or in life, produces the rigid or the bland. The denials of origin that America has asked is not unlike the denial of color once accepted by blacks—Negro, never black, until the end of this decade. Still, as W. E. B. Du Bois first pointed out, the only genuinely American music has its origins in slavery, and the "sorrow songs," which bred the spiritual and then jazz and which have a poor relation in rock and roll, were a precise meeting of an ethnic condition with its American fate. We are on our way to getting such a rich encounter in the American novel now, where the ethnic condition becomes internal, comic, heroic or antiheroic. Nineteenth-century white American culture was born from an honest use of tension—in Thoreau, Hawthorne, Dickinson, Melville, James—as the Puritan tradition gave way to a liberal skepticism. No true culture, no true life, can be born without tension and its use.

But we have let our tensions work mainly for success, rather than for an imaginative life. In our national life, more than other Western nations, we are undernourished. William Butler Yeats has told us well: "How but in custom and in ceremony/Are innocence and beauty born?" The search for custom, for ceremony, for aesthetics in life, so desperate and often so pitiful in America, is so because we have so little past to grasp. When before the poverty of immigrants America dangled the rewards of money and success, perhaps little could be kept. Yet the need for a past is inevitable. Ethnic and early American, it inevitably catches us, takes us in unawares. Witness youth today, of varying ethnic backgrounds, parading in the beards and paraphernalia of frontiersmen, of gold prospectors, electricity providing a geiger-counter music. While old cultures fade, a cross-pollination of cultures breaks through. The physical freedom and tempo of blacks is a romantic influence on the behavior of white youth. Yet without a sense of one's own identity, America reels off endlessly on fads and is now in search of life-styles. The blandness and massiveness in American life is not only proving ethnic identity more necessary but more attractive, an oasis of identity. Perhaps a new identity is already being struck, in third and fourth generation Americans, in whose lives tensions, naturally used, produce gaiety and originality.

Material success has made possible changed car styles, hair styles, fashion styles, decoration schemes, while in fact the immigrant experience of all Americans has left an American vacancy. The building of an American self needs the rich and diverse sources that made us if we are not to be plastic and destructive. The search for an American identity can look to the New England green with houses grouped around it (read cluster plan) and open space left intact. We need only look at the plan of our older towns if we wish to preserve what is left of the spectacularly beautiful American countryside. While religion has declined, ethnic customs—candle lighting and prayers on a Sabbath eve—can escape religious severity and soften the present. America is more tolerant of differences than organized religion used to be, but that tolerance is only real when we are not ashamed of them. A way out of concrete, as some city planners and neighborhood groups know, ought to be the specific rehabilitation of the old—the wooden row houses in many cities with grass in front and gardens behind, which make many a black ghetto look blissful at first glance and which were the small pride of the established immigrant. The economics of such rehabilitation could be overcome if we let the old American idea of community enterprise and self-help take hold. If we become confident of ourselves or uncomfortable enough, the melting pot need not produce uniformity; a pluralistic society need not be single-minded. If America is a set of paradoxes, we had better use them, each his own, rather than melt individuality away into foam rubber.

Perhaps America is on the verge of an honest meeting of the old and the new. As immigrant experience has brought a new vitality into American writing, so in American politics a new vitality has come from second and third generation Americans. The Kennedy years are examples of a force ready to develop, choked off by American violence. The assassins, in both cases, came from compounded uprootings. Illness or health, immigrant experience is a national experience, and the American vacancy shows the common disease. Hard-hats are in high office as well as on high buildings; are old-line Protestants as well as new-stock Americans. Blue-collar workers rally to the flag more in opposition to students whose privileges they never had than in support of the war itself.

If America is to come together, opportunity must not only become more equal, but opportunity must allow for the diversity and dignity different occupations can bring. The cult of success has meant the denigration of work by the hand, of labor itself. Television, celebrating endless consumption, defines the self in terms of sleek ownership. It is for status, not merely wages and benefits, that workers are striking today. Status, a term the young deride, puts an ill-fitting halo on the white-collar executive, whose life may be hollow enough. John A. Williams writes of his father, "He was a day laborer; the label 'nonskilled' bears a stigma today, but it didn't then. I live in New York City now and I don't often see men dressed in the clothes of a laborer—gray trousers, bulky, colorless sweaters, dust-lined faces, and crumpled caps or felt hats bent out of shape; nor do I smell honest sweat anymore, strong and acrid, as I used to smell it on my father and later on myself."

If the worker knew what the sons of the affluent, the controversial young, know, they would see in American affluence the immense sacrifices of self it all too often requires. The worker may sense this. The quiet revolution the young are leading, against a culture of consumption, against pollution not only of the air but of the self, has every chance of changing America, not only because that revolution is spreading but because the young, deeply committed to a simpler style of life, become the majority of tomorrow; and in *The Greening of America* Charles A. Reich has made us see the profound implications of the youth culture. The young in every generation in America have known, and now know more widely, with more anguish, that a man is to be judged not by what he possesses, but by what he is. The frustration of the young, and of the ethnic worker, is great because the real American promise, learned by every school child, is so high. Jefferson changed the then accepted phrase "life, liberty, and property" to "life, liberty, and the pursuit of happiness." America will not rest until the mirage, at least, comes in sight. And the young will not stop until happiness comes with meaning—meaning in work, meaning in personal relationships. In the young of today, the old and the new may have found a meeting. If they reform a culture of consumption, simply by consuming less, by turning more to craft and public service, by rejecting mass organization, the economy may be revolutionized—but at the cost of dislocation and unemployment. If the immediate political consequences could be repression and turmoil, the final solution will be a more human life. For America is a nation of myth; the myth of individuality and self-fulfillment has not died in the age of mass organization and a brutal, irrational war. Instead the myth has grown stronger. And the Vietnam War has been the telescope through which not only our insanity abroad but our waste and destruction at home has come clear.

Out of our present crisis of materialism and war, the true American character may be born. Tenuous in our gropings toward the past, Americans have sent roots, always, into the continent itself. Indigenous American customs—sports, camping, the craze for outdoor living—spring from the American land. The realization that we surrendered to industrialism, that massiveness wars on individuality, is not only marked in the young, but vague and incipient in all age groups. The young, who talk of beauty with a touching sincerity, can find in our past more than Indian beads if they will look less at television, more at our written culture. The America they rightly criticize may have made some of them, in their quest for instant joy, victims too. America will have to fight the machine not only around us, but in us.

In this book, the uprooting is painful, but partial; the writers, critical of the technological age, maintain many of the values—without the artifices—of the past. While some are skeptical of the young or more exactly the extremist young, all are held by the dream of a more human America. The black and Puerto Rican writers, both urging greater self-respect, both in that sense militant, give the America of the European immigrants and the founding fathers the chance of coming through with its promise. The most optimistic view of America, though laced with pessimism, comes from the two current immigrants—intellectuals, recent arrivals from Europe and England. Coming to America from England was, for Alan Pryce-Jones, "a little like getting out of the schoolroom into real life." Both remind us, troubled though we are, that American openness and vitality contrast brightly with European rigidity and convention. That was the contrast that brought immigrants here in the first place, and it is refreshing, restorative to know that even with doubts there can be "amazement that there is something like America." The contrast may be more than one can bear, for convention in Europe makes tradition and national character possible. Happily, some of European civilization has immigrated to America, in music, in museums, in taste, some of it in the "immigration of talents" represented here. Europeans comment on the energy and worry Americans give to their problems; we, because of a heritage of social conscience and a surplus of problems, worry that we do not worry and work on them enough.

Czeslaw Milosz, coming to America from Eastern Europe after a decade in Western Europe, finds an underlying humanism in American life, side by side with modern evils. "Perhaps that mentality, so often ridiculed, is that of the Bible-reading American entrenched in self-righteousness; and yet the fact that America is still the country of the Bible cannot but have lasting consequences. No matter how deeply religious beliefs have been eroded, the King James version is still the very core of the language and a determinant factor in its literary development. The work of Whitman and Melville and their successors always takes us back to it, the Scripture is the common property of believers, agnostics, atheists. Whoever has verified empirically, as I have, how much depends on hidden human qualities will not frivolously call a certain heavy decency and disinterestedness just plain stupidity. . . . Nor will he shrug off the contrast of goodness and wickedness originating in the Bible. In spite of arguments to the contrary, in spite of the paradox of brutal and cruel deeds . . . or perhaps just because of that paradox, America is the legitimate heir to Judaeo-Christian civilization. . . ." Not only have immigrants of all races and times brought a spirit of hope and endeavor with them, but it has drifted into our thought, our basic institutions, and rooted there. The humanism that agitates us now may allow America to become more human.

1
Pride and Poverty

AN IRISH INTEGRITY
William Alfred

My great-grandmother, Anna Maria, lived in a "city house," in the part of Brooklyn between Red Hook and Brooklyn Heights then called the Point, but recently rechristened Cobble Hill by real-estate agents. City houses were houses which fell to the borough by foreclosure for nonpayment of taxes, and which were rented out at nominal rents as a form of patronage. At this point, I must in honesty say investigable fact leaves off and legend begins. Born though I was in 1922, I am a child of the nineteenth century, for it was Anna Maria who raised me until I was four years old, that is, took care of me while my parents were out working. It is mostly her memories I propose to retell. But memories make uncertain evidence. Moreover, in many cases, I cannot rightly say where her memories leave off and my embroidering of them begins.

Anna Maria was the name I was conditioned to call her. I avoid "taught" advisedly. You learned what you were not to say to her as you learned not to lay hands on the ruby-red, cylindrical kerosene stoves scattered through that house of hers, which, now I look back on it, she deliberately allowed to fall to ruin. She never struck but with her tongue, but when she did, you winced. When the quarter-a-week insurance man, with whom she played an endless game of hide-and-seek, once flushed her out, she called him a pimp. And once in a spasm of reflex chauvinism, she called Queen Victoria, whom she rather admired, "a goddamned old water dog."

If I am a child of the nineteenth century, Anna Maria Gavin

Egan was a child of the late eighteenth. She, too, was raised by an old woman, her grandmother. With little or no education, she spoke and acted in the quirkily formal manner of a character in a Sterne novel. Her women friends she called by their last names, as they did her. Perhaps her exacting that we call her by her first name was her way of admitting the children of her blood (the kind of phrase she'd have used) to deeper intimacy.

She was born in Castlebar, Mayo, sometime between 1845 and 1850. She never knew her true age. Perhaps her birth was unregistered; perhaps the records were destroyed during the bad years. She was born sickly; and her mother separated her from her twin brother and sent her as an infant to the seashore, where her grandmother raised her until she "grew into her strength." One of her brothers became a Fenian and was forced to emigrate to the states. After his emigration, it was impossible to make a go of the small bakeshop her mother ran. British soldiers harried the shop and dwelling with nuisance raids, bayoneting the flour bags and even the featherbeds in mock searches for the absent brother. In 1866 or 1867, she and her mother made the "eight weeks' voyage in a sailing vessel" which brought her to New York.

Of Ireland she rarely spoke, save to recall that she was often hungry there and that for her main meal she often ate cress out of the brooks on oaten bread with a bit of lard. Although she always used to say she had no desire to return to Ireland to live, she lived out of a trunk to her dying day, and taught her children to do the same. I myself, till well on in my twenties, felt that Ireland, which I had never seen, was my true country. When, over eighty, she died in the early thirties, it did not seem strange six months afterward to receive a clipping from an Irish newspaper, which read: "Died in Exile: Anna Maria Gavin Egan."

Of her first years here, she never tired of speaking. She and her mother landed at Castle Garden and walked up Broadway to City Hall, with bundles of clothes and pots and featherbeds in their arms. The singing of the then exposed telegraph wires frightened them, as did the bustle of the people in the streets. They lost their fear when they met an Irish policeman who directed them to a rooming house on Baxter Street.

It must have been spring or summer when they arrived. The

windows were open; and she was wakened often in the night by the sound of drunken voices singing:

> We'll hang Jefferson Davis
> On a sour apple tree.

Her training as a "manty-maker" (mantua-maker, in other words, dressmaker) gave her an advantage over other girls of her age. She got a job fast. No woman would wear black satin, she remembered, because Mrs. Suratt, the lady in whose rooming house the murder of Lincoln had been plotted, was hanged in a dress of that material. On her way from work the first year, she nightly passed a house in whose tall, lit first-floor windows sat the most beautiful women she had ever seen, dressed to the nines, their hair as trimly curled, their faces painted fresh as new French china dolls. After weeks of gawking, she built up the courage to hazard a smile. "Come up here, you blonde bitch," one of the women called to her, "and we'll wipe that smile off your face." Years after she was married, she was finally reunited with her brother, who had gone West in a vain quest for a fortune and returned without even the wife he had married in California. "What happened to her?" Anna Maria asked. "She ran off with another fellow," he answered. "Why?" said she. "Because," said he, "I've but a little bit of a thing."

The raciness of these stories, which she told me when I was eight, would make her seem atypical. But all of her women friends, even the pious ones, were as free-spoken. There was not a Mother Machree among them. Free-spoken though she was about human matters, Anna Maria was a sphinx of reserve when it came to religion. She never went to mass, although she prayed the rosary nightly. Nor would she ever allow a priest in her house. Visiting priests, she said, brought bad luck. Why, she would not say, for it also was unlucky "to talk against the cloth."

The city house she rented for eighteen dollars a month was an abandoned mansion, let to her because my dead great-grandfather had "done favors at the Hall" to someone dead even longer than he. Churchill's mother was born five minutes' walk from it. The

Protestants, for that was what she called native-born Americans, moved out as the immigrants moved in. The first wave of immigrants must have been German and Scandinavian: there were still a few families of them left in my day. Then from the backyard tenement houses on the other side of Court Street in Brooklyn, the Irish began to move in. They were succeeded by the Italians, with whom they lived in uncertain amity.

Her house was a narrow brownstone, two windows to every floor except the ground, where the place of one window was taken by a double door of solid walnut plated with layers of dust-pocked cheap black enamel. Its shallow stoop, with ornate, Gothic-arched wrought-iron railings eaten away by rust, was fronted by a long area (pronounced "airy"). A path of slate slabs led up to the stoop past an unkempt grass plot surrounded by overgrown privet hedges. Under the stoop was the blocked up front entrance to the basement kitchen. And to the side of that, the cellar door, which boys would try to steal every election eve to feed the bonfire up on Union Street.

A stationery store had nibbled into the basement of the brownstone on the corner of Clinton Street. It dealt in penny wares, lousy-heads (nonpareils), twisted wires with red and white propellers on them, seasons of decalcomania stamps, and sweet wax buckteeth and marbles. It was run by the Wechslers, the only Jews in the neighborhood. They were beloved by Irish and Italians alike, because of their kindness to children, and because they had the only phone on the block, and would walk the block's length to call a person to it.

Little Siberia, my mother called the house. Its center was the volcano of a coal stove in the basement kitchen. No comfort was to be won of a winter's night more than eighteen inches from it; and the butter had to be set on the mantel over it to prevent having to split it with a cleaver. Little Siberia—the full sense of being an alien and poor was also in the phrase.

In earlier years the two top floors were let out to aging Irish spinsters. But in the late twenties, there were only two left, a bedridden saint of seventy and her sister, both living on Old Age. All the other rooms were shut off. The house itself has always stood in my mind as a convenient symbol of what happened to the first two generations of my mother's family under the impact of immigration, each closed room standing for failed or refused chances.

In her late twenties, Anna Maria married a widower years her senior, who died long before I was born. His first wife had been a Sheridan, a distinction which the family rejoiced in as being theirs by osmosis. Whether he had children by that marriage, I do not know. I suspect not, because the legend that was made of him pictures him as lavishing more love on a scapegrace niece than on any of his children by Anna Maria. He comes down to me as a silent man in a tasseled smoking cap, who slept apart from his wife in the front room of the basement, and who, when his niece would scratch at the basement door at three in the morning, legless (drunk) and scared to go home, would relinquish his bed to her, bundling himself in his overcoat to keep fitful watch over her from a creaking rocker in the stoveless room.

Anna Maria seems to have been as much her own woman in the 1880s as she was in the 1920s and 1930s. From time to time she would disappear from the house for days at a time. On one of these occasions, my great-grandfather was asked "Where's Egan?" "I don't know," he answered, "I think she ran away with a soldier." That was the nearest anyone came to solving the mystery.

The Dad, as his children called him, was a junkman, a canny one, with party and institutional connections that let him in on the ground floor of any major demolition. He could read or write nothing but numbers; but those he must have been able to manage with profitable shrewdness. Poverty did not empty the table or close the doors of the house until after his death.

Anna Maria had four children by him: my grandmother, Agnes, her twin, Martin, William, and Gertrude. Since Martin was a frail baby, Anna Maria gave Agnes to her mother to raise, thereby repeating the pattern of her own rearing. When my grandmother Agnes was in her early teens, Anna Maria took her to Ireland where she met her cousin, Stanislaus Bunyan, who as thoroughly loathed her at first sight as she did him. When he later emigrated to America with his sister, Katherine, he stayed with Anna Maria, 'ell in love with Agnes, and married her. She was eighteen at the time; he twenty-seven.

Impatient, dangerously temperamental, my grandfather earned his living by sketching for newspapers and by taking roles in the second- and third-string Frohman road companies. He was said to have drawn for *World* and *Puck,* and to have played the lead in *Dr. Jekyll and Mr. Hyde.* In those simpler days the transformation from Jekyll to Hyde was achieved by a foaming tumbler of Seidlitz powder and a fast fall into a wooden armchair with an open tin of green greasepaint nailed upside down under one broad arm. The sizzling glass once drunk, Jekyll would writhe in the chair, dig his hand to the wrist in the greasepaint, pass the hand over his face as if to wipe away the cold sweat, then shoot up again toward the footlights, green as a beached corpse. Men in the audience gulped; women thudded to the floor.

My grandfather's life was hard, his habits wild; and he shaped his wife in his image. "He had her dancing day and night; and she'd sew sleighbells in the hems of her skirts so the men would be looking at her ankles." Six months after she bore my mother, early in her twentieth year, she died of "congestion of the lungs," a euphemism for tuberculosis, which then was considered stark and certain evidence of a shameless life.

My grandfather left my mother, then six months old, with the owner of a boardinghouse and her daughter and went on the road. That set off a series of custody suits which produced the only heritage I have from him, a copy of "a typewritten letter," hurled at the head of the boardinghouse keeper. The threat of sending someone "a typewritten letter" was in those days as terrifying a sanction as the threat of calling the police. The letter reads:

New York, February 23rd, 1901.

Mrs. E. Walsh,

Madam:

In answer to your letter of the 21st inst, I must say that I am more than astonished to think that any sane person should be so imprudent as to dare make the proposal to me that you have done, for you should be aware by this time that I would no more think of placing my dear child in the clutches of a woman of your stamp than I would in the jaws of a wild beast.

You, who dragged my innocent babe into open court on two occasions have also dared to cast reflections on the way that she is being cared for. Permit me to tell you although it is no business of yours, that my dear child is now stronger, healthier and better in every way than she has ever been, which is a marked contrast to the half starved condition she was in when I rescued her from you.

You have all along endeavored to force yourself on my family and you have interfered and intermeddled in my family affairs. Furthermore both you and your daughter have heaped the vilest kind of insult on my people and myself although you are complete strangers to us.

Now I hereby warn you that this must *cease*. I have already placed your letters in the hands of my lawyers, and if you still persist in your letter writing and annoyance I shall at once take steps to have you arrested and punished. My lawyers have advised me repeatedly to adopt this course and I shall act on their advice if you continue to interfere in my affairs.

Your daughter . . . has also several times endeavored to force her way into the house of my child's grand-parents and has even gone as far as to defy and threaten my people. I have taken steps to have her apprehended and dealt with according to law the very next attempt she makes in this direction.

I will take no further notice of any communication you may make other than to place it in the hands of my lawyers.

Yours truly,

S. J. Bunyan

My mother went back to Anna Maria. Her only memory of her father dated from what must have been her fourth year. On a dark, cold Saturday, when she was lemon-oiling the balusters of the stair-

case, she heard a heavy step in the hall below. A hatted man in the
carefully pressed one good suit of an unsuccessful actor was staring
at her as if to commit her to memory. His handsome face was thin
and white as paper, and the jaunty walking stick which actors then
affected bore his whole weight like a cripple's cane. He broke his
gaze and walked silently down the back stairs to the kitchen. She
did not know who he was until long afterward, when she was told
that he had come to say good-bye to Anna Maria on his way back
home to die. He died in Dublin in his thirtieth year, and is said to
be buried in Glas Nevin.

His sister, Katherine, also married a cousin, her first, and did
so expressly against the admonitions of the family. She and her
husband lied to the priest about the degree of kindred (then you
needed a dispensation to marry within the fourth degree of kindred). When Anna Maria threatened to tell the priest to prevent
the marriage, Katherine pulled a bottle of iodine from her purse,
drank all of it, and collapsed to the kitchen floor. Katherine managed to pull through, Anna Maria swore never to interfere again,
and the cousins were married.

Like my grandfather (her brother), Katherine believed she
had it in her to make America her own. She took courses at Cooper
Union and was reputedly the first woman telegrapher to be hired
by the *New York Times*.

After her marriage, however, she fell to pieces. She lived in a
flat rather than a house, which was slightly disreputable in those
days. She kept house out of half-unpacked barrels of crockery and
pans in rooms uncarpeted and bare of wall (her pictures were still
in crates). She seems to have felt that something had played her
false, either her new country, her husband, or herself, or her dreams
about all three. Like her brother, her embittered heart was more and
more deeply set on going home to Ireland. She drank heavily
from breakfast to bedtime and died of a broken neck from a fall
down her own front stairs. In a prolonged agony of grief, her husband destroyed his business and himself. Every few months he
would drink himself furious and hurl pried-up cobblestones through
the windows of his own saloon. With nothing to hold on to, his
inwards gone, he died in 1910 on the top floor of the city house, at
the tactless mercy of his impoverished relatives. In 1937, his

irreconcilably reproachful ghost was said to have passed my great-aunt on the stairs "without so much as a beck or a nod."

Of Anna Maria's sons, neither Martin nor William went far in school. Martin left off after the eighth grade, and William, in the course of his first year at St. Francis Preparatory; Martin out of pride and wildness, William out of incapacity. That incapacity was usually blamed on his having fallen off a trolley as a boy and fractured his skull, an accident which was the frequent source of brutal laughter for Anna Maria and the rest of the family. William adored her, but she had eyes for no one but Martin, to whom she gave her highest accolade, a mordant nickname, Mortyeen Hungry Jaws, in sardonic appreciation of his appetite.

Such nicknames were the family's strongest terms of endearment. There was, besides, a Mohawk chariness about addressing anyone by his given name. Anna Maria had recourse from time to time to an old minstrel-show song to take the curse off our directly naming her:

> Anna Maria, Anna Maria,
> Anna Maria Jones,
> She can play the banjo,
> The piccolo,
> And the bones.

Address was awkward until you had earned your sobriquet. I earned mine, Four-Alls, when I was a crawling baby. My mother earned hers in her fifteenth year, when to measure up to the stricter standards of cleanliness in the outside world (she had just gone out to work), she undertook to do her own laundry:

> Clotty Malotty
> Who lives in our lane,
> Every day washing,
> And ne'er a day clean.

People had more than one nickname. Martin was called Mutton as well as Mortyeen Hungry Jaws; William was called Wally to his face, and the more malicious Miggsy behind his back ("Miggs!" is what you cried, holding your thumbs, when you had the misfortune of meeting a person with cockeyes).

The tortuousness of the show of affection generally underlying the choice of these epithets always seemed to me to spring from the bleak Irish terror of "overlooking" those one admired, of giving them, that is, the evil eye, calling the Devil's attention to them by imprudent praise. Love was never easily expressed in word or gesture. Kissing and hugging were as dangerous as they were vulgar. Honey, darling, sweetheart, and dear were words clowns used in books. In the family, they would have raised hoots of derision. "You" was the most intimate form of address. It could be used with crippling fury or devastating tenderness.

There was another form of address, the dreaded third person, reserved for "plugs" and "villains," those who had "presumed," who had "gone too far." For that kind of discourse you needed an intermediary off whom to ricochet your remarks: "Tell the other one that's the last time he'll put the bottle on his head in this kitchen" (i.e., drink out of the bottle); or "You're to tell that one this isn't the first time he's come into this house with the one arm as long as the other" (i.e., without the conventional call-paying gift). The intermediary generally remained silent; he was there only "for the sake of common decency." This periphrastic socialization was more frequently practiced for long periods than on an ad hoc basis and was much in evidence at wakes. My mother never spoke directly to her Aunt Gertrude or Uncle Martin for over twenty years.

It was Anna Maria's second son, Wally, God help him (in Irish usage this is as much a dismissal as a blessing), on whom the sanction of indirect address was most often invoked. His only sojourns in the family's good graces were when he served as a convenient sucker or the butt of a passing joke. He was that most perfect of patsies, an easy victim, slow on the uptake, but once having caught on, a dervish of hurtless fury. For one whole year, every Monday morning, his older brother Mutton would hairpin Wally's trunk open and take his Sunday suit out to pawn for extra spending money. Every Friday afternoon he would redeem it with his new wages. When Wally at last discovered what had been happening, he flew into the Rumpelstiltskin rage his kin found so diverting and doublelocked the trunk. From that time on, he locked up everything, even the cheap treats he occasionally bought himself. He once presented the family with a quarter-eaten French apple pie so tainted with camphor not even a pig with a headcold could have been brought to nose it. He meant the gesture kindly. When they refused it, he ate it himself.

In his late thirties, Wally married a plain, good-hearted, second-generation Newfoundland woman, whom he met at the weekly dances on Ninth Street where people used to go to "meet their own kind." He was a skilled florist and worked for years in the shop and greenhouse of a German on Stuyvesant Avenue. He added to his income by buying various job lots of odds and ends from stores under the Myrtle Avenue El and repeddling them for at least triple what they had cost. Like his brother Mutton, he prided himself on that quality which the Irish call cuteness, an aggressive sharp-dealing which takes more pleasure in outwitting people than in profit. "It will blacken before the hour is out," he once boasted of a gardenia he had just sold a high-school boy for his date's corsage.

It was not that Wally was heartless. He certainly was not. He was always faithful to the Irish precept " 'Will you?' was never a good fellow" (asking if someone wants something, rather than giving it to him unasked). He always gave unasked. But only to his own. He had a tribal sense of the outside world as fair game. Business to him was hunting: its only joy lay in the kill.

It was his generosity which kept the family's head above water in dirty times. Yet to them, perhaps because he seemed a distorting mirror of themselves, he was always the plug of plugs, a problem creature to be disowned by ridicule or exiled by contempt. He had the quarter-inch brow and ape's lip of the Paddies with grass hair they sell in florist shops on St. Patrick's Day. Like all of us, his opinions were three-quarters prejudice and one-quarter notions. His grasp of language was haphazard. He prefaced most remarks with the old Bowery expletive, "Wuh-now." Because she had been an orphan, he always introduced my mother as "this poor unfortunate." When his wife died of peritonitis, he brought the wake to a standstill by an impromptu keen in which he asked the Almighty why "her testicles got tied in knots" (he meant intestines). When he was being ragged or crossed, he would fix his tormentor with a squint-eyed look and bellow "Wuh-now, refer!" His worst term of abuse was "Communist," which he pronounced "commonness." "Wuh-now, refer! You goddam Commonness," he once yelled at a cop who told him to stop smoking on the subway. That set-to cost him thirty days in a cell on Welfare Island.

Stunted though he was from his childhood accident and lack of schooling, half-blind from a boiler explosion in the navy during the first World War, brutalized by family callousness, Wally flourished with the eccentric vitality of a trodden weed. There was a dignity in his refusal to hate or seek vengeance which moved the most vehement of his belittlers. That dignity saw him through the rebuffs of the non-Irish world as it had seen him through the rejections of his family and helped to transfigure banishment to liberation. His achievements were as modest as his desires; but of all his generation, he lived the longest and fared the best.

Mutton, Anna Maria's white-haired boy, was less lucky. He was the Yellow Kid grown up, Mayor Walker without an education. Tall and handsomely aquiline in a world of faces and bodies softened and shrunk by hard times and bad fare (the phrase was "All swollen up from water and potatoes"), he was the prince of the family and the neighborhood.

He had Anna Maria's testy sense of what life owed him. He took over the Dad's failing junk business rather than take jobs that would as a matter of course lead to moderate advancement. He worked, for instance, less than a week on the coveted subway-maintenance job which political pull had got him. He always said he left it out of shame: the first day he reported to work the only whole shoes in the house he could find to wear were a pair of ladies' patent leather boots which belonged to Katherine. That may have been the immediate cause, but the deeper one was the sense of insult to his dreams he felt at having to make do with an ordinary lot. Those who have been poor, like those who have been sick, often expect impossible compensation.

And crippling poor is what the family was. The reason usually given was that a bit of real-estate speculation had cost them all that the Dad had left. It cost them more than that; it cost them their trust in America.

Mutton bought a handsome Federal house from a woman who had been a trained nurse. She reserved one room to store some possessions in; and Mutton let the house. The tenants turned out to be deadbeats, and after a year or so had to be evicted. When they had gone, Mutton inspected the house and found the door of the room the nurse had reserved pried open. What he saw were piles of clothes on various pieces of furniture and chests, covered with muslin sheets. Since nothing seemed missing, he simply reclosed the jimmied door and contented himself with locking the two front doors.

A month or so later, the nurse was murdered, and the police took the broken-open room as a possible motive on Mutton's part. The room contained, among other things, some signed letters from George Washington, chests of eighteenth-century silver pots and pitchers, and a good deal of furniture and clothing which had belonged to Dolly Madison, of whom the nurse was a collateral descendant. Mutton was cleared of suspicion of murder through the help of the nurse's lawyer. A year or so later, the lawyer was arrested for the murder of a Polish countess at Greenwood Lake. When he confessed to that crime, he also confessed to the murder of the nurse.

In that experience, the family's deep-seated fears were realized and confirmed. That is what came of forming permanent ties here. That is what came of dealing with Protestants. Taboos previously allowed to lapse were reinforced. Stigmatized as unlucky, the house was left untenanted and untended till it was lost for nonpayment of taxes.

That course of action fulfilled two needs the family felt. The first was to make an expiatory sacrifice: after all, they couldn't say they hadn't always known in the bone that their graves in Holy Cross were the only property they were meant to own. The second was to make a proper show of contempt to the powers that were. They dealt with Fate as they dealt with unjust friends: they refused to "give it the satisfaction" of noticing its treachery.

Such a muddle of propitiation and pride underlay most of their behavior to fortune, whether it was bad or good. They reacted to fortune as wild creatures react to changes of light or sound. They fled or they froze.

Good fortune made them weep with apprehension. Sing before breakfast, weep before supper. There is no blessing unblackened by a curse. They were more themselves with trouble than with ease. Bad fortune turned them stupidly noble like characters from heroic cycles. If life was that unfair, they would face the worst it had to offer. They would sooner die than cry out for mercy or relief.

What made their stand puzzling was the sense you knew they had of what was owed them for having measured up heroically to their lot, for having been at one and the same time insulted champions and the obedient children of God. It was not the American Dream that nourished their conviction of private dignity. Its cast-iron deer values held nothing for them. Success was not to be measured in material terms, but in terms of inner fulfillment. Failing that, in terms of spiritual endurance. Their combat was not with social conditions but with "principalities and powers" or, perhaps, "the ungovernable sea."

Mutton, accordingly, all his life conceived of himself as an unrealized conqueror in voluntary exile. At nearly forty, he married a widow and settled in a rented house behind a stable on the other side of Court Street, a block or so from the Gas House and the Gowanus. With a sullen and mysterious purpose, he retraced the family's steps back to poverty. When his wife broke down, he made a comic saga out of it, though it tore him in two. When he himself lost control of his bowels and bladder, he joked about his body's vagaries, as if it belonged to someone else.

His gaze arrested you with that compelling reproach you see in the eyes of dying men. His fidelity to intimate values so self-evident to him he believed it unnecessary to state them made the pursuit of happiness that my mother and father and I were, with the rest of our generations, engaged in seem trivial prostitution and self-indulgence. He was, like Anna Maria, literally larger than life. Like her, he believed in the inviolability of his own body. She died of a cancer she had hidden for years rather than let a doctor see or touch her; he died hopelessly crippled rather than undergo a comparatively simple operation.

It was more than the peasant fear of hospitals that held them to that stand. Their attitude was a sensible and outward sign of their conviction that any tampering with mind or body would inevitably lead to a loss of wholeness worse than death. They were virgin martyrs by disposition: they relinquished the charm of life as they had relinquished the charm of the American experience in order to keep their unquestioned selves impossibly intact. Mutton dying said to me, "You'll never be the man your grandfather was." I winced at what that meant to him and to me.

It is true that Mutton recoiled from "becoming American" for fear he should lose the sense of who he was. And that the older he got, the narrower, the more ignorantly reclusive he became. And that the pride in nationality which had saved Anna Maria from going under in the bleak days after the Civil War, when the Irish were held little better than the vermin that infested their tenements, had in him become a killing reflex. And that he lived in a ghetto of his own making, and the genuine gifts which were his were lost to his generation. All those things are true. But it is also true that no Irish of my generation will ever see his like again.

2
Choosing a Dream

ITALIANS IN HELL'S KITCHEN
Mario Puzo

As a child and in my adolescence, living in the heart of New York's Neapolitan ghetto, I never heard an Italian singing. None of the grown-ups I knew were charming or loving or understanding. Rather they seemed coarse, vulgar, and insulting. And so later in my life when I was exposed to all the clichés of lovable Italians, singing Italians, happy-go-lucky Italians, I wondered where the hell the moviemakers and storywriters got all their ideas from.

At a very early age I decided to escape these uncongenial folk by becoming an artist, a writer. It seemed then an impossible dream. My father and mother were illiterate, as were their parents before them. But practising my art I tried to view the adults with a more charitable eye and so came to the conclusion that their only fault lay in their being foreigners; I was an American. This didn't really help because I was only half right. I was the foreigner. They were already more "American" than I could ever become.

But it did seem then that the Italian immigrants, all the fathers and mothers that I knew, were a grim lot; always shouting, always angry, quicker to quarrel than embrace. I did not understand that their lives were a long labor to earn their daily bread and that physical fatigue does not sweeten human natures.

And so even as a very small child I dreaded growing up to be like the adults around me. I heard them saying too many cruel things about their dearest friends, saw too many of their false embraces with those they had just maligned, observed with horror their paranoiac anger at some small slight or a fancied injury to their pride. They were, always, too unforgiving. In short, they did not have the careless magnanimity of children.

In my youth I was contemptuous of my elders, including a few under thirty. I thought my contempt special to their circumstances. Later when I wrote about these illiterate men and women, when I thought I understood them, I felt a condescending pity. After all, they had suffered, they had labored all the days of their lives. They had never tasted luxury, knew little more economic security than those ancient Roman slaves who might have been their ancestors. And alas, I thought, with new-found artistic insight, they were cut off from their children because of the strange American tongue, alien to them, native to their sons and daughters.

Already an artist but not yet a husband or father, I pondered omnisciently on their tragedy, again thinking it special circumstance rather than a constant in the human condition. I did not yet understand why these men and women were willing to settle for less than they deserved in life and think that "less" quite a bargain. I did not understand that they simply could not afford to dream, I myself had a hundred dreams from which to choose. For I was already sure that I would make my escape, that I was one of the chosen. I would be rich, famous, happy. I would master my destiny.

And so it was perhaps natural that as a child, with my father gone, my mother the family chief, I, like all the children in all the ghettos of America, became locked in a bitter struggle with the adults responsible for me. It was inevitable that my mother and I became enemies.

As a child I had the usual dreams. I wanted to be handsome, specifically as cowboy stars in movies were handsome. I wanted to be a killer hero in a world-wide war. Or if no wars came along (our teachers told us another was impossible), I wanted at the very least to be a footloose adventurer. Then I branched out and thought of being a great artist, and then, getting ever more sophisticated, a great criminal.

My mother, however, wanted me to be a railroad clerk. And that was her *highest* ambition; she would have settled for less. At

the age of sixteen when I let everybody know that I was going to
be a great writer, my friends and family took the news quite calmly,
my mother included. She did not become angry. She quite simply
assumed that I had gone off my nut. She was illiterate and her
peasant life in Italy made her believe that only a son of the nobility
could possibly be a writer. Artistic beauty after all could spring
only from the seedbed of fine clothes, fine food, luxurious living.
So then how was it possible for a son of hers to be an artist? She was
not too convinced she was wrong even after my first two books were
published many years later. It was only after the commercial success of my third novel that she gave me the title of poet.

My family and I grew up together on Tenth Avenue, between
Thirtieth and Thirty-first streets, part of the area called Hell's
Kitchen. This particular neighborhood could have been a movie
set for one of the Dead End Kid flicks or for the social drama of
the East Side in which John Garfield played the hero. Our tenements were the western wall of the city. Beneath our windows were
the vast black iron gardens of the New York Central Railroad,
absolutely blooming with stinking boxcars freshly unloaded of
cattle and pigs for the city slaughterhouse. Steers sometimes escaped and loped through the heart of the neighborhood followed by
astonished young boys who had never seen a live cow.

The railroad yards stretched down to the Hudson River, beyond whose garbagey waters rose the rocky Palisades of New Jersey. There were railroad tracks running downtown on Tenth Avenue itself to another freight station called St. Johns Park. Because
of this, because these trains cut off one side of the street from the
other, there was a wooden bridge over Tenth Avenue, a romantic-
looking bridge despite the fact that no sparkling water, no silver
flying fish darted beneath it; only heavy dray carts drawn by tired
horses, some flat-boarded trucks, tin lizzie automobiles and, of
course, long strings of freight cars drawn by black, ugly engines.

What was really great, truly magical, was sitting on the bridge,
feet dangling down, and letting the engine under you blow up
clouds of steam that made you disappear, then reappear all damp
and smelling of fresh ironing. When I was seven years old I fell
in love for the first time with the tough little girl who held my hand
and disappeared with me in that magical cloud of steam. This

experience was probably more traumatic and damaging to my later relationships with women than one of those ugly childhood adventures Freudian novelists use to explain why their hero has gone bad.

My father supported his wife and seven children by working as a track man laborer for the New York Central Railroad. My oldest brother worked for the raiload as a brakeman, another brother was a railroad shipping clerk in the freight office. Eventually I spent some of the worst months of my life as the railroad's worst messenger boy.

My oldest sister was just as unhappy as a dressmaker in the garment industry. She wanted to be a school teacher. At one time or another my other two brothers also worked for the railroad—it got all six males in the family. The two girls and my mother escaped, though my mother felt it her duty to send all our bosses a gallon of homemade wine on Christmas. But everybody hated their jobs except my oldest brother who had a night shift and spent most of his working hours sleeping in freight cars. My father finally got fired because the foreman told him to get a bucket of water for the crew and not to take all day. My father took the bucket and disappeared forever.

Nearly all the Italian men living on Tenth Avenue supported their large families by working on the railroad. Their children also earned pocket money by stealing ice from the refrigerator cars in summer and coal from the open stoking cars in the winter. Sometimes an older lad would break the seal of a freight car and take a look inside. But this usually brought down the "Bulls," the special railroad police. And usually the freight was "heavy" stuff, too much work to cart away and sell, something like fresh produce or boxes of cheap candy that nobody would buy.

The older boys, the ones just approaching voting age, made their easy money by hijacking silk trucks that loaded up at the garment factory on Thirty-first Street. They would then sell the expensive dresses door to door, at bargain prices no discount house could match. From this some graduated into organized crime, whose talent scouts alertly tapped young boys versed in strong-arm. Yet despite all this, most of the kids grew up honest, content with fifty bucks a week as truck drivers, deliverymen, and white-collar clerks in the civil service.

I had every desire to go wrong but I never had a chance. The Italian family structure was too formidable.

I never came home to an empty house; there was always the smell of supper cooking. My mother was always there to greet me, sometimes with a policeman's club in her hand (nobody ever knew how she acquired it). But she was always there, or her authorized deputy, my older sister, who preferred throwing empty milk bottles at the heads of her little brothers when they got bad marks on their report cards. During the great Depression of the 1930s, though we were the poorest of the poor, I never remember not dining well. Many years later as a guest of a millionaire's club, I realized that our poor family on home relief ate better than some of the richest people in America.

My mother would never dream of using anything but the finest imported olive oil, the best Italian cheeses. My father had access to the fruits coming off ships, the produce from railroad cars, all before it went through the stale process of middlemen; and my mother, like most Italian women, was a fine cook in the peasant style.

My mother was as formidable a personage as she was a cook. She was not to be treated cavalierly. My oldest brother at age sixteen had his own tin lizzie Ford and used it to further his career as the Don Juan of Tenth Avenue. One day my mother asked him to drive her to the market on Ninth Avenue and Fortieth Street, no more than a five-minute trip. My brother had other plans and claimed he was going to work on a new shift on the railroad. Work was an acceptable excuse even for funerals. But an hour later when my mother came out of the door of the tenement she saw the tin lizzie loaded with three pretty neighborhood girls, my Don Juan brother about to drive them off. Unfortunately there was a cobblestone lying loose in the gutter. My mother dropped her black leather shopping bag and picked up the stone with both hands. As we all watched in horror, she brought the boulder down on the nearest fender of the tin lizzie, demolishing it. Then she picked up her bag and marched off to Ninth Avenue to do her shopping. To this day, forty years later, my brother's voice still has a surprised horror and shock when he tells the story. He still doesn't understand how she could have done it.

My mother had her own legends and myths on how to amass a fortune. There was one of our uncles who worked as an assistant chef in a famous Italian-style restaurant. Every day, six days a week, this uncle brought home, under his shirt, six eggs, a stick of butter, and a small bag of flour. By doing this for thirty years he was able to save enough money to buy a fifteen-thousand-dollar house on Long Island and two smaller houses for his son and daughter. Another cousin, blessed with a college degree, worked as a chemist in a large manufacturing firm. By using the firm's raw materials and equipment he concocted a superior floor wax which he sold door to door in his spare time. It was a great floor wax and with his low overhead, the price was right. My mother and her friends did not think this stealing. They thought of it as being thrifty.

The wax-selling cousin eventually destroyed his reputation for thrift by buying a sailboat; this was roughly equivalent to the son of a Boston brahmin spending a hundred grand in a whorehouse.

As rich men escape their wives by going to their club, I finally escaped my mother by going to the Hudson Guild Settlement House. Most people do not know that a settlement house is really a club combined with social services. The Hudson Guild, a five-story field of joy for slum kids, had ping pong rooms and billiard rooms, a shop in which to make lamps, a theater for putting on amateur plays, a gym to box and play basketball in. And then there were individual rooms where your particular club could meet in privacy. The Hudson Guild even suspended your membership for improper behavior or failure to pay the tiny dues. It was a heady experience for a slum kid to see his name posted on the billboard to the effect that he was suspended by the Board of Governors.

There were young men who guided us as counselors whom I remember with fondness to this day. They were more like friends than adults assigned to watch over us. I still remember one helping us eat a box of stolen chocolates rather than reproaching us. Which was exactly the right thing for him to do; we trusted him after that. The Hudson Guild kept more kids out of jail than a thousand policemen. It still exists today, functioning for the new immigrants, the blacks, and the Puerto Ricans.

There was a night when the rich people of New York, including the Ethical Culture Society, attended a social function at the Hudson Guild in order to be conned into contributing huge sums of money for the settlement house program. I think it was a dinner and amateur theater presentation that was costing them a hundred bucks a head. Their chauffeurs parked the limousines all along the curbs of Twenty-seventh Street and Tenth Avenue. Us deprived kids, myself the leader, spent the night letting the air out of our benefactors' tires. *Noblesse oblige.*

But we weren't all bad. In our public schools one year an appeal was made to every child to try to bring a can of food to fill Thanksgiving baskets for the poor. The teachers didn't seem to realize *we* were the poor. We didn't either. Every kid in that public school, out of the goodness of his heart, went out and stole a can of food from a local grocery store. Our school had the best contributor record of any school in the city.

Some of the most exciting days in my life were spent at the Hudson Guild. At the age of eleven I became captain of my club football team for seven years, and president of the Star Club, an office I held for five. I enjoyed that success more than any other in my life. And learned a great deal from it. At the age of fifteen I was as thoroughly corrupted by power as any dictator until I was overthrown by a coalition of votes; my best friends joining my enemies to depose me. It was a rare lesson to learn at fifteen.

The Star Club was made up of boys my own age, a gang, really, which had been pacified by the Hudson Guild Settlement House. We had a football team, a baseball team, a basketball team. We had a yearbook. We had our own room, where we could meet, and a guidance counselor, usually a college boy. We had one named Ray Dooley whom I remember with affection to this day. He took us for outings in the country, to the Hudson Guild Farm in New Jersey for winter weekends where we hitched our sleds to his car,

towed at thirty miles an hour. We repaid him by throwing lye into
his face and almost blinding him. We thought it was flour. He never
reproached us and it wound up OK. We idolized him after that. I
liked him because he never tried to usurp my power, not so that I
could notice.

The Hudson Guild was also responsible for absolutely the hap-
piest times of my childhood. When I was about nine or ten they
sent me away as a Fresh Air Fund kid. This was a program where
slum children were boarded on private families in places like New
Hampshire for two weeks.

As a child I knew only the stone city. I had no conception of
what the countryside could be. When I got to New Hampshire,
when I smelled grass and flowers and trees, when I ran barefoot
along the dirt country roads, when I drove the cows home from
pasture, when I darted through fields of corn and waded through
clear brooks, when I gathered warm brown speckled eggs in the
henhouse, when I drove a hay wagon drawn by two great horses—
when I did all these things—I nearly went crazy with the joy of
it. It was quite simply a fairy tale come true.

The family that took me in, a middle-aged man and woman,
childless, were Baptists and observed Sunday so religiously that
even checker playing was not allowed on the Lord's day of rest.
We went to church on Sunday for a good three hours, counting
Bible class, then again at night. On Thursday evenings we went
to prayer meetings. My guardians, out of religious scruple, had
never seen a movie. They disapproved of dancing, they were no
doubt political reactionaries; they were everything that I came
later to fight against.

And yet they gave me those magical times children never forget. For two weeks every summer from the time I was nine to
fifteen I was happier than I have ever been before or since. The man
was good with tools and built me a little playground with swings,
sliding ponds, seesaws. The woman had a beautiful flower and vegetable garden and let me pick from it. A cucumber or strawberry in
the earth was a miracle. And then when they saw how much I loved
picnics, the sizzling frankfurters on a stick over the wood fire, the
yellow roasted corn, they drove me out on Sunday afternoons to
a lovely green grass mountainside. Only on Sundays it was never

called a picnic, it was called "taking our lunch outside." I found it then—and now—a sweet hypocrisy.

The Baptist preacher lived in the house a hundred yards away and sometimes he, too, took his lunch "out" with us on a Sunday afternoon, he and his wife and children. Outside of his church he was a jolly fat man, a repressed comedian. Also a fond father, he bought his children a great many toys. I borrowed those toys and on one late August day I sailed his son's huge motor launch down a quiet, winding brook and when it nosed into a wet mossy bank I buried the toy there to have the following year when I came back. But I never found it.

There came a time, I was fifteen, when I was told I was too old to be sent away to the country as a Fresh Air Fund kid. It was the first real warning that I must enter the adult world, ready or not. But I always remembered that man and woman with affection, perhaps more. They always bought me clothing during my visits, my very first pajamas. They sent me presents at Christmastime, and when I was about to go into the army I visited them as a young man of twenty-one. The young were excessively grateful then, so I did not smoke in their house nor did I follow up on a local maid who seemed promising.

I believed then, as a child, that the State of New Hampshire had some sort of gates at which all thieves and bad guys were screened out. I believed this, I think, because the house was left unlocked when we went to church on Sundays and Thursday nights. I believed it because I never heard anyone curse or quarrel with raised voices. I believed it because it was beautiful to believe.

When I returned home from these summer vacations I had a new trick. I said grace with bowed head before eating the familiar spaghetti and meat balls. My mother always tolerated this for the few days it lasted. After all, the two weeks' vacation from her most troublesome child was well worth a Baptist prayer.

From this Paradise I was flung into Hell. That is, I had to help support my family by working on the railroad. After school hours of course. This was the same railroad that had supplied free coal and free ice to the whole Tenth Avenue when I was young enough to steal with impunity. After school finished at 3 P.M. I went to work in the freight office as a messenger. I also worked Saturdays and Sundays when there was work available.

I hated it. One of my first short stories was about how I hated that job. But of course what I really hated was entering the adult world. To me the adult world was a dark enchantment, unnatural. As unnatural to the human dream as death. And as inevitable.

The young are impatient about change because they cannot grasp the power of time itself; not only as the enemy of flesh, the very germ of death, but time as a benign cancer. As the young cannot grasp really that love must be a victim of time, so too they cannot grasp that injustices, the economic and family traps of living, can also fall victim to time.

And so I really thought that I would spend the rest of my life as a railroad clerk. That I would never be a writer. That I would be married and have children and go to christenings and funerals and visit my mother on a Sunday afternoon. That I would never own an automobile or a house. That I would never see Europe, the Paris and Rome and Greece I was reading about in books from the public library. That I was hopelessly trapped by my family, by society, by my lack of skills and education.

But I escaped again. At the age of eighteen I started dreaming about the happiness of my childhood. As later at the age of thirty I would dream about the joys of my lost adolescence, as at the age of thirty-five I was to dream about the wonderful time I had in the army which I had hated being in. As at the age of forty-five I dreamed about the happy, struggling years of being a devoted husband and loving father. I had the most valuable of human gifts, that of retrospective falsification: remembering the good and not the bad.

I still dreamed of future glory. I still wrote short stories, one or two a year. I still *KNEW* I would be a great writer but I was beginning to realize that accidents could happen and my second choice, that of being a great criminal, was coming up fast. But for the young everything goes so slowly, I could wait it out. The world would wait for me. I could still spin out my life with dreams.

In the summertime I was one of the great Tenth Avenue athletes but in the wintertime I became a sissy. I read books. At a very early age I discovered libraries, the one in the Hudson Guild and the public ones. I loved reading in the Hudson Guild where the librarian became a friend. I loved Joseph Altsheler's (I don't even have to look up his name) tales about the wars of the New York State Indian tribes, the Senecas and the Iroquois. I discovered Doc Savage and the Shadow and then the great Sabatini. Part of my character to this day is Scaramouche, I like to think. And then maybe at the age of fourteen or fiteen or sixteen I discovered Dostoevsky. I read the books, all of them I could get. I wept for Prince Myshkin in *The Idiot*, I was as guilty as Raskolnikov. And when I finished *The Brothers Karamazov* I understood for the first time what was really happening to me and the people around me. I had always hated religion even as a child but now I became a true believer. I believed in art. A belief that has helped me as well as any other.

My mother looked on all this reading with a fishy Latin eye. She saw no profit in it but since all her children were great readers she was a good enough general to know she could not fight so pervasive an insubordination. And there may have been some envy. If she had been able to she would have been the greatest reader of us all.

My direct ancestors for a thousand years have most probably been illiterate. Italy, the golden land, so loving to vacationing Englishmen, so majestic in its language and cultural treasures (they call it, I think, the cradle of civilization), has never cared for its poor people. My father and mother were both illiterates. Both grew up on rocky, hilly farms in the countryside adjoining Naples. My mother remembers never being able to taste the ham from the pig they slaughtered every year. It brought too high a price in the marketplace and cash was needed. My mother was also told the family could not afford the traditional family gift of linens when she married and it was this that decided her to emigrate to America to marry her first husband, a man she barely knew. When he died in a tragic work accident on the docks, she married my father, who assumed responsibility for a widow and her four children perhaps out of ignorance, perhaps out of compassion, perhaps out of love. Nobody ever knew. He was a mystery, a Southern Italian with blue eyes who departed from the family scene three children later when I was twelve. But he cursed Italy even more than my mother did. Then again, he wasn't too pleased with America either. My mother never heard of Michelangelo; the great deeds of the Caesars had not yet reached her ears. She never heard the great music of her native land. She could not sign her name.

And so it was hard for my mother to believe that her son could become an artist. After all, her one dream in coming to America had been to earn her daily bread, a wild dream in itself. And looking back she was dead right. Her son an artist? To this day she shakes her head. I shake mine with her.

America may be a fascistic, warmongering, racially prejudiced country today. It may deserve the hatred of its revolutionary young. But what a miracle it once was! What has happened here has never happened in any other country in any other time. The poor who had been poor for centuries—hell, since the beginning of Christ—whose children had inherited their poverty, their illiteracy, their hopelessness, achieved some economic dignity and freedom. You didn't get it for nothing, you had to pay a price in tears, in suffering, but why not? And some even became artists.

Not even my gift for retrospective falsification can make my eighteenth to twenty-first years seem like a happy time. I hated my life. I was being dragged into the trap I feared and had foreseen even as a child. It was all there, the steady job, the nice girl who would eventually get knocked up, and then the marriage and fighting over counting pennies to make ends meet. I noticed myself acting more unheroic all the time. I had to tell lies in pure self-defense, I did not forgive so easily.

But I was delivered. When World War II broke out I was delighted. There is no other word, terrible as it may sound. My country called. I was delivered from my mother, my family, the girl I was loving passionately but did not love. And delivered WITHOUT GUILT. Heroically. My country called, ordered me to defend it. I must have been one of millions, sons, husbands, fathers, lovers, making their innocent getaway from baffled loved ones. And what an escape it was. The war made all my dreams come true. I drove a jeep, toured Europe, had love affairs, found a wife, and lived the material for my first novel. But of course that was a just war as Vietnam is not, and so today it is perhaps for the best that the revolutionary young make their escape by attacking their own rulers.

Then why five years later did I walk back into the trap with a wife and child and a civil service job I was glad to get? After five years of the life I had dreamed about, plenty of women, plenty of booze, plenty of money, hardly any work, interesting companions, travel, etc., why did I walk back into that cage of family and duty and a steady job?

For the simple reason, of course, that I had never really escaped, not my mother, not my family, not the moral pressures of our society. Time again had done its work. I was back in my cage and I was, I think, happy. In the next twenty years I wrote three novels. Two of them were critical successes but I didn't make much money. The third novel, not as good as the others, made me rich. And free at last. Or so I thought.

Then why do I dream of those immigrant Italian peasants as having been happy? I remember how they spoke of their forebears, who spent all their lives farming the arid mountain slopes of Southern Italy. "He died in that house in which he was born," they say enviously. "He was never more than an hour from his village, not in all his life," they sigh. And what would they make of a phrase like "retrospective falsification"?

No, really, we are all happier now. It is a better life. And after all, as my mother always said, "Never mind about being happy. Be glad you're alive."

When I came to my "autobiographical novel," the one every writer does about himself, I planned to make myself the sensitive, misunderstood hero, much put upon by his mother and family. To my astonishment my mother took over the book and instead of my revenge I got another comeuppance. But it is, I think, my best book. And all those old-style grim conservative Italians whom I hated, then pitied so patronizingly, they also turned out to be heroes. Through no desire of mine. I was surprised. The thing that amazed me most was their courage. Where were their Congressional Medals of Honor? Their Distinguished Service Crosses? How did they ever have the balls to get married, have kids, go out to earn a living in a strange land, with no skills, not even knowing the language? They made it without tranquillizers, without sleeping pills, without psy-

chiatrists, without even a dream. Heroes. Heroes all around me.
I never saw them.

But how could I? They wore lumpy work clothes and handlebar
moustaches, they blew their noses on their fingers and they were so
short that their high-school children towered over them. They spoke
a laughable broken English and the furthest limit of their horizon
was their daily bread. Brave men, brave women, they fought to live
their lives without dreams. Bent on survival they narrowed their
minds to the thinnest line of existence.

It is no wonder that in my youth I found them contemptible.
And yet they had left Italy and sailed the ocean to come to a new
land and leave their sweated bones in America. Illiterate Colombos,
they dared to seek the promised land. And so they, too, dreamed a
dream.

Forty years ago, in 1930, when I was ten, I remember gas light,
spooky, making the tenement halls and rooms alive with ghosts.

We had the best apartment on Tenth Avenue, a whole top
floor of six rooms, with the hall as our storage cellar and the roof as
our patio. Two views, one of the railroad yards backed by the Jersey
shore, the other of a backyard teeming with tomcats everybody shot
at with BB guns. In between these two rooms with a view were three
bedrooms without windows—the classic railroad flat pattern. The
kitchen had a fire escape that I used to sneak out at night. I liked
that apartment though it had no central heating, only a coal stove
at one end and an oil stove at the other. I remember it as comfort-
able, slum or not.

My older brothers listened to a crystal radio on homemade
headsets. I hitched a ride on the backs of horses and wagons, my
elders daringly rode the trolley cars. Only forty years ago in calendar time, it is really a thousand years in terms of change in our
physical world. There are the jets, TV, penicillin for syphilis, cobalt
for cancer, equal sex for single girls; yet still always the contempt of
the young for their elders.

But maybe the young are on the right track this time. Maybe
they know that the dreams of our fathers were malignant. Perhaps
it is true that the only real escape is in the blood magic of drugs. All
the Italians I knew and grew up with have escaped, have made their

success. We are all Americans now, we are all successes now. And yet the most successful Italian man I know admits that though the one human act he never could understand was suicide, he understood it when he became a success. Not that he ever would do such a thing; no man with Italian blood ever commits suicide or becomes a homosexual in his belief. But suicide has crossed his mind. And so to what avail the finding of the dream? He went back to Italy and tried to live like a peasant again. But he can never again be unaware of more subtle traps than poverty and hunger.

There is a difference between having a good time in life and being happy. My mother's life was a terrible struggle and yet I think it was a happy life. One tentative proof is that at the age of eighty-two she is positively indignant at the thought that death dares approach her. But it's not for everybody that kind of life.

Thinking back I wonder why I became a writer. Was it the poverty or the books I read? Who traumatized me, my mother or the Brothers Karamazov? Being Italian? Or the girl sitting with me on the bridge as the engine steam deliciously made us vanish? Did it make any difference that I grew up Italian rather than Irish or black?

No matter. The good times are beginning, I am another Italian success story. Not as great as DiMaggio or Sinatra but quite enough. It will serve. Yet I can escape again. I have my retrospective falsification (how I love that phrase). I can dream now about how happy I was in my childhood, in my tenement, playing in those dirty but magical streets—living in the poverty that made my mother weep. True, I was a deposed dictator at fifteen but they never hanged me. And now I remember, all those impossible dreams strung out before me, waiting for me to choose, not knowing that the life I was living then, as a child, would become my final dream.

3
Pioneers to Eternity

NORWEGIANS ON THE PRAIRIE
Eugene Boe

In contrast to the smiling social democracy it is today, Norway in the last century was an overpopulated land of sharp class distinctions. The government, an insular monarchy, allowed only a privileged few any political expression. The clergy were aloof to the blunt realities of poverty and injustice. Nature had yielded her blessings in scant measure, but nothing was done to help or encourage the tens of thousands struggling to survive on little scraps of barren soil. Neighbor had quarreled with neighbor for every square foot of those steep, stony, stumpy upland meadows and the plots staked out were too small to support a family. Indebtedness was inevitable, the grip of creditor on debtor strangulating. Stills on the farms were legal and too many of the luckless could find their only consolation in drink.

In the early decades of the nineteenth century reports began drifting in from across the Atlantic that painted the New World in the colors of the Promised Land. A trickle of migrations from Norway to America started in the 1830s. Most of these emigrants set out for the frontiers of Illinois and Wisconsin, where land was available. Their letters home and the eyewitness accounts of visiting missionaries fanned the flames of discontent back in the Old Country and provoked new waves of emigration.

The Indian treaties of 1851 opened up fresh lands for settlement. By the late 1850s Norwegians were swarming into Iowa and the southern counties of Minnesota. When Minnesota shed its territorial status in 1858 for statehood, it early on established an Immigration Department that employed Norwegian-American journalists to prepare pamphlets for circulation in Norway. This literature praised the exhilarating climate, the beauties of prairie and woodland and lakes, and the potential riches of the new state. Verily, the publicists sang, this was the Land of Canaan, a "glorious new Scandinavia."

In 1862 President Lincoln signed the Homestead Act. After January 1, 1863, any person who was twenty-one years old and was either a citizen or had applied for citizenship could file a claim for a quarter section (160 acres) of land and come into ownership of that land after five years' occupation of it. A claimant need have only fourteen dollars for the filing fee.

The government land offices and transportation packagers spread the word throughout the Scandinavian countries and the urge to emigrate became epidemic. The Norwegian government and church opposed any exodus of its people. Massive leave-takings were a reproach—and a shout to the world that much was wrong in the little kingdom. They also threatened the country with a kind of self-inflicted genocide, since only the strongest and the youngest of its sons and daughters—the perpetuators of the race—would take up the challenge to escape. The antimigrationists pictured America as a land ridden with poisonous snakes, bloodthirsty animals, and dangerously wild men. In a song called "Oleana" they ridiculed Ole Bull, the distinguished Norwegian violinist who had tried to build an ideal community of emigrants in Pennsylvania:

> Salmon hopping from brook to kettle,
>   Cakes that rained out of the heavens,
> And the little roasted piggies
>   That politely asked one to have some ham. . . .

Emigration Fever was called "the most dangerous disease of our time, a bleeding of the Fatherland, a Black Death."

Osten and Henrik Boe (Bö) were two young men who caught the fever. With their parents and three sisters they lived on a tiny *gaard* (farm) near the village of Vang. Vang is in the district of Valders, on the southeastern coast of Norway. Behind it the land sweeps upward steeply into a wide, flat sugarloaf of mountains.

The Boes, like their neighbors, subsisted on a little patch of ground that also had to nourish a cow and a few chickens. Finding enough food for mere survival consumed most of the family's energies. The limited rations of milk, eggs, and potatoes were supplemented only by fish taken from a lake nearby.

In the spring of 1864 Osten and Henrik were twenty-five and twenty-one years old, respectively. Since childhood they had heard the tales of a big open country far across the seas. It is doubtful that word of the Homestead Act had reached their hamlet. It was enough for them to be told of a land where bread and meat were plentiful, where neighbor helped neighbor and there was the chance to breathe and stretch. They had also heard the shocking accounts of the way the red man had slain many of their countrymen in the southern counties of Minnesota. But that uprising had occurred two years earlier and the Indians were peaceful again.

For years the brothers had been saving the trifling sums they were paid for helping local fishermen. Now they had enough put by for the modest fare to take them on their long voyage. A group of Valders folk were setting sail from the port of Drammen and Osten and Henrik would be on that boat.

The brothers were leaving with the blessing of their parents. (Later the daughters were also to go.) The moment of parting must have been painful all around. These farewells were as final as a funeral. Parents and children alike knew they would not lay eyes upon one another again in this world. For the old folks the New World was as fabled and elusive as the lost Atlantis or the Kingdom of Heaven itself. Only the young had any chance of surviving the journey and they would never take that long, long trail back to the Old Country.

One can only imagine that parting. . . .

All morning the parents of emigrating sons have been carrying provisions aboard a sailboat bobbing in the little harbor under a cheerful April sun. Now it is high noon, the boat is loaded, and the captain is eager to set sail.

Osten and Henrik pick up the crude rucksacks that contain all their worldly trappings. The two young Vikings stand sturdy and straight as a brace of Norwegian spruce. Each is as blond as the sun. Osten has a curve of scar on his forehead; it looks like the souvenir of a Heidelberg duel but was actually inscribed by a skate. (In a turn of exhibition skating he had leapt over a horse but the point of one skate stuck in the ice and then flew back to gash him over the right eye.) He walks up the ramp with a slight limp incurred in a skiing accident. Both of these minor imperfections will be with him the rest of his long life.

The sailboat skims across the fjord toward the open sea. It rounds a peninsular cliff and the harbor with the waving parents is lost. Now the old folks must reverse the path back to their village and lonely huts. Fortunately it is spring and the light will hold nearly around the clock until the end of summer. Now, too, is the busiest time, and with fewer hands to help, those left behind will be too burdened to sorrow. The acute sense of loss will not be felt until the long black winter night sets in.

The sailboat hugs the coastline, pitching around those southernmost extremities of land curved like the tip of a tongue. Sweeping off to starboard—fleetingly—is the magnificent fjord-serrated western coast. Then the fjords, the high wooded cliffs, the silvery cascades of waterfall, and finally the long vertebrate of snow-crowned mountains slip away into the mists. The boat becomes a solitary sail on the North Sea.

Later the voyage would bring terror and prayers for God's deliverance. But as Norway fell back from them irrevocably, the voyagers were filled with the anguish of leaving. As one dialect poet of Telemark wrote:

> Farewell now, o valley of Soljord
> Farewell to church and woods and home.
> Farewell to parson and parish clerk,
>   To kith and kin, and the lovely gardens of home.
> Would to God this were undone!
>   For the old home lies there grieving.
> Turn about, hasten, hasten away.

But with this anguish sometimes went expressions of criticism for a fatherland that had failed its neediest. In the words of one peasant bard:

Farewell, thou Mother Norway, now I must leave thee!
  Because thou fostered me,
  I must give thee many thanks.
All too sparing were thee in providing food
  For the throng of thy laborers,
Though thou givest more than enough
  To thy well-schooled sons.

Those who made the crossing by sailboat (steamboats became the usual mode after the late 1860s) spent long wretched weeks on the high seas. Winds were contrary. Storms nearly overturned the vessels time after time and dumped almost enough water inside to sink them. Mold formed on all the rations. The flat bread, or *skriva brod* (a thin-sliced, yellowish-brown bread), dried mutton and ham, *primost* (a brown cheese in cake form made of whey, sugar, and cream), and *gjatost* (goat's cheese) had to be scraped and dried regularly. Seasickness, pneumonia, dysentery, and typhoid fever were common ailments. It was an unusual voyage that didn't have death itself for a fellow traveller. When someone died, the body was wrapped in sails (or a big stone was tied to the feet) and consigned to the ocean.

Each evening the captain of the boat, as devout as all the poor peasants aboard, conducted devotionals. The wooden masts might be creaking and the boat listing dangerously to windward but the good captain would be heard. "We should all be grateful to God," he intoned, "for all His gifts to us, who are so unworthy. We should be grateful to our Lord and Creator that He lets His sun rise on us so many times. It is the Almighty Who decides everything for the best. As long as He gives life and strength, we shall not fear the future. . . ."

The boat carrying Osten and Henrik took eight weeks to arrive in Quebec City. To the brothers it was stranger than a dream, this first breath of the New World. They had never been near a real city before. Why, this Quebec with its bustling waterfront must be as big and busy as Kristiania (today's Oslo) or Bergen! So many people, thousands of them, chattering away in a language you couldn't understand. Such strange people, too! Especially those

black-faced men loading and unloading the boats. Neither teacher
nor pastor had ever told them the world had people with black skins.
Caroline Soliah, who was to meet and marry Osten Boe on the
prairies of western Minnesota, made the voyage from Norway the
following year and she always recalled her terror as a nine-year-
old child seeing those black men on the Quebec waterfront.

The two young men slept on the wharves under the open sky
for two nights. Then they were herded like swine into a canalboat
that took them 150 miles down the St. Lawrence to Montreal. In
Montreal they boarded the immigration car—with its steerage ac-
commodations—of a westward-bound train. Crowded and caged,
they rattled for days through the Canadian forest and across the
breadth of Michigan. At Grand Haven a steamboat took them over
Lake Michigan to Milwaukee. Another train, also equipped with
an immigrant box car—and then wagons—carried them across Wisconsin to the old French fur-trading town of Prairie du Chien and
finally to Decorah, in the northeastern corner of Iowa.

Decorah had been settled a few years earlier by immigrant
Norwegians from Voss, Telemark, Sogn, and Valders. New arrivals
from those districts always found a welcome there. They joined the
households of the earlier immigrants, whose hospitality had no
limits. Here the newcomers got their first real indoctrination into
the ways and possibilities of America. From their hosts they might
pick up a few words of English to help them in any dealings with
Yankee tradesmen or civil servants. Visitors shared the labors of
the family and able-bodied males could usually earn day's wages
working as peripatetic hired hands. It was a marking-time inter-
lude in a kind of staging area that gave the emigrant a chance to
get his bearings and to plan his next move.

Osten and Henrik soon became restless in the Decorah settlement. They were too late for it. It was a little too formed, too
picked over. Stories of a newer colony of Norwegians had been
reaching their ears. These most recent emigrants were settling the
village of Northfield, in the new state of Minnesota.

Eager to break fresh ground, the brothers quit Decorah one
day in the late spring of 1865 and began the northwesterly trek
of 150 miles to Northfield. They traveled the entire distance on
foot. For Henrik it would be the end of the journey. For the sixty-

odd remaining years of his life, Northfield was home. There he prospered as a hardware merchant. There he married, established a home, and fathered three children who all entered professions. And there, one day in 1876, he was eyewitness to the hair-raising robbery of the Northfield bank by the Jesse James gang.

The charms of the pleasant little Norwegian-American community wore thin on Osten. Village life lacked something vital. He dreamed of land . . . of a plot of ground he could call his own, of taming it, growing things on it. He listened intently to the tales of homesteading to the north and west, of rich farmland in an open country.

One April day in 1868, when the snow was off the ground at last, he set off on foot for St. Cloud. To reach this little town on the Mississippi River he followed oxcart trails in a north-by-north-westerly direction. It took him nine days to hike the 125 miles of rough terrain. As a prospective homesteader he went to the government land office in St. Cloud, where he was shown maps of surveyed areas. Now he must decide where he wanted to settle and go to inspect the quarter sections in that area that were available for claim. When he came back and paid his filing fee, the land he had chosen would be registered in his name. Six months later he could take possession of his land. If he never left it for five years, he could have a deed to the land.

Osten chose the township of Aastad, Minnesota, because it was the farthest point out of the immigrant thrust in 1868. Only two settlers had filed claims there and no land had been broken beyond it. Aastad lies some 135 miles north and west of St. Cloud. It measures 6 miles square with 36 sections of 640 acres each. Its soil is rich black alluvial loam. The township is a gently rolling prairie punctuated with marshes, creeks, thickets, and thirty clear lakes. Its western edge flattens out and sweeps into the rich valley of the Red River of the North.

The Great Northern and Northern Pacific railroads had not put down their tracks yet. It would be a decade before those caravans of prairie schooners would come creeping like a fleet through the endless sea of green and golden grasses, their canvas tops gleaming brightly in the shimmering light. There was only the old Red River oxcart trail, the St. Paul-Pembina artery of a diminished fur-trading industry. The landscape was a trackless wilderness, immense, beautiful, uncluttered.

Again Osten is on foot. The rucksack and quilt are strapped to his back and he carries an axe to clear the jungle of undergrowth, the snarls of hazel and plum brush and vines. The air is filter-pure and the sky as blue as if it had just been scoured and painted. He passes forests primeval and lakelets and sloughs that hold a mirror to the sky, mounds and relics of prehistoric people, wild roses entwining with the grasses in a thick carpet. As he walks through the deserted land the spirits of antiquity seem to keep him company. His trail takes him closer and closer to the geographical heart of this vast continent, past the point where there is any tree, house, or living creature to break the terrain. The cathedral-like silence deepens as the path bears westward. At night he lies down with the vaulted heavens for a roof overhead. The moon swings above the landscape in solemn grandeur and the North Star is his guiding light. Finally, one sweet morning in May, there is *his* prairie . . . billowing into slopes, rising in low hills, then leveling off to sink into the interminable plain.

This last, roughest segment of his four-hundred-mile hike from Decorah has taken a fortnight of hard pushing. Now Osten is home —at last. But for him the end of the emigrant journey is only the beginning of the immigrant pioneer ordeal.

In the nineteenth century and the early decades of the twentieth century a million Norwegians emigrated to America. Most of them followed in the tracks of Osten and Henrik, pressing westward. (To immigrants, as Archibald MacLeish has remarked, America was "the west and the winds blowing.") When the valley of the Red River of the North was settled, it had the largest concentration of Norwegians outside of Norway. Its great bonanza farms began to harvest millions of bushels of wheat annually and it became known as the Breadbasket of the World.

The wonder is not that so many of these first settlers succumbed, but that so many survived. A partial catalogue of the trials that beset them would show such entries as grasshopper plagues, blizzards, long Arctic winters, stupefyingly hot shadeless summers, prairie fires, earthquakes, cyclones, tornadoes, electrical storms, the devastation of blackbirds and gophers and the chinch bug, hail storms, torrential rains that turned the grain to rot, poor seed and ignorance of good farming practices, oxen running wild, horses and cattle driven insane by mosquitoes, nerve-shattering winds, droughts, crop failures, money panic ("Need brings dogs into bondage," said the bankers), lost or stolen livestock, stem rust in the spring wheat, the constant threat of attack by Indians, killing strikes by pneumonia and influenza and tuberculosis and black diphtheria and typhoid fever, death by freezing, back-breaking labor without end, and the aching loneliness.

For many, the challenge exceeded the limits of human endurance. Perhaps of all the groups who became Americans only our black brothers—those involuntary immigrants who were brought here in chains—were more sorely tested. Many who could not endure the life simply lay down and died. Others took their own lives. (My grandparents and their neighbors could swap horror tales of going into their barns and finding strangers hanging from the hayloft.) Still others found the release of madness.

But those who neither perished, nor committed suicide nor went mad achieved a kind of indestructibility. They lived on and on and on, many of them into their tenth decade and beyond, active, alert, and cheerful. They truly believed it was God's will that had kept them alive so long and that it would have been profane to be idle or to have wished for an earlier grave.

Not long ago a pair of old settlers who had homesteaded in Otter Tail County celebrated their eightieth wedding anniversary. They were 105 and 102 years old. To the best of all available records, they had been married longer than any other couple in the history of the United States.

The first child born on the Aastad prairie recently granted the *Fergus Falls Daily Journal* an interview. She was ninety-six years old at the time and still presiding over her home. Nothing that the reporter could ask her, nothing in the flow of reminiscences that the question unleashed, could distract the sprightly little lady from the fact that she had a cake in the oven. Three times in the course of the interview she went to the kitchen to check on its progress.

Osten stood on the treeless prairie. The buffalo grasses brushed against the calves of his legs. The plain was so wide that the rim of the heavens cut down on it in a 360-degree circle. He might have wished for some woodlands to remind him of home. But this land was *his* and it would always have a value beyond any riches it might yield. Possession of land made him one with the Norse chieftains. Land had dignity and stability. It stood for the permanence of family and it was something that could be handed down through the centuries.

First he must have a roof over his head. There was only one ripple in the terrain. Into the tough sod he plunged his axe. He hacked out pieces of earth a foot or so wide and began piling these on top of one another to make his dugout in the side of the hillock. It was a one-room sod hut, a home built of dirt, literally a hole in the ground. The walls were dirt, the roof was dirt, and the floor beneath him was dirt. Time brought a few refinements. Tamarack poles supported the roof. Rough windows and doors were cut in the sod walls. Clay steps led to the entrance. The walls, after several years, were boarded up and whitewashed and a floor was put in.

The furnishings were primitive. For sleeping there were mattresses of straw and the used straw was taken out regularly and burned. Benches for eating were made of logs split in half, their legs fastened on with wooden pegs. There was a table and eventually a cupboard with shelves and an open hearth.

Osten lived in this earth house for ten years. Then he built a one-room log house and three years later a large frame house. To the sod hut he brought his bride, the spirited seventeen-year-old girl he had met at Sunday services in a neighbor's granary during his fourth summer on the prairie. Here four of his nine children were born—and died: two in infancy, and two young daughters who, as victims of the dreaded black diphtheria, choked to death in his arms.

In winter blizzards the snow often packed against the door and drifted over the roof, imprisoning the family for days. In the spring, before there were floors, the earth beneath them would give a jar, then another jar, and gophers and garter snakes would surface to share their humble quarters.

When he looked back on that experience, Osten's fondest memories of that first home in the new country were of the winter nights when he lay warm under Caroline's patchwork quilts. A candle burned in the hollowed-out turnip and the hearth ablaze with cow dung gave off the most beautiful colors. Lying there awake he'd gaze out through the wooded slats at the moonlight putting its dazzling shine on the boundless white sea of crusted snow.

So simple were the earliest tools of the prairie that the Egyptian farmers of two thousand years ago would have been quite at home there.

In the custom of penniless immigrants, Osten helped his neighbors for two years before touching his own quarter section. The few dollars earned bought a team of oxen. By giving a neighbor another helping hand, he was able to borrow a one-bottom walking plow. The sod was extremely tough of fiber and fought hard against uprooting. Yielding finally, it gleamed and glistened under the summer sun, a rich black substance that promised great fertility.

His first growing season Osten seeded five acres of wheat. The grain was sown broadcast by hand and when it was mature it was cut with a scythe. When it was bound he carried it by wagon fifty miles over the roadless void to Alexandria, where the nearest grist mill was. The journey took three days each way and at night he slept in the wagon. In Alexandria the "liquid gold" turned into flour, which he bartered for food staples, items of clothing, and a couple of crude farming tools.

The next season he plowed and planted a few more acres. And so the process continued in successive years. The new acres were put to barley, oats, rye, clover, flax, and potatoes as well as wheat. Summers, when the grain was growing, Osten—walking with a wagon—would make several trips to Ten Mile Lake to cut down trees that would be hauled back to build the log barn, to be planked for fences, and to be used for fuel. These trips took a day of travel each way and a day to fell the trees.

After he had prospered beyond the bartering stage, Osten sold his wheat to elevator operators who shipped it to the flourishing new flour mills in Minneapolis. When he acquired cows, butter was churned on the farm and shaped into pound slabs that were stamped with lovely flowered figures made from a wood press. These were sold to the creamery in town.

Threshing machines, reapers, binders, separators, and other laborsaving implements came along. But for Osten and his fellow homesteaders the farming life remained an unremitting burden from dawn to darkness. Always there were the farmerly chores of plowing, seeding, cultivating, harvesting, threshing, binding, milking, building fences and planting trees, feeding and doctoring the livestock, horses, and oxen.

But a farmer like Osten had to wear many other hats. He had to be carpenter enough to build his own home and furniture, sleds, skis, ox yokes, and harrows. He had to be something of a cobbler to make and repair the family's shoes and boots. And he must hunt and fish—not recreationally, as a sportsman, but from need to fatten the family larder. (Long before tall "fish stories" became an entertainment, Osten, who was as incapable of an exaggeration as of a lie, would tell about going to the slough on the edge of his property and pulling up messes of pike and pickerel by the pitchfork.)

In later years Grandma Caroline spent long hours in quite advanced crocheting, embroidering, and crewel work. Watching the needle flicking away, I'd sometimes tease her, "Grandma, I guess you've always had it easy, haven't you? Even back on the farm?" The fun of it was her serious denial. "Oh, no. Surely I was busy."

Surely she was busy, indeed. Besides feeding five children and a husband three meals a day and morning and afternoon "lunches," she spun yarn, wove cloth, sewed and darned and knitted and patched the family's wardrobe, made rugs and bedding, washed and ironed, kept the home sparkling clean, tended the orchard, put up preserves and dried fruits, took care of the chickens, often did the milking, churned the butter, baked, and made the candles (by dipping a wick of twisted cord into melted tallow) and soap (from ashes and greases and lye). Then, too, vast reservoirs of energy—and time—always had to be allocated to treating her children's ailments and superintending their religious training.

With all their industry and persistence, many homesteaders like Osten and Caroline were rather accidental farmers. They knew so little about what they were doing. Help from sources like agricultural extension colleges was decades away. Their only strategy was trial and error. They did not learn about crop rotation, for instance, until their soil was nearly exhausted. They were blessed with some of the richest farm land in the world, but what they had gained in natural resources was so frequently offset by disasters they could neither predict nor control. . . .

They came like dive bombers out of the west. They came by the millions with the rustle of their wings roaring overhead. They came in waves, like the rolls of the sea, descending with a terrifying speed, breaking now and again like a mighty surf. They came with the force of a williwaw and they formed a huge, ominous, dark brown cloud that eclipsed the sun. They dipped and touched earth, hitting objects and people like hailstones. But they were not hail. These were *live* demons. They popped, snapped, crackled, and roared. They were dark brown, an inch or longer in length, plump in the middle and tapered at the ends. They had transparent wings, slender legs, and two black eyes that flashed with a fierce intelligence.

So came the grasshoppers, like one of the seven plagues of Egypt, and the devastation they wrought was homeric.

Blanketing the ground like snow, they devoured everything in sight but the implements in the fields. They ate every blade of grass, every stalk of grain, the roots of vegetables, the bark on the trees, the clothes on the line, the hickory handles on forks, even leather saddles and boots. Boys who went barefoot and barelegged had their feet and legs eaten raw.

The hoppers left only the holes in the ground. Before calling it a season they seeded the plowed fields with tiny eggs that looked like a fine, dry sawdust, laying enough of them to pollute a continent. Next summer a fresh invasion ravaged the countryside. And the summer after that.

Osten and his neighbors set up smudge pots. They put coal tar on sheet iron. Two men would walk through the fields holding either end of a long stick scooping the hoppers into burlap sacks held open by a wooden barrel hoop. Bounties were paid according

to weight. But the hoppers—which were really Rocky Mountain
locusts—were seemingly as unconquerable as the cockroaches that
infest urban dwellings today. Osten remembered that they were so
thick in the wagon ruts that the juice from their crushed bodies
would run in streams down the wagon tires. Only chickens and
ducks could eat them, but a diet of hoppers turned the yolks of
eggs red and gave the eggs such a strong taste they were nearly
inedible.

So critical was the situation that Governor Pillsbury proclaimed a day of prayer in April of 1878. The next day, as history
still records, a polar wave struck and froze every grasshopper in the
state stiff. And no replacements ever flew in.

The devout, among them my grandparents, always cited this
as irrefutable proof of the power of prayer.

Inside the dugout Osten heard the raging wind. The howl and
whine terrified his young wife and set their infant daughter to
screaming. In its fury he could see it driving waves of snow across
the fields. He knew what was happening and he knew that before
it got any worse he must somehow find his way to the barn and milk
the cows.

The barn was no more than fifty yards from the dugout. But so
great were the clouds of driving snow that he could not dimly locate
it. In fact, he could scarcely see his hand in front of him. He took a
coil of rope from inside, fastened one end of it to the door, and began
walking in the direction of the barn. If he could just hold onto the
rope, he would be able to retrace his steps to the hut.

The foaming, fuming storm blasted him off his feet again and
again. The snow stabbed his face like icy needles and slashed his
clothing with the force of nails. He wandered for hours, losing all
sense of time, before finding the barn. Then it took all the strength
of his mighty arms to open the door against that maniacal wind.

Osten was trapped in the barn for three days and three nights.
The wind howled across the open plain at seventy-five miles per
hour and the temperature dropped to forty degrees below zero. He
drank the milk from the cows and jumped up and down and beat
himself to keep from freezing to death. There were times, he con-

fessed later, when he thought how nice it would be if he could bring himself to kill the animals and wrap himself up in their skins.

Such were his memories of the Great Blizzard of 1876.

The cold was always an overpowering fact of life, as inevitable as the coming of those long, gray, sunless, skyless days of winter itself. It still is. But nowadays there are ways of sidestepping it (Hawaii and Arizona being two popular options among the natives). The snow often comes in early October and keeps falling sometimes until May. There can be a month of days when the thermometer never makes it up to the freezing mark, while plummeting to thirty-five or forty below at night.

The cold dominates my father's earliest recollections of life on the farm and school. It was always dark when he got up and made his way with a kerosene lantern to the barn to help with chores. Sometimes he put on two suits of long underwear, two flannel shirts, two pairs of pants, a vest, a heavy coat, and two or three pairs of woolen mittens. Even so, it was impossible to keep warm. He walked the mile or so, sometimes through deep drifts, to the one-room schoolhouse, slapping his hands and jumping in place. But frequently his fingers and toes were frozen on arrival, and a good part of the school day would be spent thawing them by rubbing them with snow and ice water.

Dad recalls being trapped in the school overnight by a blizzard and that the teacher and children chopped up the pine desks and benches and burned them to keep warm. As the flames lowered, they threw in all their books to keep the fire going.

The snow fell and fell and fell, piling up to the top of the roof so that all that was visible in this great universe of whiteness was the smoking chimney. The breath hung frozen in the air and skin that touched an iron implement would be ripped off. Livestock and horses lost during a blizzard were not found until the spring thaw uncovered their frozen corpses. When Osten and Caroline's daughters died of black diphtheria, they were buried in the snow and not brought to their permanent gaves until spring softened the earth again.

The spring thaw, when it came, often flooded the fields like a reenactment of the biblical rain of forty days and forty nights.

Nothing sustained the tension in life like the threat of the "fairen," or prairie fire. It struck usually in the autumn, when the grasses were dry. Anything could set it off—a hunter dropping a match, a bolt of lightning, even a spark from a chimney or passing train. Fanned by a good breeze, it became a holocaust. It blazed across the countryside, scorching hay, fences, cattle, poultry, clothing, faces, bodies, homes. The flames leaped ten and twelve feet high. They painted the sky red and sped across the horizon like a race horse. The roar of the fire sounded like an express train or the thundering of an angry Thor.

When Osten and his neighbors had frame houses to protect, they plowed a series of furrows around their homes as a firebreak. The furrows were broken some yards apart and the grasses between them were burned to keep the fire away. Further afield they fought the fires with wet grain sacks, flailing away rather futilely at the speeding monster.

Burns, frostbites, diseases, and all other ailments were treated with home remedies. These *landnamsmen* and their families survived without doctors. They had no alternative. Doctors did not exist in that part of the country in those days. Later, when they were available, my grandparents and their children still seemed to get along without them very well. To this day my father, a robust seventy-seven year old, thinks doctors should be visited only in time of real emergency, as with a broken leg or an attack of smallpox. Live right, keep moving, and stop thinking there's anything wrong with you, according to Dad, and you won't need to be running to doctors' offices.

Children of those early settlers even got themselves born without a doctor's helping hand. The women all took turns serving one another as midwives, and they seemed to have remarkable antennae for detecting when an expectant mother's time was nigh.

All nine of Grandma Caroline's children were delivered with the help of midwives.

The nearest thing to a doctor was the itinerant "medicine man" who traveled from farm to farm with a line of salves, oils, "inhalers" for catarrh, liniments, and other health aids. He traveled his route with wagon and horse and made the rounds about once a month when the weather was good. His arrival always created excitement because he was not only company but a glamorous stranger who came from far beyond the horizon. In the practice of frontier hospitality he was always given supper and shelter for the night.

Dad has vivid memories of Naftalin, a Jewish peddler, whose grandnephew was a recent mayor of Minneapolis. Besides "medical" supplies, Naftalin's wagon was loaded with objects of fascination such as combs, shoelaces, handkerchiefs, reading glasses, pocket knives, and mouth organs. When supper was over, Naftalin entertained the family with a mouth organ recital.

Grandma had quite fixed notions of how to deal with common complaints. Goose grease was rubbed on the neck and chest for sore throats and chest congestion and a wool cloth was wrapped around the greased areas to induce heat. Severe chest colds called for a rubdown with skunk oil. Carbuncles and boils got treated with poultices of sweet cream and flour or of dried bread that was crumbled, softened, and mixed with sweet milk and crushed herb leaves. Ginger tea was drunk "to bring out" measles and a multi-herbal tea was administered for "building blood" and curing flu. Castor oil was taken for stomachaches, constipation, and cleaning out the system.

Dentistry was as unknown as medicine. To ease the pain of an exposed nerve, a tiny wad of cotton saturated with strong liniment was rubbed on the cheek and put near the infected area. When teeth became badly infected, they were yanked out, usually with a shoemaker's or carpenter's pincers.

In the wake of a good rain mosquitoes arrived by the millions. Grandma always applied sweet cream to relieve the itching and bandaged badly bitten arms and legs.

Suffering was borne with remarkable fortitude. This might in part be attributed to the fatalism of the Norse mind. But it more reflected the conviction that everything that happened in this world was in accordance with the will of God. To complain would be to invite the wrath of the Lord, who would send a punishment that would really be something to complain about.

The settlements were all homogeneous and self-contained. The immigrant invasion of that part of the country was overwhelmingly Scandinavian, but the separate components of Scandinavia did not become a melting pot in the New World. A township like Aastad remained exclusively Norwegian. The Swedes and Danes and Finns kept to themselves in communities that had names like Swedish Grove and Dane Prairie and Finlandia. The different groups could have made themselves understood to one another and might have found they had much in common. But these exchanges did not occur.

Even those first settlers who eventually left their farms to live in town—as did my grandparents after thirty-four years—managed to reestablish this separateness in a new community. The county seat, Fergus Falls, in the early 1900s was a polyglot village of Poles, Germans, Irish, Scotsmen, New England Yankees, and Dutch, as well as Scandinavians. But the various Scandinavian populations touched no other group but themselves. Each had its own Lutheran churches, newspapers, and social fraternities, with little or no cross-pollination. My grandfather and my grandmother lived more than sixty and eighty years, respectively, in this country, but there's no evidence they had more than glancing contact with anyone who was not Norwegian.

Ironically, the most contact my grandparents had with non-Norwegians was with the Chippewa Indians. Grandma, especially, was not fond of the Indians, but it had nothing to do with the pigmentation of their skin. An old Indian trail meandered close to the edge of their fields and during summers nomadic Chippewas wandering across the prairie would lay themselves down to sleep near the barn or even pitch a skin tent beside the slough, with half-naked children dancing around the evening fire.

They were a peaceful people, but Grandma would be terrified to hear them creeping up behind her when she was busy at the kitchen stove. Always they asked for pancakes and coffee. Grandma did not begrudge them the food and drink they begged. But trespassing on other people's property! Stealing into homes without knocking! Once it was pointed out to Grandma that these were minor impertinences compared with what the white man had done —and was still doing—to the red man. But Grandma was having none of this argument. She had not contributed to any ill treatment of Indians. Right was right. And that was that.

But the Indians got off lightly compared with the Swedes. How Grandma could have formed her impressions of the Swedes is difficult to imagine, because to the best of our knowledge she had never known a Swede in her life. Nonetheless, her warning could not have been firmer: never trust a Swede. At this remove it is impossible to recall any of her exact quotes on the subject. But the essence of her counsel was that the Swedes were a strange, cold, selfish, sneaky lot and that any contact with them could only have unhappy consequences.

Had Grandma been the only one with an anti-Swedish bias, it could have been dismissed as a personal idiosyncracy. But the prejudice was general. I remember walking in Fergus Falls one day with my uncle and stopping to talk with a man who served with him on the hospital's board of directors. At some point in the conversation the man good-naturedly remarked, "The trouble with you Swedes—." Reddening, my uncle interrupted, "Please don't call us Swedes."

When the Nazis invaded Norway at the beginning of World War II, the Norwegian community was stunned and outraged. It soon became apparent that Sweden had no intention of compromising its cool neutrality to come to the aid of her neighbor and the wrath of the Norwegians fixed as much on the Swedes as on the occupying enemy.

Grandma accepted the fact of Swedish noninvolvement with resignation. She closed her eyes and shook her head knowingly. What else, after all, could you expect from the Swedes?

In the midst of excruciating hardship, Osten and Caroline could see God's blessings all around them. When drought or hail or prairie fire or insect war had taken the food out of their mouths, they could still articulate the twenty-third Psalm and believe it. "The Lord is my shepherd, I shall not want. . . ." Even when poverty, disease, or death overtook them, they could see divine purpose being fulfilled. They must thank God, for God governed best. He sent them suffering and tribulations only to test their faith.

Their faith was their abiding comfort, and that faith alone enabled them to endure the perversities of fate. This time on earth was but a preparation for the heavenly home which would be their eternal abode. While they struggled through this mortal phase, a welcome was being prepared for their arrival in heaven. Ultimately they would assemble with God in the eternal mansion, where they would find everlasting joy and contentment in beholding God's face.

In the years before the first church was built, the little colony of settlers gathered each Sunday in one another's dugouts. The host would read a passage from the Bible and give his interpretation of it. Then there would be prayers and hymns. When the group came to my grandparents' hut, there was always the singing of Osten and Caroline's favorite hymn, "Den Store Kvede Flok" ("The Big White Flock," signifying angels).

As years passed, the growing community had the services of a *klokker*. The *klokker* was not an ordained minister but a kind of peddler of spiritual wares who carried the Good Word from farm to farm. He knew the Bible, he could give sermons, and he had the authority to baptize.

The coming of the *klokker* was a great event. This was God's emissary on earth. Nothing was too good for him. The devoutness and hospitality of the family must shine forth so that God would receive a good report of them. They might be living on *grot* (a mixture of flour and water) and eggs, but one of the laying chickens must be killed to feed the *klokker*. Taking his leave, he would often say, "I'll be at your house next Friday if not Providentially detained." The coy reference suggested that at any moment God might see fit to recall him for some heavenly mission. But the *klokker's* gift for survival on this planet proved quite as remarkable as that of his flock's.

The church, when it was built, was like an oasis in the desert. All week long Osten and Caroline and their neighbors were sustained by the thought of Sunday, when they would travel three

miles to gather in the little wooden structure and hear the Word
of God proclaimed. Nobody ever felt "not up to" attending these
services and no inclemency of weather could deter anybody. In sub-
zero temperatures, with the wind lashing against their faces and
driven snow blinding the vision, they crossed the countryside by
open sleigh to perform their sacred duty. In the church they sat en-
thralled for two hours or more while God's spokesman described the
rosy hereafter that awaited the pious, and, in even more vivid detail, the fires of hell that would consume infidels and transgressors.

Grandpa was in his eighties when I was born. My memories of
him are dim but they mostly seem to involve religion. For much of
his waking time in those last years he studied the Bible and his
hus postil, which was a book of sermons and devotionals. He also
read every word of the *Decorah-Posten*, a Norwegian-language
daily which is still being published, and the *Ugeblad*, a local
weekly. Both these publications ran prayers and inspirational essays and news of the Norwegian Synod of the Lutheran Church.

At family dinners it was the custom for the youngest to give the
blessing for the food. For a while I was the youngest grandchild and
in my five-year-old mind I'm sure I thought I had found one all-
purpose grace that would see me through all those family dinners.
It went:

> God is great, God is good.
>   We will thank Him for this food.
> By His hand we all get fed,
>   Give us Lord our daily bread.

Grandpa suffered this grace a few times before taking up the matter
with my mother one Sunday. "Doesn't he ever learn any other
blessings? he asked. The tone of reproof was not lost on Mother,
who saw to it that I learned some new ones.

Mother herself had discovered early on just where Grandpa's
values lay. Not long after she and Dad were married, Grandpa
summoned the family to a conference in his home. He indicated
that he had important business to discuss and no one should be
absent. Mother assumed it could only mean that the children were
about to receive some portion of their inheritance. Like most young

newlyweds, she and Dad could have used any financial help that came their way.

Indeed, when the family was assembled around the dining room table, Grandpa said he had a special gift for each of them. Then, with all the majesty of a feudal lord dispensing parcels of a fiefdom to deserving vassals, he handed out copies of a paperbound book he had bought through a mailorder house. The title of the book was *All Through Grace*. Across the span of nearly half a century, Mother can still savor the disappointment that nearly reduced her to tears. She never opened her copy of *All Through Grace*.

Religious fervor coalesced with social hunger. These first immigrants were starved for companionship. Neighbor was separated from neighbor by too much space and the workday was too consuming to allow for visits back and forth. But Sundays all the community met at church and after services were over no one was in a hurry to start home. In nice weather the congregation lingered for hours on the grounds, socializing and sharing with one another the food each family had brought. In winter if a blizzard should trap them in the unheated church overnight, it was an adventure rather than a catastrophe. They had their devotion, their singing, and their fellowship, after all, to keep them warm.

Otherwise only a funeral could break the week-long isolation. There were those who even attended funerals in churches outside the township, where they mourned the deaths of people they had never known in life. To some this might suggest a morbid streak in their natures, but a more plausible explanation was that funerals promised human contact. After the deceased was put to rest, the mourners moved from the graveside to the survivors' home where there would be refreshments and conversation, however subdued.

In the time of harvest everyone came together to give one another a helping hand. One day they would all be at Hans's farm and the next at Eric's and then Olaf's. While the men were busy in the fields, the women chatted over their sewing and quilting and crocheting. The men hunted and fished together to fatten the provender. As time went on, and there were additional hands around the farm to help with the work, there might be an occasional berry-picking expedition in summer or a brilliant winter day that would inspire a cross-country skiing jaunt to a neighbor's house or a skating party on the slough. May 17 was Norwegian Independence Day, a holiday always commemorated with folk songs and dances and feasting.

But the seventeen days of Christmas was the time of the year that brought everyone together in sustained revelry. All work came to a halt except for such inescapable chores as milking the cows and feeding the animals and chickens. Neighbors visited back and forth in a kind of festival of open houses. A major feature of these celebrations was the practice of *Yulebooking*, which translates as "Christmas fooling." Adults and children alike tried to disguise themselves in strange-looking odds and ends of clothing and homemade masks. Then they'd present themselves at their neighbors' houses and it would be up to their hosts to guess who in the world these visitors could be.

Thomas Sajord was an immigrant born in the same hamlet in Norway as my grandfather. He came to America in 1870 and worked as a farm hand for a time before becoming a private secretary to a United States senator. In 1899, from Washington, he wrote an open letter to the *St. Paul Pioneer Press* which was addressed to the Valderses (people from the district of Valders in Norway) of the Twin Cities. "Couldn't these good people have a reunion some time this spring?" he asked. "These good people" welcomed the idea. In June of that year a reunion was held in Minneapolis at which there were songs and speeches, feasting and games, and much informal visiting among long-separated fellow clansmen. This was the beginning of the Valders Lag and the entire *lag* movement.

The Valderses met again the next year and in 1901 a permanent society called the Valdris Samband was organized. Natives of other districts began similar organizations. Andrew Veblen, a professor of physics at the University of Iowa, became the first president of the Valdris Samband. In his *Valders Book* he characterized the *lags* as "for auld lang syne societies." But they were more than that. Over the years they published thousands of pages of biographical and historical material about their members and origins and they collected charitable and memorial gifts to be given to their ancestral community.

When the Valders Lag was held in our town, my grandfather's house—like the houses of the other local Valderses—would be open to Lag members who came from other parts of the state, Iowa, or the Dakotas. Nobody ever had to stay at a hotel. The same was true wherever this *lag* or any of the other *lags* were held.

Today the *lags* are fading from the scene. Their founders are dead and so are most of their children. Succeeding generations, for the most part, have never bothered to learn the language and simply do not have that much interest in perpetuating their ties to the Old Country.

It was the church that provided most of the opportunities for social outlets. There were, however, purely fraternal organizations, such as the Sons of Norway. A story, perhaps apocryphal, is told of the troubles one community had in getting a Sons of Norway chapter started. Supposedly the charter ruled that it was necessary to have one hundred members signed up before a chapter could be formed. This community had ninety-nine candidates pledged. Everybody hunted and hunted for that hundredth Norwegian that would put them in business. But he couldn't be found. It remained for an Irishman to supply the solution. "Why not take the ninety-nine Norwegians," he suggested, "and add one Swede and just change the name to Sons of Bitches?"

However these people got together, it was always without the social lubricant of drink. They were rigidly opposed to the use of alcohol for any purpose whatsoever. It's a safe speculation that my grandparents—and everybody they knew—went to their graves without a drop of hard liquor ever having moistened their lips. If a doctor had prescribed whiskey to alleviate some pain or affliction, they would have ignored the prescription and suffered in silence.

The evils of drink were promulgated, of course, from the pulpit. But why had the clergy fixed on this one transgression to underscore so emphatically? The Bible warns against drunkenness, among other sins of excess. But it also extols the salubrious effects of wine taken in moderation and it makes clear that the fermented juice of the grape flowed at the marriage at Cana and many another occasion. But these men of the cloth could not be softened by such references. Many of them, ironically, were grossly overweight because they were always ready to eat when food was set before them, and this could be many times a day in making their rounds. But it didn't seem to occur to them that they were guilty of gluttony, another sin deplored in the Good Book.

According to an old Christmas custom in Norway, the lady of the house gave wine to each member of the family Christmas morning while everyone was still in bed. For this ceremony my grandmother used chokecherry wine made from berries gathered on the farm. The amount of wine each of us received was a mere soupçon—as symbolic as the taking of Communion—and hardly enough to relax the central nervous system of an ant. A bottle of wine in Grandma's house lasted longer than the bottle of vermouth of someone who drinks his martinis very, very dry.

Just before my father went off to World War I, he daringly brought home a case of beer from the local brewery and invited Grandpa to drink a farewell bottle with him. To his surprise, Grandpa accepted. "And I'll have another one with you when you come back," said Grandpa. But probably nothing short of sending a son off to foreign battlefields could have persuaded him to down anything as heady as even that insipid local beer.

There was one member of the family who did like his drop. But excuses were made for him. During a prairie fire he had risked his life to save some newly born calves from a burning barn. He carried to the grave the scars of his bravery. And being both a man of God and a man of substance, Uncle Eric could be forgiven if he sometimes refreshed himself from the bottles he kept up in the attic.

As a young bride my mother was unwittingly introduced to one of those bottles during a family picnic. A bee had stung her and she was crying from the pain. Uncle Eric was the one who had something more than sympathy to offer. "Come with me, little girl," he said, "I've got some special medicine for bee sting." He took her up to the attic. There on a long table was a row of decanters apparently containing magic elixirs for the cure of various afflictions. Each had a different label: Croup, Catarrh, Summer Complaint, Appendicitis, Gallopping Consumption, Gout, etc.

From the decanter labeled Bee Sting Uncle Eric poured a

generous dosage of the "medicine" into a glass of lemonade he had carried upstairs and told her to drink it slowly.

Mother immediately began to feel better and soon she was telling Uncle Eric what a wonderful time she was having. She says she was never afraid of being stung again by a bee at Uncle Eric's, remembering how pleasurable could be the cure.

The groaning board known as the smorgasbord came long after the early prairie years. In the beginning the immigrants had simple, monotonous diets. They ate whatever they could raise or catch or maybe barter in exchange for a hogshead of flour. Early menus featured bread, oatmeal, smoked fish and fish soups, cheeses like *primost* and *gjatost,* pemmican (dried meat mashed into a paste with fat), buttermilk, sour milk on boiled potatoes, and *spky kjot*—the shavings off a leg of lamb or beef that had been dried and smoked and were almost too tough a challenge for a regular knife.

In season game was plentiful, as there were always quail and pheasants and prairie chickens to be flushed out of the long grasses and ducks in the slough. On special occasions there was (and still is) *lutefisk,* a dried cod whose odor in the cooking has sent strong men fleeing from the house. When a family could afford to eat into its capital, so to speak, a chicken was killed or a hog or a cow was butchered for home consumption. Two meat specialties were *lub,* a blood sausage, and *rulapulsa,* a meat roll made of beef flank stuffed with pork steak and usually sliced cold. Dried apricots and prunes and apples formed the basis of the fruit soups so dear to the palates of all Scandinavians. Lingonberries and herring, two other staples of the Norwegian diet, were imported from the Old Country. Lingonberries were bought by the barrel.

By modern nutritional standards, the immigrant diet was "heavy" and deficient in key vitamins and minerals. Meat and potatoes became the essential table. Cream, butter, and milk high in dairy fat content were consumed daily in large quantities, but nobody had heard of cholesterol counts and nobody ever seemed to die from hardening of the arteries. Orange juice, leafy green vegetables, and salads were unknown to my grandparents.

In common with most people who abstain from alcohol, each of my grandparents developed a prominent sweet tooth. When she could afford the time and a few conveniences, Grandma developed into an accomplished bread and pastry chef. Some of the confections that came from her kitchen—such as the delicate rosettes with their topping of Devonshire-thick cream and lingonberries and her *Krumkage* and *Berliner Kranser* —can't be found anywhere today. Her *flot brod* was renowned. So was her *lefse,* a potato-flour pastry which is eaten half-raw and speaks eloquently for the sturdiness of the Norwegian digestive system.

It was said of Grandma that she kept things so clean you could eat off her floors. It's been said of others, of course. But it was said of her even when her floor was the smooth earth of the dugout.

Cleanliness was a virtue held in high esteem by all her contemporaries. It ranked just behind godliness, where the Bible had placed it. "Cleanliness is next to godliness. . . ." For them it was a virtue unto itself, unrelated to hygiene. The Scriptures recommended it and that was sufficient reason to practice it.

Some higher judge will have to rate Grandma on her godliness. But with cleanliness, it was almost possible to root for the dirt, so uneven was the contest. "Everything should be so clean," she often said, "that the king could come and visit and there would be no room for shame." (Grandma never entirely adapted to the sea change that had borne her from a monarchy to a republic.)

On the farm no domestic chore took precedence over her making of the soap. She scrubbed and scrubbed at everything. When each object and surface in the house had been scoured, she went outside and scrubbed down the cows with a brush. She said this was a practice brought over from the Old Country but many thought she invented it. She had different skirts for scrubbing, dusting, and cooking and these she'd change during the course of the day as she moved from one task to the next. Whatever else she might be doing, the dust cloth was rarely out of her sight.

Grandma spent the last years of her life in a house that was far too big for one person. She was on everybody's mind, but there didn't seem to be any solution to the problem. She was determined

to hold her ground and not move in with any member of the family.
Hiring a housekeeper to live with her was out of the question because of Grandma's standards of immaculateness. Several attempts
were made to install a married couple in an upstairs apartment
who would live there rent free in exchange for keeping an eye on
Grandma. But the lodgers had barely unpacked their bags before
the family began hearing reports of untidiness and accumulating
filth.

I was last in Minnesota for any extended time in the spring
of 1946. I had just come out of the army and was catching my
breath before going back to college in the East. Grandma was in
her ninetieth year then and still in charge. But we worried about
her, especially her being alone at night. It was decided, as a makeshift solution for those weeks while I was at home, that I would
sleep at her house.

For the first night's vigil I came armed with what I thought
were newsy tidbits that would interest her. I would tell her about
meeting her pastor on the street, how Mother's flowers were progressing, and the results of Dad's fishing trip. But Grandma's attention was hard to hold. We sat in the living room and the inevitable dust cloth was in her hand. In mid-sentence I would be deserted by Grandma's sudden flights from the room. Dim as was the
light, her sharp eye had spied a speck of dust on the bannister in
the hallway or on the rungs of one of the dining-room chairs. And
of course it had to be erased that instant.

I finally gave up and retreated to my book. But I could feel
Grandma's eyes on me and knew she had something on her mind.

"Eugene," she said (she always pronounced it Jew-gin),
"come. You must help me."

The problem was in the kitchen. When she mopped the floor,
she could only reach so far underneath the refrigerator. Her bones
were too brittle now for her to get down on her hands and knees
and push the mop all the way back. But she knew there must be dirt
way under, against the baseboard.

"But Grandma," I said, bending over, "it looks spotless."

No, there had to be dirt way back there.

"But if you can't see it, Grandma, and I can't see it, what
does it matter?"

Like Hilary's Mt. Everest, it was there—and had to be con-
quered.

Down on hands and knees, pushing the mop hard against the
baseboard, I felt the top of my head being patted. Grandma had
never been demonstrative and this uncharacteristic stroke of affection surprised me. When I looked up, she was beaming her
gratitude.

"Oh, I wish I could do that," she sighed. It was the only time
I ever heard an expression of envy from her.

A thrift born of early poverty was natural among these people.
But here again Grandma set rather a record. Long after circumstances had rendered such economies ridiculous, she was patching
and repatching ten-cent washcloths. She saved every piece of string
and tin foil and every paper bag that came into the house. She
salvaged bits and pieces from worn-out clothing items, even socks
and mittens. No piece of wrapping paper was ever discarded; if
it had contained fish or meat from the market she scrubbed it until
it was clean and odorless. Even when he was going to high school
in town, my father says he was still wearing underwear made out
of flour sacks.

Her eyes opened wide with wonder when she saw something
new in anybody's house. It might be just a lamp or a whatnot shelf
but she would always remark, "Surely that must be expensy." To
save ourselves the implied criticism of extravagance—and Grandma
any fears she might have of our impending bankruptcy—we learned
to play down new acquisitions. A wise strategy was to infer that
something had been gotten cheap at a fire sale, through coupons,
won in a contest, or as a birthday present. One could almost hear
Grandma's sigh of relief.

Social security was still decades away. But Osten was able
to retire in 1902 when he was in his early sixties. Though he might
not have looked or felt it, he was—by any reasonable standards
of the day—a prosperous man. He owned two farms, which he
rented out. He moved his family into a house he had built on the

edge of town with enough land for gardens and an orchard and to keep a few cows, chickens, and horses.

"Town" was Fergus Falls, six miles from the original homestead. Fergus Falls is one of the loveliest small cities in the middle of America. Set in a natural amphitheater of low hills, it is a green, green city lavishly endowed with parks and groves and tree-lined avenues and flowers (even the street lamps sprout nosegays). The city has five lakes and is bisected by a meandering tributary of the Red River of the North.

In common with so many heirs of the landed immigrants, not one of the five children of Osten and Caroline who lived had any desire to remain on the farm, though one of the daughters was to marry a farmer. America must hold out something different from the grueling experiences their parents had been through. They themselves had suffered enough hardships to know that a farmer's life, in that time and place, promised little more than an ordeal.

Moving to town meant moving into a peopled world. It meant activity and excitement, companionship with other young persons, learning English, completing their schooling, careers . . . getting on with the process of Americanization. The two sons were interested in business—and eventually both would reap modest fortunes as merchants. Unlike so many of the Scandinavian girls who emigrated to those parts on their own or who were the daughters of laborers, my aunts were spared the necessity of becoming servant girls in the homes of the well-to-do burghers. (Such girls worked out as either a *barnepige*—someone who took care of the children—or as a *tjenestepige,* one who worked as a maid-of-all-service.) Osten's daughters could think of taking up nursing or secretarial work or hat making, because the means were available for their training.

Thus, the children of Osten and Caroline found a larger landscape. At about the same time, the children of Osten's brother and sisters were doing the same. And the children of all these children extended themselves further. The progression is typically American and what, in essence, most of us think America is all about. The sociological wordsmiths of our day call it upward mobility.

More than a century has passed since the April morning on which the two young brothers set out from that forgotten hut five thousand miles away. Their quest was mainly for meat and bread. In their wildest fantasies they could not possibly have dreamed that the seed from their family tree—flowering now unto its fifth generation—would be so fruitful in the New World . . . that it would bear surgeons, lawyers, writers, musicians, professors, farmers with large landholdings, politicians, successful businessmen, a college president, and a state governor.

In his ebbing years Osten occupied himself quietly. Much of the time when he wasn't studying God's Word he was marveling at God's wonders in the physical world around him. He especially loved birds and developed an almost encyclopedic knowledge of those birds that were indigenous to that area. He talked to the robins, people said, and the robins sat in his lap and talked right back to him.

He was also devoted to the animals he kept. Of these he had a particular fondness for a pair of white mares named Nancy and Lady, who pulled him in the buggy on his errands downtown. Nancy and Lady were a pair of sluggish beasts, but Osten had taught them the one trick of rearing up on their hind legs. And somehow he had trained them to do this the moment he untied them from the hitching post in front of the creamery or the feed mill store or wherever. The idea, as my father explains it, was that some passerby would assume that Osten had a pair of high-spirited, runaway horses on his hands and would come hollering, "Whoa, whoa!" But in all truth, says Dad, Nancy and Lady were so fat and overindulged they could not have been goaded into running anywhere. Such was the ingenuousness of Osten's deceits!

Osten fretted that his youngest grandson was not learning Norwegian. Not because knowledge of the language would enable them to communicate better or because the boy was being culturally deprived. No, Osten's concern was that without facility in the language, this grandson could not be confirmed in Norwegian at the Bethlehem Lutheran Church.

I was just starting school then and nothing was less enticing than the study of Norwegian. To be able to speak Norwegian, I reasoned, meant you were going to speak English with a Norwegian accent. And that would be fatal. To speak with an accent of any kind was to invite the mockery and abuse of one's peers—a punishment far outweighing all possible benefits.

I never regretted not having been confirmed in Norwegian any more than I would regret it if I had never been confirmed at all. But the neglected opportunity to learn the language of my fore-bears now seems like such a high price to have paid for a silly con-formity.

Osten died in the summer of 1928, at eighty-nine. Death came simply from the accumulation of years. Caroline, who was seventeen years his junior, lived nearly another twenty years; she died a few months short of her ninety-first birthday in April of 1947.

The death of Osten shattered Caroline as no other blow ever had. Years later, as her daughter lay dying of cancer—a beautiful woman, taken in her prime, whose sunshine made the flowers bloom in January—she could stand by the deathbed and say quite matter-of-factly, "Now, Berte [Bertha], you must make your peace with the Lord." Once more she could acquiesce to the Divine Will, though this was the daughter who had stayed home, who gave up marriage to care for her parents in their old age, and whose death would deprive her of that support and companionship. Nobody could remember ever having seen Caroline cry before, but with Osten's death the tears of a lifetime flowed openly. This tribulation was nearly more than she could bear. This time God had tested her and found her wanting.

They had been through so much together, these two parallel pillars, and had borne it all without a whimper. Except for the Great Blizzard and the times Osten went to the lake forest for logs, they had never in the fifty-five years of their marriage been out of each other's sight longer than two hours. Never had they raised their voices to each other in argument or anger. Together these constant companions had survived so many disasters, so many varieties of privation and discomfort. And it had all been suffer-able because of their faith—and each other.

The obituaries of Osten and Caroline—and so many other pioneers of that time and place—praised their kindness, courage, charity, and "fine Christian character." Their patience, honesty, and stamina might also have been noted. The faces on the faded photographs shine with goodness; they are open and guileless and have a touching, childlike innocence.

What eclipses the memory of my grandparents' wondrous piety is the fact that they actually managed to live so much of their religion. They inherently abided by the Golden Rule. No one can recall any word or deed of theirs that would have given them anguish had it been turned back upon themselves. With their children they were severe disciplinarians, but when punishment was dispensed, the pain was clearly mutual.

And how industrious they were! Now industry is no longer necessarily synonymous with virtue. We must question the consequence of industriousness, whether the result of an effort is truly serving man or just adding to the glut of production that threatens to poison man's body and stifle his spirit. But there can be no questioning the end of *their* industriousness, which was the maintenance of life itself through the growth of the soil.

If lightness and laughter were not their dominant assets, their experiences had hardly been the sort to promote levity. Humor came to them late in life and then quietly. Not much that had happened to them had been a laughing matter. Nor would it have crossed their minds that they were expected to find anything in this world funny. Their duty, as they conceived it, was to endure what must be endured—uncomplainingly.

The corner of the world they touched is a more civilized place for their having passed this way.

And so they came and went, the first sons and daughters of that cruel prairie. The long, hard day's journey into night had a stop—finally—and they are all gone now, these builders and tamers, gone gently into that last wakeless sleep, where surely they dream of the eternal mansion with gates flung open, its towers resplendent in the celestial morning.

4
Halfway to Dick and Jane

A PUERTO RICAN PILGRIMAGE
Jack Agueros

My father arrived in America in 1920, a stowaway on a steamer that shuttled between San Juan and New York. At sixteen, he was through with school and had been since thirteen or fourteen when he left the eighth grade. Between dropout and migrant, the picture is not totally clear, but three themes dominate: baseball, cockfighting, and cars. At sixteen, my father had lived in every town of Puerto Rico, had driven every road there in Ford Models A and T, had played basketball, baseball, studied English and American History, hustled tourists, and had heard the popular and classical music of two cultures.

With a superficial knowledge of America, wholly aware that the streets were not paved in gold, interested specifically in neither employment nor education, my father visited New York in the same spirit in which a family might drive out in the country on a Sunday afternoon. But it was winter 1920, and my father's romantic picture of snow was shattered. His clothes were inadequate for cold weather, and he himself was not prepared either physically or emotionally for cold. The light English patter he had charmed the tourists with was no match for the rapid-fire slurred English of New York's streets. His school English, with its carefully pronounced "water" and "squirrel," seemed like another language compared to "wudder" and "squaral."

It was a three-day winter for my father. In seventy-two hours, he thought he understood New York: the flatness of its geography and humanity, the extreme cold of climate and character, the toe to toe aloneness. On the fourth day, Joaquin Agueros went back to San Juan.

He came back "north" again in his early twenties, but again there is an unclear time span. There appears to have been a short hitch in the Puerto Rican National Guard, and during this time, there was an upheaval in island and mainland politics. Governors of Puerto Rico were appointed by the White House and had considerable powers over the island's economy and politics. The new governor began a thorough shake-up of the civil service, and as a result, my father left the National Guard and my grandfather, Ramon Agueros, was relieved of his title and duties of police captain. My father's family, composed of my grandparents, three brothers, a sister, and one or two *hermanos de crianza* (literally, "brothers of upbringing," or children brought up as if brothers), was plunged into total poverty. My grandfather was not and had never been a landowner. His policeman's pay was the only source of income. Joaquin was the oldest son, and unemployed. The family was spared starvation by the Order of the Masons, which delivered trucks full of food once or twice a month (Grandpa was a master).

The tyranny of the new gringo governor was causing serious repercussions on the island. Puerto Rico was an extraordinarily underdeveloped country, very poor and depressed, without a unanimity of affection for America. There was a massacre of civilians at Ponce by the police. This was blamed on the new governor, as were all the island's problems. My father has told me that talk and rumors of assassination were common. Many people expected to hear of the governor's death. Nevertheless, the governor was not assassinated, and there were no more Ponce massacres. Capitan Ramon Agueros was readmitted to the force but not reinstated in rank. Soon thereafter, his eldest son Joaquin also became a policeman.

In my youth, I loved to look at the pictures of Father and Grandfather in their police uniforms. Of Ramon, bald and clean shaven in his *capitan's* jacket, I remember a large chest, a strong jaw, and tough eyes. Set in a gilded oval frame with an American eagle at the top, it hung under glass in my parents' bedroom. Of

my father, I remember a patched-up photo, probably torn up by
my mother after a spat. In it a tall, very handsome young man
was standing full length with hat and riding boots. Face not stern
like Ramon's, but with a look of forced seriousness. Joaquin bore
a resemblance to Rudolf Valentino and to Carlos Gardel, the Ar-
gentinian singer and film star.

"Are you still a policeman?"

"No," my father says. He is sitting in a rocking chair, stroking
his mustache idly, enjoying the nightingale in the cage hanging between rooms. "No, I am not a cop." He pauses, strokes, rocks,
gives a big smile as if enjoying some inside joke, and says, "I had
a bad revolver. Used to chew up the bullets, chack, chack, chack;
finally, bang." Then he stops smiling.

"Why did you have such funny shoes?"

"Your father was a mounted police," my mother tells me from
the kitchen. (One day I told a cop on a horse in Central Park, "My
father was a mounted policeman." "So what?" shot back the cop.)
"He was very skinny, but very tall in the saddle, and a good rider."

"Those are riding boots. I had a big red, sixteen hands, so alive
he couldn't walk." (Furious rocking.) "I'd take him down to the
beach and let him go. It was illegal, but we both loved it, and we'd
wash down in the ocean. . . ."

My father, once animated, would and does go on telling stories.
Most of high adventure, with chase-escape climaxes, and every one
peppered with mischief.

I was told that my father left the police force because he had
shot and wounded a moonshiner in a raid on a still. (Not very unlikely, for such raids were common: there is a photo, sepiaed by
time, Grandpa and Father, guns pointing at a group of desperados
with hands held high up against a wall of vats, jugs, and plumbing.)
The wounded moonshiner turned out to be a member of high society, and my father was accused of misconduct and promiscuous
use of a firearm—the chack chack story had its undivulged point.

Joaquin, like many Puerto Ricans, has always been proud to
a fault. Standing departmental hearings, he was exonerated of the
charges. But the exoneration was meaningless; outraged that his integrity had been questioned at all, he resigned from the force.

This pride and value of integrity is ancient. You can find it in

El Cid, in the plays of Lope de Vega, in *Don Quixote.* And you find it among the Puerto Ricans today. In America it debilitates them, it keeps them from filing complaints of violation of human and civil rights, from contesting employers' decisions before state referees, and it keeps them from insisting upon full service from city and state agencies.

That's what I know about my old man's early life—he was a picaresque character from a Spanish novel. It is a collage of information, some of it concrete and verifiable, most of it gathered haphazardly and connected by conjecture. Does it matter what the governor's name is? Does it matter whether any or all of it is fact or fiction? What matters is that I thought my old man enjoyed life, let no grass grow under his feet, and it also matters that he came back to New York.

I was born in Harlem in 1934. We lived on 111th Street off Fifth Avenue. It was a block of mainly three-story buildings—with brick fronts, or brownstone, or limestone imitations of brownstone. Our apartment was a three-room first-floor walk-up. It faced north and had three windows on the street, none in back. There was a master bedroom, a living room, a kitchen–dining room, a foyer with a short hall, and a bathroom. In the kitchen there was an air shaft to evacuate cooking odors and grease—we converted it to a chimney for Santa Claus.

The kitchen was dominated by a large Victorian china closet, and the built-in wall shelves were lined with oilcloth, trimmed with ruffle, both decorated by brilliant and miniature fruits. Prominent on a wall of the kitchen was a large reproduction of a still life, a harvest table full of produce, framed and under glass. From it, I learned to identify apples, pumpkins, bananas, pears, grapes, and melons, and "peaches without worms." A joke between my mother and me. (A peach we had bought in the city market, under the New Haven's elevated tracks, bore, like the trains above, passengers.)

On one shelf of the kitchen, over the stove, there was a lineup of ceramic cannisters that carried words like "nutmeg," "ginger," and "basil." I did not know what those words meant and I don't know if my mother did either. "Spices," she would say, and that was that. They were of a yellow color that was not unlike the yellow of the stove. The kitchen was itself painted yellow, I think, very pale. But I am sure of one thing, it was not "Mickey Moused." "Mickey Mousing" was a technique used by house painters to decorate the areas of the walls that were contained by wood molding. Outside the molding they might paint a solid green. Inside the wood mold, the same solid green. Then with a twisted-up rag dipped in a lighter green they would trace random patterns.

We never used wallpaper or rugs. Our floors were covered with linoleum in every room. My father painted the apartment every year before Christmas, and in addition, he did all the maintenance, doing his own plastering and plumbing. No sooner would we move into an apartment than my father would repair holes or cracks, and if there were bulges in the plaster, he would break them open and redo the area—sometimes a whole wall. He would immediately modify the bathrooms to add a shower with separate valves, and usually as a routine matter, he cleaned out all the elbow traps, and changed all the washers on faucets. This was true of the other families in the buildings where I lived. Not a December came without a painting of the apartment.

We had Louis XIV furniture in the living room, reflected in the curved glass door and curved glass sides of the china closet. On the walls of the living room hung two prints that I loved. I would spend hours playing games with my mother based on the pictures, making up stories, etc. One day at Brooklyn College, a slide projector slammed, and I awoke after having dozed off during a dull lecture to see Van Gogh's "The Gleaners" on the screen. I almost cried. Another time I came across the other print in a book. A scene of Venice by Canaletto.

The important pieces of the living room, for me, were a Detrola radio with magic-eye tuning and the nightingale, Keero. The nightingale and the radio went back before my recollection. The bird could not stop singing, and people listened on the sidewalk below and came upstairs offering to buy Keero.

The Detrola, shaped like a Gothic arch with inlaid woodwork, was a great source of entertainment for the family. I memorized all the hit songs sung by Libertad Lamarque and Carlos Gardel. Sundays I listened to the Canary Hour presented by Hartz Mountain Seed Company. Puppy, a white Spitz, was my constant companion. Puppy slept at the foot of my bed from the first day he came to our house till the day he died, when I was eleven or twelve and he was seven or eight.

My *madrina* lived on the third floor of our building, and for all practical purposes, her apartment and ours formed a duplex. My godmother really was my second mother. Rocking me to sleep, playing her guitar, and singing me little songs, she used to say, "I'm your real mother, 'cause I love you more." But I knew that wasn't so.

Carmen Diaz, my mother, came to New York in 1931. Her brother, a career soldier, had sent for her with the intention of taking her up to Plattsburg, where he was stationed. Like my father, she arrived in New York on a steamer. My uncle had planned to show his kid sister the big city before leaving for Plattsburg, but during a week in New York my mother was convinced to stay. More opportunities, and other Spanish-speaking people, were the reasons that changed her mind.

Carmen had had a tough time all her life in Puerto Rico. Her mother had died when she was only two. Her father, a wealthy farmer and veterinarian, remarried and began paying less and less attention to his business affairs. The stepmother was not very fond of the children. Thus, when her older sister married a policeman, Carmen accepted the invitation to live with the newlyweds, acting as a sort of housekeeper-governess. After many years in this role, which my mother describes as "rewarding, but not a life for a young girl," came the offer to "go north."

On the island, my mother had had two serious suitors. One was a schoolteacher who had an ailing mother and could not afford to marry on his salary. The other was a rookie cop who had arrested her brother-in-law for carrying a concealed weapon. The brother-in-law took the arrest in good humor, and after proving that he was an off-duty cop, invited the rookie home for dinner. The rookie became a frequent visitor, twirling apples for Carmen's delight, but one day he came to visit and said he was going north, to find a good job. He said he would write, but no letter ever came from Joaquin.

Carmen had big plans for her life in America, intending to go to school and study interior decorating. But the Puerto Ricans who came to New York at that time found life in the city tough. It was the Depression, and work was hard to come by. My mother went from job to job for about six months and finally landed a job in the garment district as a seamstress. Twenty years later, she retired from the ILGWU, her dream of becoming a decorator waylaid by bumping into my father on a Manhattan street and reviving the old romance. My father had been back in America since the mid-twenties. In America he remembers working a long day to earn $1.25. After a time, he found a job in a restaurant that paid nine dollars a week and provided two meals a day. That was a good deal, even at a six-day week, twelve to fifteen hours a day.

I am an only child. My parents and I always talked about my becoming a doctor. The law and politics were not highly regarded in my house. Lawyers, my mother would explain, had to defend people whether they were guilty or not, while politicians, my father would say, were all crooks. A doctor helped everybody, rich and poor, white and black. If I became a doctor, I could study hay fever and find a cure for it, my godmother would say. Also, I could take care of my parents when they were old. I liked the idea of helping, and for nineteen years my sole ambition was to study medicine.

My house had books, not many, but my parents encouraged me to read. As I became a good reader they bought books for me and never refused me money for their purchase. My father once built a bookcase for me. It was an important moment, for I had always believed that my father was not too happy about my being a bookworm. The atmosphere at home was always warm. We seemed to be a popular family. We entertained frequently, with two standing parties a year—at Christmas and for my birthday. Parties were always large. My father would dismantle the beds and move all the furniture so that the full two rooms could be used for dancing. My mother would cook up a storm, particularly at Christmas. *Pasteles, lechon asado, arroz con gandules,* and a lot of *coquito* to drink (meat-stuffed plantain, roast pork, rice with pigeon peas, and coconut nog). My father always brought in a band. They played without compensation and were guests at the party. They ate and drank and danced while a victrola covered the intermissions. One year my father brought home a whole pig and hung it in the foyer doorway. He and my mother prepared it by rubbing it down with oil, oregano, and garlic. After preparation, the pig was taken down and carried over to a local bakery where it was cooked and returned home. Parties always went on till daybreak, and in addition to the band, there were always volunteers to sing and declaim poetry.

My mother kept an immaculate household. Bedspreads (chenille seemed to be very in) and lace curtains, washed at home like everything else, were hung up on huge racks with rows of tight nails. The racks were assembled in the living room, and the moisture from the wet bedspreads would fill the apartment. In a sense, that seems to be the lasting image of that period of my life. The house was clean. The neighbors were clean. The streets, with few cars, were clean. The buildings were clean and uncluttered with people on the stoops. The park was clean. The visitors to my house were clean, and the relationships that my family had with other Puerto Rican families, and the Italian families that my father had met through baseball and my mother through the garment center, were clean. Second Avenue was clean and most of the apartment windows had awnings. There was always music, there seemed to be no rain, and snow did not become slush. School was fun, we wrote essays about how grand America was, we put up hunchbacked cats at Halloween, we believed Santa Claus visited everyone. I believed everyone was Catholic. I grew up with dogs, nightingales, my godmother's guitar, rocking chair, cat, guppies, my father's occasional roosters, kept in a cage on the fire escape. Laundry delivered and collected by horse and wagon, fruits and vegetables sold the same way, windowsill refrigeration in winter, iceman and box in summer. The police my friends, likewise the teachers.

In short, the first seven or so years of my life were not too great a variation on Dick and Jane, the school book figures who, if my memory serves me correctly, were blond Anglo-Saxons, not immigrants, not migrants like the Puerto Ricans, and not the children of either immigrants or migrants.

My family moved in 1941 to Lexington Avenue into a larger apartment where I could have my own room. It was a light, sunny, railroad flat on the top floor of a well-kept building. I transferred to a new school, and whereas before my classmates had been mostly black, the new school had few blacks. The classes were made up of Italians, Irish, Jews, and a sprinkling of Puerto Ricans. My block was populated by Jews, Italians, and Puerto Ricans.

And then a whole series of different events began. I went to junior high school. We played in the backyards, where we tore down fences to build fires to cook stolen potatoes. We tore up whole hedges, because the green tender limbs would not burn when they were peeled, and thus made perfect skewers for our stolen "mickies." We played tag in the abandoned buildings, tearing the plaster off the walls, tearing the wire lath off the wooden slats, tearing the wooden slats themselves, good for fires, for kites, for sword fighting. We ran up and down the fire escapes playing tag and over and across many rooftops. The war ended and the heavy Puerto Rican migration began. The Irish and the Jews disappeared from the neighborhood. The Italians tried to consolidate east of Third Avenue.

What caused the clean and open world to end? Many things. Into an ancient neighborhood came pouring four to five times more people than it had been designed to hold. Men who came running at the promise of jobs were jobless as the war ended. They were confused. They could not see the economic forces that ruled their lives as they drank beer on the corners, reassuring themselves of good times to come while they were hell-bent toward alcoholism. The sudden surge in numbers caused new resentments, and prejudice was intensified. Some were forced to live in cellars, and were then characterized as cave dwellers. Kids came who were confused by the new surroundings; their Puerto Ricanness forced us against a mirror asking, "If they are Puerto Ricans, what are we?" and thus they confused us. In our confusion we were sometimes pathetically reaching out, sometimes pathologically striking out. Gangs. Drugs. Wine. Smoking. Girls. Dances and slow-drag music. Mambo. Spics, Spooks, and Wops. Territories, brother gangs, and war councils establishing rules for right of way on blocks and avenues and for seating in the local theater. Pegged pants and zip guns. Slang.

Dick and Jane were dead, man. Education collapsed. Every classroom had ten kids who spoke no English. Black, Italian, Puerto Rican relations in the classroom were good, but we all knew we couldn't visit one another's neighborhoods. Sometimes we could not move too freely within our own blocks. On 109th, from the lamp post west, the Latin Aces, and from the lamp post east, the Senecas, the "club" I belonged to. The kids who spoke no English became known as Marine Tigers, picked up from a popular Spanish song. (The *Marine Tiger* and the *Marine Shark* were two ships that sailed from San Juan to New York and brought over many, many migrants from the island.)

The neighborhood had its boundaries. Third Avenue and east, Italian. Fifth Avenue and west, black. South, there was a hill on 103rd Street known locally as Cooney's Hill. When you got to the top of the hill, something strange happened: America began, because from the hill south was where the "Americans" lived. Dick and Jane were not dead; they were alive and well in a better neighborhood.

When, as a group of Puerto Rican kids, we decided to go swimming to Jefferson Park Pool, we knew we risked a fight and a beating from the Italians. And when we went to La Milagrosa Church in Harlem, we knew we risked a fight and a beating from the blacks. But when we went over Cooney's Hill, we risked dirty looks, disapproving looks, and questions from the police like, "What are you doing in this neighborhood?" and "Why don't you kids go back where you belong?"

Where we belonged! Man, I had written compositions about America. Didn't I belong on the Central Park tennis courts, even if I didn't know how to play? Couldn't I watch Dick play? Weren't these policemen working for me too?

Junior high school was a waste. I can say with 90 per cent accuracy that I learned nothing. The woodshop was used to manufacture stocks for "homemades" after Macy's stopped selling zip-guns. We went from classroom to classroom answering "here," and trying to be "good." The math class was generally permitted to go to the gym after roll call. English was still a good class. Partly because of a damn good, tough teacher named Miss Beck, and partly because of the grade-number system (7-1 the smartest seventh grade and 7-12, the dumbest). Books were left in school, there was little or no homework, and the whole thing seemed to be a holding operation until high school. Somehow or other, I passed the entrance exam to Brooklyn Technical High School. But •

I couldn't cut the mustard, either academically or with the "American" kids. After one semester, I came back to PS 83, waited a semester, and went on to Benjamin Franklin High School.

I still wanted to study medicine and excelled in biology. English was always an interesting subject, and I still enjoyed writing compositions and reading. In the neighborhood it was becoming a problem being categorized as a bookworm and as one who used "Sunday words," or "big words." I dug school, but I wanted to be one of the boys more. I think the boys respected my intelligence, despite their ribbing. Besides which, I belonged to a club with a number of members who were interested in going to college, and so I wasn't so far out.

My introduction to marijuana was in junior high school in 1948. A kid named Dixie from 124th Street brought a pack of joints to school and taught about twelve guys to smoke. He told us we could buy joints at a quarter each or five for a dollar. Bombers, or thicker cigarettes, were thirty-five cents each or three for a dollar. There were a lot of experimenters, but not too many buyers. Actually, among the boys there was a strong taboo on drugs, and the Spanish word "motto" was a term of disparagement. Many clubs would kick out members who were known to use drugs. Heroin was easily available, and in those days came packaged in capsules or "caps" which sold for fifty cents each. Method of use was inhalation through the nose, or "sniffing," or "snorting."

I still remember vividly the first kid I ever saw who was mainlining. Prior to this encounter, I had known of "skin-popping," or subcutaneous injection, but not of mainlining. Most of the sniffers were afraid of skin-popping because they knew of the danger of addiction. They seemed to think that you could not become addicted by sniffing.

I went over to 108th Street and Madison where we played softball on an empty lot. This kid came over who was maybe sixteen or seventeen and asked us if we wanted to buy Horse. He started telling us about shooting up and showed me his arms. He had tracks, big black marks on the inside of his arm from the inner joint of the elbow down to his wrist and then over onto the back of his hand. I was stunned. Then he said, "That's nothing, man. I ain't hooked, and I ain't no junky. I can stop anytime I want to."

I believe that he believed what he was saying. Invariably the kids talking about their drug experiences would say over and over, "I ain't hooked. I can stop anytime."

But they didn't stop; and the drug traffic grew greater and more open. Kids were smoking on the corners and on the stoops. Deals were made on the street, and you knew fifteen places within a block radius where you could buy anything you wanted. Cocaine never seemed to catch on although it was readily available. In the beginning, the kids seemed to be able to get the money for stuff easily. As the number of shooters grew and the prices went up, the kids got more desperate and apartment robbing became a real problem.

More of the boys began to leave school. We didn't use the term drop out; rather, a guy would say one day, after forty-three truancies, "I'm quitting school." And so he would. It was an irony, for what was really happening was that after many years of being rejected, ignored, and shuffled around by the school, the kid wanted to quit. Only you can't quit something you were never a part of, nor can you drop out if you were never in.

Some kids lied about their age and joined the army. Most just hung around. Not drifting to drugs or crime or to work either. They used to talk about going back at night and getting the diploma. I believe that they did not believe they could get their diplomas. They knew that the schools had abandoned them a long time ago— that to get the diploma meant starting all over again and that was impossible. Besides, day or night, it was the same school, the same staff, the same shit. But what do you say when you are powerless to get what you want, and what do you say when the other side has all the cards and writes all the rules? You say, "Tennis is for fags," and "School is for fags."

My mother leads me by the hand and carries a plain brown shopping bag. We enter an immense airplane hangar. Structural steel crisscrosses on the ceiling and walls: large round and square rivets look like buttons or bubbles of air trapped in the girders. There are long metallic counters with people bustling behind them. It smells of C.N. disinfectant. Many people stand on many lines up to these counters; there are many conversations going on simultaneously. The huge space plays tricks with voices and a very eerie combination of sounds results. A white cabbage is rolled down a counter at us. We retaliate by throwing down stamps.

For years I thought that sequence happened in a dream. The rolling cabbage rolled in my head, and little unrelated incidents seemed to bring it to the surface of my mind. I could not understand why I remembered a once-dreamt dream so vividly. I was sixteen when I picked up and read Freud's *The Interpretation of Dreams*. One part I understood immediately and well, sex and symbolism. In no time, I had hung my shingle: Streetcorner Analyst. My friends would tell me their dreams and with the most outrageous sexual explanations we laughed whole evenings away. But the rolling cabbage could not be stopped and neither quack analysis nor serious thought could explain it away. One day I asked my mother if she knew anything about it.

"That was home relief, 1937 or 1938. You were no more than four years old then. Your father had been working at a restaurant and I had a job downtown. I used to take you every morning to Dona Eduvije who cared for you all day. She loved you very much, and she was very clean and neat, but I used to cry on my way to work, wishing I could stay home with my son and bring him up like a proper mother would. But I guess I was fated to be a workhorse. When I was pregnant, I would get on the crowded subway and go to work. I would get on a crowded elevator up. Then down. Then back on the subway. Every day I was afraid that the crowd would hurt me, that I would lose my baby. But I had to work. I worked for the WPA right into my ninth month."

My mother was telling it "like it was," and I sat stupefied, for I could not believe that what she said applied to the time I thought of as open and clean. I had been existing in my life like a small plant in a bell jar, my parents defining my awareness. There were things all around me I could not see.

"When you were born we had been living as boarders. It was hard to find an apartment, even in Harlem. You saw signs that said 'No Renting to Colored or Spanish.' That meant Puerto Ricans. We used to say, 'This is supposed to be such a great country?' But with a new baby we were determined not to be boarders and we took an apartment on 111th Street. Soon after we moved, I lost my job because my factory closed down. Your father was making seven or eight dollars a week in a terrible job in a carpet factory. They used to clean rugs, and your father's hands were always in strong chemicals. You know how funny some of his fingernails are? It was from that factory. He came home one night and he was looking at his fingers, and he started saying that he didn't come to this country to lose his hands. He wanted to hold a bat and play ball and he wanted to work—but he didn't want to lose his hands. So he quit the job and went to a restaurant for less pay. With me out of work, a new apartment and therefore higher rent, we couldn't manage. Your father was furious when I mentioned home relief. He said he would rather starve than go on relief. But I went and filled out the papers and answered all the questions and swallowed my pride when they treated me like an intruder. I used to say to them, 'Find me a job—get my husband a better job—we don't want home relief.' But we had to take it. And all that mess with the stamps in exchange for food. And they used to have weekly 'specials' sort of—but a lot of things were useless—because they were American food. I don't remember if we went once a week or once every two weeks. You were so small I don't know how you remember that place and the long lines. It didn't last long because your father had everybody trying to find him a better job and finally somebody did. Pretty soon I went into the WPA and thank God, we never had to deal with those people again. I don't know how you remember that place, but I wish you didn't. I wish I could forget that home relief thing myself. It was the worst time for your father and me. He still hates it.

(He still hates it and so do many people. The expression, "I'd rather starve than go on welfare" is common in the Puerto Rican community. This characteristic pride is well chronicled throughout Spanish literature. For example, one episode of *Lazarillo del Tormes*, the sixteenth-century picaresque novel, tells of a squire who struts around all day with his shiny sword and pressed cape. At night the squire takes food from the boy, Lazarillo—who has begged or stolen it—explaining that it is not proper for a squire to beg or steal, or even to work! Without Lazarillo to feed him, the squire would probably starve.)

"You don't know how hard it was being married to your father then. He was young and very strong and very active and he wanted to work. Welfare deeply disturbed him, and I was afraid that he would actually get very violent if an investigator came to the house. They had a terrible way with people, like throwing that cabbage, that was the way they gave you everything, the way we used to throw the kitchen slop to the pigs in Puerto Rico. Some giving! Your father was, is, *muy macho*, and I used to worry if anybody says anything or gives him that why-do-you-people-come-here-to-ruin-things look he'll be in jail for thirty years. He almost got arrested once when you were just a baby. We went to a hospital clinic —I don't remember now if it was Sydenham or Harlem Hospital— you had a swelling around your throat—and the doctor told me, 'Put on cold compresses.' I said I did that and it didn't help. The doctor said, 'Then put hot compresses.' Your father blew up. In his broken English, he asked the doctor to do that to his mother, and then invited him to transfer over to the stable on 104th Street. 'You do better with horses—maybe they don't care what kind of compresses they get.'

"One morning your father tells me, 'I got a new job. I start today driving a truck delivering soft drinks.' That night I ask him about the job—he says, 'I quit—bunch of Mafia—I went to the first four places on my list and each storeowner said, "I didn't order any soda." So I got the idea real fast. The Mafia was going to leave soda in each place and then make the guys buy from them only. As soon as I figured it out, I took the truck back, left it parked where I got it, and didn't even say good-bye.' The restaurant took him back. They liked him. The chef used to give him eggs and meats; it was very important to us. Your father never could keep still (still can't), so he was loved wherever he worked. I feel sorry for people on welfare—forget about the cabbage—I never should have taken you there."

Pity was not a universal emotion provoked by welfare recipients in Harlem—East Harlem—residents. One old man on whom I used to gingerly test my developing notions despised welfare and people on it. Don Pedro had pure white hair, his back was rounded into a slight hump, and he was not very tall—at sixteen I was taller than he. He had come to America looking for something he did not find. He was bitter about people who did not work, and he did not work. He was for me the local wiseman, historian of Harlem and American commentator, willing to discuss anything with me—so long as I remembered my place—*los niños hablan cuando las gallinas mean* (the Puerto Rican version of children should be seen and not heard, literally, "children speak when chickens urinate"). That small saw quickly ended conversations, for it indicated annoyance—and I was taught never to be disrespectful in any way to an elder.

Don Pedro never said whether he had been on welfare, but everything about it was mind-bending for him. His pride would have prohibited him from accepting welfare, and if life had been cruel enough to force him to it, his pride would have kept him from such an admission. He was the contemporary starving squire. And the racist and conservative arguments that I came to hear as an adult from White America, I first heard as a teenager from Don Pedro. "Lazy bastards. I see them every day playing dominoes, drinking beer. Late in the afternoons going off to buy parts for their cars. Healthy as me. Have two or three women pregnant, children running around like savages, no discipline, no education [meaning in Spanish not school, but manners and morals]. And the other ones, you think they like to answer so many questions? You think they like to buy on credit, wait for checks? Why shouldn't they have a TV? What government has the right to tell me I can't give a person a TV as a gift? [Welfare families were not allowed to buy or receive as gifts TV sets. On the day the investigator was due, the tenements were like a scene from a Beatles movie—many doors open—out come people with TVs, carrying them all into one door. End of day back go people with their TV sets.] And what about those investigators? Where do they find people who take such jobs? They don't ask so many questions if you work out an 'agreement.' A few bucks from your miserable check to them every month and they won't look under the bed. Bastards! But they all deserve what they get. You know what—I have more respect for a thief than any of them. A thief has—well I don't mean I would be a thief—I mean if it came to welfare or stealing—I'd steal. I'd steal before I would become an investigator, let alone a client."

And welfare was not the only thing Don Pedro was turned off on. He didn't believe in voting. "Fixed, the whole thing is fixed. First they decide who they want for anything. Take the judges. All of a sudden you have a bunch of names for a judge. Their names on all the parties. Well hell, if the guy is both a Republican and a Democrat, what's the sense of voting? He is an automatic winner! Then, I've seen them take the machines and turn them around. Or else somebody conveniently forgets to turn the little key, so no votes register. Or else they get you on technicalities. You changed your address. You gotta take the literacy test again. You can't vote—you got two last names. [In Puerto Rico, children assume the father's surname followed by a hyphen and then the mother's maiden name, but this causes so much confusion in New York that most Puerto Ricans eventually drop the usage.] Then they get you the other way. You sit and read about the candidates and what they stand for. You go down and vote for what you think is right. Meanwhile they take a truck up to the Bowery and pick up fifteen or twenty guys, tell them how to vote, and then give 'em a pint of whiskey for their troubles. I've seen them buy a whole family with a bag of groceries, and I've seen dead men vote, if you know what I mean."

If there was one thing that Don Pedro believed about America, it was that it was a thoroughly corrupt nation. There was not one bureaucracy, not one establishment that he dealt with, that didn't have somebody on the make. The problem for the poor, he said, "is that they didn't have any money to bribe people."

"You know how many jobs, how many apartments I lost because I couldn't fix somebody? Some goddamned Irish could go to a super and give him twenty-five dollars for an apartment, but if you were Puerto Rican you had to give fifty dollars for the same apartment."

Why shouldn't I believe him? By sixteen I had my own collection of anecdotes supporting discrimination. Police telling me to "move on" for no reason, to get off the stoop of the building where I lived, being called fag and spic, stopped and searched on the streets, in hallways, in candy stores, and anywhere that we congregated. Called fag because in a time of crew cuts the Puerto Rican male took pride in his long hair. With the postwar movies of American heroes in Germany, Gestapo and Nazi were familiar figures, and for me they were our police. Who could you complain to about police? Hitler?

In school, Mr. Miller, goddamn him to hell forever, took a Puerto Rican boy named Luis and kept him under the teacher's desk during class periods. When Luis would moan, Miller would kick him. Between periods, Miller walked Luis around the school, keeping him in a painful armlock. Mr. Flax, the principal, laughed. And Diamond, the algebra teacher, either sent us to play basketball or asked us to lay our heads on our desks while he checked the stock market reports in the *New York Times*. To whom did you complain about a teacher—a laughing principal?

But in the process of discrimination, different attitudes are produced. Don Pedro, prejudged in housing, employment, and health services, hated the Puerto Ricans who made slums, the Puerto Ricans who would not work, the Puerto Ricans who did not respect the Gestapo. And he hated Luis under the desk as much as Mr. Miller. And when I tried to tell Don Pedro, "Baby, who you really hate is you," he would say, "When chickens urinate."

My father and I are walking through East Harlem, south down Lexington from 112th toward 110th, in 1952. Saturday in late spring, I am eighteen years old, sun brilliant on the streets, people running back and forth on household errands. My father is telling me a story about how back in nineteen thirty something, we were very poor and Con Ed light meters were in every apartment. "The Puerto Ricans, maybe everybody else, would hook up a shunt wire around the meter, specially in the evenings when the use was heavy —that way you didn't pay for all the electric you used. We called it *'pillo'* (thief)."

We arrive at 110th Street and all the cart vendors are there peddling plantains, avocados, yams, various subtropical roots. I make a casual remark about how foolish it all seemed, and my father catches that I am looking down on them. "Are they stealing?" he asks. "Are they selling people colored water? Aren't they working honestly? Are they any different from a bank president? Aren't they hung like you and me? They are *machos*, and to be respected.

Don't let college go to your head. You think a Ph.D. is automatically better than a peddler? Remember where you come from—poor people. I mopped floors for people and I wasn't ashamed, but I never let them look down on me. Don't you look down on anybody."

We walk for a way in silence, I am mortified, but he is not angry. "One day I decide to play a joke on your mother. I come home a little early and knock. When she says 'Who?' I say 'Edison man.' Well, there is this long silence and then a scream. I open the door and run in. Your mother's on a chair, in tears, her right arm black from pinky to elbow. She ran to take the *pillo* out, but in her nervousness she got a very slight shock, the black from the spark. She never has forgiven me. After that, I always thought through my jokes."

We walk some more and he says, "I'll tell you another story. This one on me. I was twenty-five years old and was married to your mother. I took her down to Puerto Rico to meet Papa and Mama. We were sitting in the living room, and I remember it like it happened this morning. The room had rattan furniture very popular in that time. Papa had climbed in rank back to captain and had a new house. The living room had double doors which opened onto a large *balcon*. At the other end of the room you could see the dining table with a beautiful white handmade needlework cloth. We were sitting and talking and I took out a cigarette. I was smoking Chesterfields then. No sooner had I lit up than Papa got up, came over, and smacked me in the face. 'You haven't received my permission to smoke,' he said. Can you imagine how I felt?" So my father dealt with his love for me through lateral actions: building bookcases, and through tales of how he got his wounds, he anointed mine.

What is a migration? What does it happen to? Why are the Eskimos still dark after living in that snow all these centuries? Why don't they have a word for snow? What things are around me with such high saturation that I have not named them? What is a migration? If you rob my purse, are you really a fool? Can a poor boy really be president? In America? Of anything? If he is not white? Should one man's achievement fulfill one million people? Will you let us come near your new machine: after all, there is no more ditch digging? What is a migration? What does it happen to?

The most closely watched migrants of this world are birds. Birds migrate because they get bored singing in the same place to the same people. And they see that the environment gets hostile. Men move for the same reasons. When a Puerto Rican comes to America, he comes looking for a job. He takes the cold as one of a negative series of givens. The mad hustle, the filthy city, filthy air, filthy housing, sardine transportation, are in the series. He knows life will be tough and dangerous. But he thinks he can make a buck. And in his mind, there is only one tableau: himself retired, owner of his home in Puerto Rico, chickens cackling in the back yard.

It startles me still, though it has been five years since my parents went back to the island. I never believed them. My father, driving around New York for the Housing Authority, knowing more streets in more boroughs than I do, and my mother, curious in her later years about museums and theaters, and reading my books as fast as I would put them down, then giving me cryptic reviews. Salinger is really silly (*Catcher in the Rye*), but entertaining. That evil man deserved to die (*Moby Dick*). He's too much (Dostoevski in *Crime and Punishment*). I read this when I was a little girl in school (*Hamlet* and *Macbeth*). It's too sad for me (*Cry, the Beloved Country*).

My father, intrigued by the thought of passing the foreman's exam, sitting down with a couple of arithmetic books, and teaching himself at age fifty-five to do work problems and mixture problems and fractions and decimals, and going into the civil service exam and scoring a seventy-four and waiting up one night for me to show me three poems he had written. These two cosmopolities, gladiators without skills or language, battling hostile environments and prejudiced people and systems, had graduated from Harlem to the Bronx, had risen into America's dream-cherished lower middle class, and then put it down for Puerto Rico after thirty plus years.

What is a migration, when is it not just a long visit?

I was born in Harlem, and I live downtown. And I am a migrant, for if a migration is anything, it is a state of mind. I have known those Eskimos who lived in America twenty and thirty years and never voted, never attended a community meeting, never filed a complaint against a landlord, never informed the police when they were robbed or swindled, or when their daughters were molested. Never appeared at the State or City Commission on Human Rights, never reported a business fraud, never, in other words, saw the snow.

And I am very much a migrant because I am still not quite at home in America. Always there are hills; on the other side—people inclined to throwing cabbages. I cannot "earn and return"—there is no position for me in my father's tableau.

However, I approach the future with optimism. Fewer Puerto Ricans like Eskimos, a larger number of leaders like myself, trained in the university, tempered in the ghetto, and with a vision of America moving from its unexecuted policy to a society open and clean, accessible to anyone.

Dick and Jane? They, too, were tripped by the society, and in our several ways, we are all still migrating.

5
Puritans from the Orient

A CHINESE EVOLUTION
Jade Snow Wong

From infancy to my sixteenth year, I was reared according to nineteenth century ideals of Chinese womanhood. I was never left alone, though it was not unusual for me to feel lonely, while surrounded by a family of seven others, and often by ten (including bachelor cousins) at meals.

My father (who enjoyed our calling him Daddy in English) was the vital, temperamental, dominating, and unquestioned head of our household. He was not talkative, being preoccupied with his business affairs and with reading constantly otherwise. My mother was mistress of domestic affairs. Seldom did these two converse before their children, but we knew them to be a united front, and suspected that privately she both informed and influenced him about each child.

From the village of Fragrant Mountains in southern Canton, my father had immigrated as a young man in 1903 to San Francisco. Many years later when I was a grown woman, he told me with sadness that when he had asked his mother, whom he adored, for permission to come to the United States, she had expressed her reluctance. When this only son had insisted that he must leave her, she had cursed him, "Go! Go! You will have the life to go, but not the life to return!"

Trained in his father's rice and lumber business, he had been offered a position as accountant for an importer of rice and other staples needed by the Chinese in San Francisco. The inhabitants of the new Chinatown clustered together for mutual protection and a degree of social life, even though most of them were employed outside the community, serving Westerners as laborers, laundrymen, waiters, cooks, or in other occupations not requiring much knowledge of the American language they hadn't mastered. It was a predominantly male group of bachelors and married men who had left their families behind while they sought fortunes in the new land, then and now dubbed in Chinese, "Old Golden Mountains," for the legend of the Forty-niner Gold Rush days had been grossly exaggerated in Canton to lure railroad workers to California.

The community lived toughly by its own code. Chinese ethics could not be honored by Western courts; they were implemented either peacefully or violently by Chinese organizations. Enterprises such as caring for the sick or providing burials for the dead were duties of "Benevolent Associations," whose members spoke a common dialect based on their various geographical Cantonese origins. Protection of property rights or from persecution was assumed by membership in a family name clan of greater power (such as all the Chans in their clan, and all the Wongs in theirs). Some clans embraced three or four names, their bearers descendants of historically friendly families. A man therefore thought twice before provoking another, depending on the relative family-name strength of his opponent.

It was the ambition of most of these men to work and save in the United States and return to China to marry or rejoin a waiting wife, buy property in their village, and enjoy rents for lifelong income. Many succeeded in doing so. But my father happened to combine free thinking with Chinese conservatism. While attending night classes at the Methodist Chinese Mission in San Francisco to learn English, he was exposed to Christian theory and the practical kindness of Christian Westerners. The Golden Rule did not conflict with the Confucian doctrines which he had carefully retained. The measure of human dignity accorded to Western women particularly impressed him. He was contemporary with Sun Yat Sen, founder of the new Chinese Republic in 1910, born in the same village district, and a follower of the new Christianity in China. As part of his revolutionary demands in forging a new nation, Dr. Sun had advocated the elimination of the bound feet that had kept Chinese women crippled house slaves.

My father's motherland was in the grip of military and political upheaval. My father wrote to his family, "In America, I have learned how shamefully women in China have been treated. I will bleach the disgrace of my ancestors by bringing my wife and two daughters to San Francisco, where my wife can work without disgrace, and my daughters shall have the opportunity of education." He was beginning his own domestic revolution. For fifty-five years, my father was to remain in San Francisco. He retained a copy of every letter he wrote to China.

To support the family in America, Daddy tried various occupations—candy making, the ministry to which he was later ordained —but finally settled upon manufacturing men's and children's denim garments. He leased sewing equipment, installed machines in a basement where rent was cheapest, and there he and his family lived and worked. There was no thought that dim and airless quarters were terrible conditions for living and working, or that child labor was unhealthful. The only goal was for all in the family to work, to save, and to become educated. It was possible, so it would be done.

My father had had only a few years of formal Chinese schooling. He taught himself garment manufacturing, from cutting the yardage in five-dozen-layer lots to fixing the machines when they broke down. A Western jobber delivered the yardage to him and picked up finished garments for sales distribution to American retailers. My father figured his prices to include thread, machine use, labor, and his overhead-profit. He was a meticulous bookkeeper, using only an abacus, brush, ink, and Chinese ledgers. Because of his newly learned ideals, he pioneered for the right of women to work. Concerned that they have economic independence, but not with the long hours of industrial home work, he went to shy housewives' apartments and taught them sewing.

Only the ambitious but poor gather their courage and tear up their roots to journey across the seas, in the hope of bettering their living abroad. In China, the winds of popular discontent were blowing, caused by the decaying old empire and the excessive concessions granted to various European powers. My father used to tell

us of insults and injuries suffered by ordinary Chinese at the hands
of East Indian mercenary police, employed by the British in Hong
Kong.

My mother still talks of the poverty in Fragrant Mountains. If
they had rice, they were fortunate. If there was salt, or oil, they were
even more fortunate. Tea made the fourth absolute necessity; anything more was luxury. Meat and fish were rarities. Sometimes a
relative would bring some fresh green vegetables. Sometimes they
bought a penny's worth of salted olives or thick, red soy, to steam
on the rice for a change of flavors. On a birthday or a feast day, there
might be a chicken. For annual grave pilgrimages to pay respect to
the dead, roast pig was first offered to the departed souls; later the
meat was enjoyed by the worshippers.

My earliest memories of companionship with my father were
as his passenger in his red wheelbarrow, sharing space with the piles
of blue-jean materials he was delivering to a worker's home. He
must have been forty. He was lean, tall, inevitably wearing blue
overalls, rolled shirt sleeves, and high black kid shoes. In his
pockets were numerous keys, tools, and pens. On such deliveries,
I noticed that he always managed time to show a mother how to sew
a difficult seam, or to help her repair a machine, or just to chat.

I observed from birth that living and working were inseparable.
My mother was short, sturdy, young looking, and took pride in her
appearance. She was at her machine the minute housework was
done, and she was the hardest working seamstress, seldom pausing,
working after I went to bed. The hum of sewing machines continued
day and night, seven days a week. She knew that to have more than
the four necessities, she must work and save. We knew that to overcome poverty, there were only two methods: working and education.
It was our personal responsibility. Being poor did not entitle us to
benefits. When welfare programs were created in the depression
years of the thirties, my family would not make application.

Having provided the setup for family industry, my father
turned his attention to our education. Ninety-five per cent of the
population in China had been illiterate. He knew that American
public schools would take care of our English, but he had to be the
watchdog to nurture our Chinese knowledge. Only the Cantonese
tongue was ever spoken by him or my mother. When the two oldest

girls arrived from China, the schools of Chinatown received only boys. My father tutored his daughters each morning before breakfast. In the midst of a foreign environment, he clung to a combination of the familiar old standards and what was permissible in the newly learned Christian ideals.

My eldest brother was born in America, the only boy for fourteen years, and after him three daughters—another older sister, myself, and my younger sister. Then my younger brother, Paul, was born. That older brother, Lincoln, was cherished in the best Chinese tradition. He had his own room; he kept a German Shepherd as his pet; he was tutored by a Chinese scholar; he was sent to private school for American classes. As a male Wong, he would be responsible some day for the preservation of and pilgrimages to ancestral graves—his privileges were his birthright. We girls were content with the unusual opportunities of working and attending two schools.

For by the time I was six, times in Chinatown were changing. The Hip Wo Chinese Christian Academy (in the same building as the Methodist Mission) had been founded on a coeducational basis, with nominal tuition. Financial support came from three Protestant church boards: the Congregational, Presbyterian, and Methodist churches contributed equal shares. My father was on the Hip Wo School Board for many years. By day, I attended American public school near our home. From 5:00 P.M. to 8:00 P.M. on five weekdays and from 9:00 A.M. to 12 noon on Saturdays, I attended the Chinese school. Classes numbered twenty to thirty students, and were taught by educated Chinese from China. We studied poetry, calligraphy, philosophy, literature, history, correspondence, religion, all by exacting memorization. The Saturday morning chapel services carried out the purposes of the supporting churches.

Daddy emphasized memory development; he could still recite fluently many lengthy lessons of his youth. Every evening after both schools, I'd sit by my father, often as he worked at his sewing machine, sing-songing my lessons above its hum. Sometimes I would stop to hold a light for him as he threaded the difficult holes of a specialty machine, such as one for bias bindings. After my Chinese lessons passed his approval, I was allowed to attend to American homework. I was made to feel luckier than other Chinese girls who didn't study Chinese, and also luckier than Western girls without a dual heritage.

We lived on both levels of our factory, which had moved out of the basement to street level. The kitchen, bathroom, and sitting–dining room were at the rear of the street floor. Kitchen privileges were granted employee seamstresses, who might wish to heat lunch or wash hands; our family practically never had privacy. Floor-boards ran the length of the factory; we were never permitted to play on them because of the danger of splinters. My mother carried each child on her back with a traditional Chinese support until he was able to walk firmly, to eliminate the necessity of crawling and the danger of injury by machine pulleys and motor belts. Only the living quarters were laid with what was known as "battleship linole-um," which was an uninspired brown, but unquestionably durable.

Bedrooms were upstairs, both in the front and the rear of the factory, to be where there were windows. Between front and rear bedrooms were more machines and the long cutting tables, which were partially lit by the skylights. I shared a room with my younger sister, and later with my baby brother, too. Windows were fitted with opaque glass to eliminate the necessity for curtains, and iron bars were installed by Daddy across the entire length of those up-stairs windows to keep out intruders and keep in peeping children.

Both my older sisters married when I was a child, and my third older sister went to live with the oldest of them, for which my father paid room and board. Thus, congestion at our factory-home was re-lieved. There was little time for play and toys were unknown to me. In any spare time, I was supplied with embroidery and sewing for my mother.

The Chinese New Year, which by the old lunar calendar would fall sometime in late January or early February of the Western Christian calendar, was the most special time of the year, for then the machines stopped for three days. Mother would clean our living quarters very thoroughly, decorate the sitting room with flowering branches, fresh oranges, and arrange candied fruits or salty melon seeds for callers. All of us would be dressed in bright new clothes, and relatives or close friends, who came to call, would give each of us a red paper packet containing a good luck coin—usually a quarter. I remember how my classmates would gleefully talk of *their* receipts. But my mother made us give our money to her, for she said that she needed it to reciprocate to others.

Yet there was little reason for unhappiness. I was never hungry. Though we had no milk, there was all the rice we wanted. We had hot and cold running water—a rarity in Chinatown, as well as our own bathtub. Others in the community used the YWCA or YMCA facilities, where for twenty-five cents, a family could draw six baths. Our sheets were pieced from dishtowels, but we had sheets. I was never neglected, for my mother and father were always at home. During school vacation periods, I was taught to operate many types of machines—tacking (for pockets), overlocking (for the raw edges of seams), buttonhole, double seaming; and I learned all the stages in producing a pair of jeans to its final inspection, folding, and tying in bundles of a dozen pairs by size, ready for pickup. Denim jeans are heavy—my shoulders ached often. My father set up a modest nickel-and-dime piecework reward for me, which he recorded in my own notebook, and he paid me regularly.

On Sundays, we never failed to attend the Methodist Church, as my father's belief in the providence of God strengthened with the years, and his wife and family shared that faith. My father's faith in God was unwavering and unshakable. (Some day, we were to hear his will, which he wrote in Chinese, and which began, "I believe in God, Jehovah. . . .") I have no statistics on the percentage of Christians in Chinatown at that time, but I am sure they were a minority. Our Methodist branch could not have had more than a hundred adult members, with less than fifty regular Sunday attendants. Many of Daddy's contemporaries scoffed at or ridiculed Christians as "do-gooders" who never gambled, when Mah-Jongg games were Chinatown's favorite pastime. Father used to chase lottery peddlers away from his factory; cards were never allowed in our home. I suppose that for him, the Christian faith at first comforted him far from his loved ones. Secondly, it promised him individual worth and salvation, when all his life in China had been devoted only to his family's continuity and glorification. Third, to this practical man who was virtually self-taught in all his occupations, Christianity suggested action on behalf of others in the community, while Confucianism was more concerned with regulating personal relationships. Daddy seldom hesitated to stick his neck out if he thought social action or justice were involved. For instance, he was on the founding board of the Chinese YMCA and fought for its present location, though he was criticized for its being on a hill, for being near the YWCA, for including a swimming pool.

Group singing and community worship in a church must have been dramatically different from the lonely worship of Chinese ancestral tablets at home. He listened to weekly sermons, expounding new ideas or reiterating old ones, and sometimes they were translated from the English spoken by visiting pastors. His daughters learned to sing in the choir and were permitted to join escorted church visits to Western churches—their only contact with a "safe" organization outside of Chinatown.

If my father had one addiction, it was to reading. He eagerly awaited the delivery of each evening's Chinese newspaper—for there had been none where he came from. His black leather-bound Testaments, translated into Chinese, were worn from constant reference. Before our Sunday morning departure for Sunday School, he conducted his own lessons at our dining table. No meal was tasted before we heard his thankful grace.

In a conservative, reactionary community, most members either peacefully avoided criticism, or if involved in controversial occupations (such as gambling, smuggling), joined the strength of the tongs for self-defense. My father was neither type. He was genial, well known to the man on the street, liked to talk in public, but he had few intimate friends. Cousins and uncles sought his counsel; he never sought theirs. He contributed to causes or to individuals when he could scarcely provide for his own family, but he never asked another for help. During China's long years of conflict, first for the sake of the Revolution, and later against the Japanese, he worked tirelessly in the name of our church, to raise funds here for China war relief.

My mother dutifully followed my father's leadership. Because of his devotion to Christian principles, she was on the path to economic security. She was extremely thrifty, but the thrifty need pennies to manage, and the old world of Fragrant Mountains had denied her those. Upon arrival in the new world of San Francisco, she accepted the elements her mate had selected to shape her new life: domestic duties, seamstress work in the factory-home, mothering each child in turn, church once a week, and occasional movies. Daddy frowned upon the community Chinese operas because of their very late hours (they did not finish till past midnight) and their mixed audiences.

Very early in my life, the manners of a Chinese lady were taught to me. How to hold a pair of chopsticks (palm up, not down); how to hold a bowl of rice (one thumb on top, not resting in an open palm); how to pass something to elders (with both hands, never one); how to pour tea into the tiny, handleless porcelain cups (seven-eighths full so that the top edge would be cool enough to hold); how to eat from a center serving dish (only the piece in front of your place; never pick around); not to talk at table, not to show up outside of one's room without being fully dressed; not to be late, ever; not to be too playful—in a hundred and one ways, we were molded to be trouble-free, unobstrusive, quiescent, cooperative.

We were disciplined by first being told, and then by punishment if we didn't remember. Punishment was instant and unceremonious. At the table, it came as a sudden whack from Daddy's chopsticks. Away from the table, punishment could be the elimination of a privilege or the blow on our legs from a bundle of cane switches. My father used the switch, but mother favored a wooden clotheshanger. Now that I have four children myself, I can see that my parents' methods insured "domestic tranquility." Once, when I screamed from the sting of his switch, my father reminded me of my good fortune. In China, he had been hung by his thumbs before being whipped by an uncle or other older family member, called to do the job dispassionately.

Only Daddy and Oldest Brother were allowed individual idiosyncrasies. Daughters were all expected to be of one standard. To allow each one of many daughters to be different would have posed enormous problems of cost, energy, and attention. No one was shown physical affection. Such familiarity would have weakened my parents and endangered the one-answer authoritative system. One standard from past to present, whether in China or in San Francisco, was simpler to enforce. Still, am I not lucky that I am alive to tell this story? Mother used to point out to me one of the old women seamstresses, tiny of build, with bound feet. She came from another village which practiced the killing of unwanted newborn females, and admitted that she had done so herself in China. But a daughter was born here to her, and I remember her. She was constantly cowed by her mother's merciless tongue-lashings, the sounds of a bitter woman who had not been blessed by any son.

Thirty-five years later, I have four children, two sons and two daughters. In principle we remain true to my father's and mother's tradition, I believe. Our children respect my husband and me, but it is not a blind obedience enforced by punishment. It is a respect won from observing us and rounded by friendship. My parents never said "please" or "thank you" for any service or gift. In Chinese, both "please" and "thank you" can be literally translated as "I am not worthy" and naturally, no parent is going to say that about a service which should be their just due. There is no literal translation for "sorry" in Chinese. If someone dies, we can say, "It is truly regrettable." But if we regret an act, we say again, "I am not worthy." Now I say "thank you," "please," and "sorry" to my children, in English, and I do not think it lessens my dignity. The ultimate praise I ever remember from my parents was a single word, "good."

We do not abhor a show of affection. Each child looks forward to his goodnight kiss and tuck-in. Sometimes one or more of them will throw his arms around one of us and cry out, "I love you so."

My son, Mark, has completed more than eight years of night Chinese school, the same one I attended. I have also served on that school board, as my father before me. Unlike my well-attended Chinese classes—nearly every Chinese child in the community of my childhood was sent to night school for some years—Mark's last Chinese grade included only a handful of students. When I enrolled my youngest boy, Lance, in first grade this fall, the principal was distressed that the entering students were half the number entering in previous years. I saw parents and grandparents proudly shepherding the little ones who were to be his classmates—obviously, these were the parents who cared. The movement of second-generation Chinese Americans has been to the suburbs or to other parts of San Francisco, and it is no longer practical to send their children, the third generation, to Chinese school in Chinatown. My husband and I cherish our Chinese ties and knowledge, and waited many years to purchase a home which would be within walking distance of Chinatown. If a child has difficulty with homework, Chinese or American, he or she can come to see us at our office-studio, and we drop everything to help.

As in my own dual education, the children are learning Chinese history, culture, or what being a member of the Chinese race means. The six-year-old learns one new ideograph a day. After a week, he knew that one writes Chinese from top to bottom, from left to right. They do not lack time for playing, drawing, reading, or TV viewing. Sometimes they do complain, because Chinese is not taught as pleasurably as subjects at American school. When they ask why they must attend Chinese school, I say firmly, "This is our standard. If you lived in another home, you could do as they do." Our children chatter among themselves in English, but they can understand and speak Chinese when desired. It is a necessity when with their grandmothers. Even this simple ability contrasts with some children of Chinese ancestry. As my mother exclaimed in dismay when such a grandchild visited her, "We were as a duck and a chicken regarding each other without understanding."

As a wife and mother, I have naturally followed my Chinese training to wait on my husband and serve my children. While ceramics is my career, the members of my family know they come first, and they do not pay any penalty for my work. Chinese men expect to be family heads, and to receive loving service from wife and children, but they are also marvelously helpful as fathers, and nearly all Chinese men I know enjoy being creative cooks on occasion. If you visit the parks of Chinatown, you are likely to see more men than women overseeing the laughing children. If you shop in Chinatown, you find as many men as women choosing the groceries. My husband has given our children from birth more baths and shampoos than I have. He has also been their manicurist and ear cleaner, for once a week, when they were smaller, there were eight ears to swab clean and eighty nails to trim.

Selective self-expression, which was discouraged in my father's household, has been encouraged in our family. About two years ago, my husband established this tradition: every Sunday evening each child presents an original verbal or verbal-visual project, based on a news article, a school project, a drawing (since the youngest can't read yet), a film. We correct diction, posture, presentation, in the hope that each will be able to think aloud on his feet someday. Each of the three older children has one or more special friend. I have met these friends at our home, preferring that they be invited here rather than have our children leave home. Seldom do we plan children's parties, but when we entertain our adult friends, our children are included. How else would they learn correct etiquette and expect to fit into an adult world some day? At their age, I used to be uncertain to the point of being terrified of "foreigners." Thanks to the hospitality of our Western friends, we and our children have been guests at their homes, their pools, their country retreats. And when they come to our home, the whole family delights in helping to prepare Chinese treats to serve them.

Traditional Chinese parents pit their children against a standard of perfection without regard to personality, individual ambitions, tolerance for human error, or exposure to the changing social scene. It never occurred to that kind of parent to be friends with their children on common ground. Unlike our parents, we think we tolerate human error and human change. Our children are being encouraged to develop their individual abilities. They all draw and can use their hands in crafts, are all familiar with our office and love to experiment with the potter's wheel or enameling supplies at our studio. Sometimes I have been asked, "What would you like your children to be?" Let each choose his or her career. The education of our girls will be provided by us as well as that of our boys. My father used to say, "If no one educated girls, how can we have educated mothers for our sons?" I hope each one will be a civilized, constructive, creative, conservative nonconformist.

During the Depression, my mother and father needed even more hours to work. Daddy had been shopping daily for groceries (we had no icebox) and my mother cooked. Now I was told to assume both those duties. The management of money, time, and cookery had to be mastered. My mother would give me fifty cents to buy enough fresh food for dinner and breakfast. In those years, twenty-five cents could buy a small chicken or three sand-dabs, ten cents bought three bunches of green vegetables, and fifteen cents bought some meat to cook with these. After American school I rushed to the stores only a block or so away, returned and cleaned the foods, and cooked in a hurry in order to eat an early dinner and get to Chinese school on time. When I came home at 8:00 P.M., I took care of the dinner dishes before starting homework. Saturdays and Sundays were for housecleaning and the family laundry, which I scrubbed on a board, using big galvanized buckets in our bathtub.

Our children are all trained to assist in elementary house-cleaning and bedmaking. Each is given an allowance commensurate with his necessary expenditures. But if anyone is occasionally loaded with homework or enchanted with a book or wishes to see his favorite TV program following dinner, I never insist that chores come first.

I had no such sympathetic guidance as an eleven-year-old in my own reign in the kitchen, which lasted for four years. I finished junior high school, started high school, and continued studying Chinese. With the small earnings from summer work in my father's basement factory (we moved back to the basement during the Depression), I bought materials to sew my own clothes. But the routine of keeping house only to be dutiful, to avoid tongue or physical lashings, became exasperating. The tiny space which was the room for three sisters was confining. After I graduated from Chinese evening school, I began to look for part-time paying jobs as a mother's helper. Those jobs varied from cleaning house to baking a cake, amusing a naughty child to ironing shirts, but wearying, exhausting as they were, they meant money earned for myself.

As I advanced in American high school and worked at those jobs, I was gradually introduced to customs not of the Chinese world. My American teachers were mostly kind. I remember my third-grade teacher's skipping me half a year. I remember my fourth-grade teacher—with whom I am still friendly. She was the first person to hold me to her physically and affectionately—because a baseball bat had been accidentally flung against my hand. I also remember that I was confused by being held, since physical comfort had not been offered by my parents. I remember my junior high school principal, who skipped me half a grade and commended me before the school assembly, to my great embarrassment.

In contrast, Chinese schoolteachers acted as extensions of Chinese parental discipline. There was a formal "disciplinarian dean" to apply the cane to wayward boys, and girls were not exempt either. A whisper during chapel was sufficient provocation to be called to the dean's office. No humor was exchanged; no praise or affection expressed by the teachers. They presented the lessons, and we had to learn to memorize all the words, orally, before the class. Then followed the written test, word for word. Without an alphabet, the Chinese language requires exact memorization. No originality or deviation was permitted and grading was severe. One word wrong during an examination could reduce a grade by 10 per cent. It was the principle of learning by punishment.

Interest and praise, physical or oral, were rewards peculiar to the American world. Even employers who were paying me thanked me for a service or complimented me on a meal well cooked, and sometimes helped me with extra dishes. Chinese often said that "foreigners" talked too much about too many personal things. My father used to tell me to think three times before saying anything, and if I said nothing, no one would say I was stupid. I perceived a difference between two worlds.

The difference was not always lovely. One day after junior high school classes (I was one of only two Chinese faces there), a tormentor chased me, taunting me with "Chinky, chinky, Chinaman . . ." and tacked on some insults. Suddenly, I wondered if by my difference, I was inferior. This question had to be resolved again and again later: when I looked for my first job, when I looked for an apartment, when I met with unexplained rejection. It was a problem I felt that I could not discuss with my parents.

It is a problem which has not diminished with the years. Only a few days ago, my two youngest children came home from their walk to the neighborhood library with the story that some boys had physically attacked them as they passed the schoolyard, insulting them because they were Chinese. Immediately I took them with me and looked for the schoolyard's director, who called the culprits. There were defensive denials and looks of surprised guilt.

But our children will not be wondering for years if being Chinese means being inferior.

By the time I was graduating from high school, my parents had done their best to produce an intelligent, obedient daughter, who would know more than the average Chinatown girl and should do better than average at a conventional job, her earnings brought home to them in repayment for their years of child support. Then, hopefully, she would marry a nice Chinese boy and make him a good wife, as well as an above-average mother for his children. Chinese custom used to decree that families should "introduce" chosen partners to each other's children—a custom which has some merits and which has not been abandoned. The groom's family should pay handsomely to the bride's family for rearing a well-bred daughter. They should also pay all bills for a glorious wedding banquet for several hundred guests. Then the bride's family could consider their job done. Their daughter belonged to the groom's family and must henceforth seek permission from all persons in his home before returning to her parents for a visit.

But having been set upon a new path, I did not oblige my parents with the expected conventional ending. At fifteen, I had moved away from home to work for room and board and a salary of twenty dollars per month. Having found that I could subsist independently, I thought it regretful to terminate my education. Upon graduating from high school at the age of sixteen, I asked my parents to assist me in college expenses. I pleaded with my father, for his years of encouraging me to be above mediocrity in both Chinese and American studies had made me wish for some undefined but hopefully brighter future.

My father was briefly adamant. He must conserve his resources for my oldest brother's medical training. Though I desired to continue on an above-average course, his material means were insufficient to support that ambition. He added that if I had the talent, I could provide for my own college education. When he had spoken, no discussion was expected. After his edict, no daughter questioned.

But this matter involved my whole future—it was not simply asking for permission to go to a night church meeting (forbidden also). Though for years I had accepted the authority of the one I honored most, his decision that night embittered me as nothing ever had. My oldest brother had so many privileges, had incurred unusual expenses for luxuries which were taken for granted as his birthright, yet these were part of a system I had accepted. Now I suddenly wondered at my father's interpretation of the Christian code: was it intended to discriminate against a girl after all, or was it simply convenient for my father's economics and cultural prejudice? Did a daughter have any right to expect more than a fate of obedience, according to the old Chinese standard? As long as I could remember, I had been told that a female followed three men during her lifetime: as a girl, her father; as a wife, her husband; as an old woman, her son.

My indignation mounted against that tradition and I decided then that my past could not determine my future. I knew that more education would prepare me for a different expectation than my other female schoolmates, few of whom were to complete a college degree. I, too, had my father's unshakable faith in the justice of God, and I shared his unconcern with popular opinion.

So I decided to enter junior college, now San Francisco's City College, because the fees were lowest. I lived at home and supported myself with an after-school job which required long hours of housework and cooking but paid me twenty dollars per month, of which I saved as much as possible. The thrills derived from reading and learning, in ways ranging from chemistry experiments to English compositions, from considering new ideas of sociology to the logic of Latin, convinced me that I had made a correct choice. I was kept in a state of perpetual mental excitement by new Western subjects and concepts and did not mind long hours of work and study. I also made new friends, which led to another painful incident with my parents, who had heretofore discouraged even girlhood friendships.

The college subject which had most jolted me was sociology. The instructor fired my mind with his interpretation of family relationships. As he explained to our class, it used to be an economic asset for American farming families to be large, since children were useful to perform agricultural chores. But this situation no longer applied and children should be regarded as individuals with their own rights. Unquestioning obedience should be replaced with parental understanding. So at sixteen, discontented as I was with my parents' apparent indifference to me, those words of my sociology professor gave voice to my sentiments. How old-fashioned was my parents' dead-end attitude! How ignorant they were of modern thought and progress! The family unit had been China's strength for centuries, but it had also been her weakness, for corruption, nepotism, and greed were all justified in the name of the family's welfare. If the system were so great, why could not China stand firm against Western violations? My new ideas festered; I longed to release them.

One afternoon on a Saturday, which was normally occupied with my housework job, I was unexpectedly released by my employer, who was departing for a country weekend. It was a rare joy to have free time and I wanted to enjoy myself for a change. There had been a Chinese-American boy who shared some classes with me. Sometimes we had found each other walking to the same 8:00 A.M. class. He was not a special boyfriend, but I had enjoyed talking to him and had confided in him some of my problems. Impulsively, I telephoned him. I knew I must be breaking rules, and I felt shy and scared. At the same time, I was excited at this newly found forwardness, with nothing more purposeful than to suggest another walk together.

He understood my awkwardness and shared my anticipation. He asked me to "dress up" for my first movie date. My clothes were limited but I changed to look more graceful in silk stockings and found a bright ribbon for my long black hair. Daddy watched, catching my mood, observing the dashing preparations. He asked me where I was going without his permission and with whom.

I refused to answer him. I thought of my rights! I thought he surely would not try to understand. Thereupon Daddy thundered his displeasure and forbade my departure.

I found a new courage as I heard my voice announce calmly that I was no longer a child, and if I could work my way through college, I would choose my own friends. It was my right as a person.

My mother heard the commotion and joined my father to face me; both appeared shocked and incredulous. Daddy at once demanded the source of this unfilial, non-Chinese theory. And when I quoted my college professor, reminding him that he had always felt teachers should be revered, my father denounced that professor as a foreigner who was disregarding the superiority of our Chinese culture, with its sound family strength. When Confucius had already established his ethics for civilized behavior, the Westerners were bloodthirstily persecuting Christ. My father did not spare me; I was condemned as an ingrate for echoing dishonorable opinions which should only be temporary whims, yet nonetheless inexcusable.

The scene was not yet over. I completed my proclamation to my father, who had never allowed me to learn how to dance, by adding that I was attending a movie with a boy I had met at college, unchaperoned.

My startled father was sure that my reputation would be subject to whispered innuendos. I must be bent on disgracing the family name; I was ruining my entire future, for surely I would yield to temptation. My mother underscored him by saying that I hadn't any notion of the problems endured by parents of a young girl.

I would not give in. I reminded them that they and I were not in China, that I wasn't going out with just anybody but someone I trusted! Daddy gave a roar that no man could be trusted, but I devastated them in declaring that I wished the freedom to find my own answers.

Both parents were thoroughly angered, scolded me for being shameless, and predicted that I would some day tell them I was wrong. But I dimly perceived that they were conceding defeat and were perplexed at this breakdown of their training. I was too old to beat and too bold to intimidate.

That stormy disagreement climaxed my departure from total acceptance of my parents' ideas and authority. In the thirty years which have intervened, my receptiveness to Western ideas has not meant my unequivocal acceptance. Each situation which arises requires its own evaluation. Sometimes the Western assumption is rejected; sometimes Chinese caution is discarded.

My present standard of values was remarkably amplified at Mills College, which offered me a general scholarship because of a good junior college scholastic record. Mills is primarily a residence college for women, and I was given a chance to live on campus by working for room and board in the home of the dean. Additional duties at her office enabled me to earn money for books and necessities.

Many classes were small in number, with less than ten students. The professors' methods here were the opposite pole from the Chinese. No longer did I memorize wise echoes of the past. The emphasis was on originating, creating, articulating. I was awkwardly unsuccessful at first. But I groped, was made to express my thinking aloud, and had my ideas discussed, rejected, or commended by an audience. I learned too to make and fire pottery and copper enamels, an art that was to become my work. My two years there for completion of my B.A. degree convinced me that education in the liberal arts was a lifetime prize well worth my four years of struggle. It was a valuable concept to learn that academic excellence and skill with one's hands were compatible. The traditional Asian scholar from China to India, even today, refuses to get his hands dirty except with ink. I also learned to lay down forever the fear of prejudice, for I learned what educated Westerners thought of the Chinese culture.

Flanking the entrance to the Mills Art Gallery were two ancient Chinese marble "Fou Dogs," also called Temple Lions. Among the courses which thrilled me most was the one on the history of Chinese art. Those years of dull Chinese evening classes had not included this subject. My art professor at Mills, a European, spoke and read the Chinese language, which led us to fascinating discussions. The instructor for my pottery course emphasized that the greatest achievements in ceramics have been Chinese, with the Sung Dynasty (960 to 1279 A.D.) known as the Golden Age of pottery.

In the field of English at Mills, my work compared the Chinese novel with the English novel—the term paper was read at a conference. For English Club, my anecdotes on Chinatown delighted my classmates and advisor. Thus I concluded that my Chinese background could be accommodated in the widening knowledge of the Western world. Together with my parents' faith in the superiority of the Chinese culture, these exposures convinced me that my background was no liability.

This conclusion was strengthened by the personal friendliness of those whom I met in the new environment. Daily living with the dean was a calm and reassuring experience. I respected her, but she was my true friend and counselor. In her home, I met famous guests, such as visiting speakers and musicians, who were sincerely interested in me. In associating with the encouraging, exacting professors, mingling with students both Chinese and Western, none of whom cared that I alone in my circle of friends had to work my way, my restricted mental confines expanded. Even learning to laugh was an uncertain new sensation.

On occasional weekend home visits, I did not attempt to tell my family of my new life and slipped into the expected behavior forms. They were therefore most surprised when they came to the campus for my graduation ceremonies. They found an exhibit of my handicrafts at the art gallery. They were also astonished when Aurelia Henry Reinhardt, the president, came up to ask to meet my family and to be photographed with me.

Pearl Harbor's destruction had occurred six months before that graduation day. It was patriotic to look for a job related constructively to the war effort. I decided that I would work for a while, to save money for graduate studies, which were necessary for a social service degree. At that time, I thought that this type of training would utilize my Chinese and Western educations for some type of effective work in Chinatown.

I moved back to my parents' home, which had been improved by a move from the basement to a second-floor location. The garment business was profiting from the war boom. My older brother did not complete his medical training, but was helping my father in his business. Moreover, we had a new baby brother, Jon.

I first worked for the Red Cross, then the shipyard, performing various secretarial duties. I thought it patriotic to work for organizations concerned with the war effort. When a San Francisco newspaper sponsored a contest to find a solution to absenteeism, I did research around our shipyard, interviewed medical authorities outside, and wrote a paper which took top prize. The reason for "absenteeism" was not complicated: human beings cannot work seven days a week to reap overtime pay, week after week, and not have to reckon with the physical inability to keep up the pace. My reward for finding this out was the honor of christening a liberty ship and a gift of a great round sterling platter. There was a good deal of newspaper fanfare, my paper was read into the Congressional Record, and the entire incident became the seven-day wonder of Chinatown and of my family.

After three years in the working world, I made some observations not in the realm of books. I was uncertain that helping people through a social service career would bring me the most rewarding work—many who needed help resented it. Traditionally, Chinese have distrusted investigators. In business and in civic work, I had no problem in getting along in a Caucasian world. If anything, people's interest and cordiality had been heightened by my difference. Yet I knew that secretarial work could never lead me to a great future.

How could I utilize my dual educations? I longed to be in some field which would someday bring me to see China. What work could I do in which I would find no prejudice as a woman? I went alone to the country, where I could think in quiet beauty, close to nature. Troubled, seeking, I had an idea. I liked making pottery and I liked writing. Could I not make a modest living for myself in this combination, which could utilize all I had learned? If I failed, I could return either to the conventional work world or to graduate studies. I was starting from nothing, so I had nothing to lose.

I was already working at my potter's wheel at home. A corner of the sewing factory was allocated for my equipment and cans of clays. At the age of twenty-four, I began a tiny business. I found a Grant Avenue shopkeeper in the heart of Chinatown who permitted me to install my wheel in one of his display windows and to sell my pottery in his store in return for a commission to him. Whenever I was throwing pottery in the window, day or night, great crowds gathered and automobiles caused traffic jams. I sold pottery, too, but not to the curious Chinese. When Chinatown's residents looked at my stoneware bowls made of California clays, they did not see the art in them. "Why, this is a rice bowl!" they would exclaim. "And not even a porcelain one. Only rough clay, suitable for coolies. How can she ask several dollars for something which would cost a few dimes in China? She will soon go out of business." I learned a peculiar human characteristic. People would talk about me as if my presence were not there, and they never thought to ask me for the explanation—that there were no porcelain clays in

California and I made one-of-a-kind pieces, not sets of rice bowls.
And when I went around Chinatown, I was jeered, "Here comes
the girl who plays with mud." They must also have thought, "Here
is a college graduate foolish enough to get her hands dirty."

Today, twenty-three years later, they do not jeer or patronize
me. A Chinese artist friend tells me that when the popular crowd
finds his calligraphy beautiful, he shudders. But when they cannot
understand, then he knows that he has risen above the common-
place. By my occupation and my interests, I have become a minority in my own community.

I soon outgrew the store window and moved into a wooden
frame building my father had purchased on the western edge of
Chinatown, after carefully agreeing to pay my father the full normal rent. Daddy became a frequent visitor, not only to check on his
property, but because he was genuinely concerned with my career.
He had told me that his father had always stressed the importance
of owning one's business, no matter how small, without partners.
Grandfather Wong also thought that anyone who knew how to use
his hands would never starve. But the kindest remark Daddy made
was that I had vindicated his promise to relatives that he "would
bleach the disgrace of our ancestors" in respect to their treatment
of women.

I discovered that it was impossible to work at pottery when I
liked and write when I liked. "The work of one day is gazed upon
a hundred days" is a familiar Chinese admonition to make that
day's work worthy for gazing. Handwork should not be rushed, fir-
ing failures had to be remedied, and a host of other nonhandwork
business details had to be handled. It took three long years before
the ceramics business promised to survive.

In achieving new forms and colors not tried before, I retained
principles of Chinese harmony, restraint, color tones. Through trial
and error, a range of shapes, sizes, and stock colors was developed
which could be sold wholesale to fine stores and retailed to visitors
at my studio. A number of exhibition prizes and museum purchase
awards brought favorable recognition.

When I had been the most distracted over the success of my
business, my mother had surprised me by a remark as I walked past
her machine, "Jade Snow, it is fine to have a career when you are

young, but it is not a complete life for a woman. When you grow older, you should have a husband to care for you in sickness, and children to relieve your loneliness."

I had assured her that I wasn't antimarriage (I had turned down several of their "introductions") but that I must marry someone right for me. As it happened, the man who was to be my husband, Woody, a childhood acquaintance, returned to Chinatown after fighting in World War II, to be amazed when he saw me working in that store window. We decided independently about our marriage and then told my father, who was pleased. Woody's mother had been one of his home seamstresses, and when I had been a visitor to their home, riding that wheelbarrow, Woody had been sufficiently enchanted to buy me my first ice cream cone.

Woody studied handicrafts, especially silversmithing, at Mills during the summer before our marriage, preparatory to joining me in business. We planned a simple wedding and were married by the chaplain at Mills, who had been one of my professors. The dean and her husband were our matron-of-honor and best man. Our guests reflected my years of independence and growth from the Chinese community, for there were more Western faces than Chinese, although both our families were present.

Just about the time I had started the pottery business, I received letters of inquiry from Harper & Bros., signed by a woman editor who had read some magazine articles, expanded, actually, from college papers, which I had written about Chinatown. She asked me to think about writing an autobiography, and when I consulted with my junior college English teacher, I received further encouragement on the project from her. The timing of our wedding was two months before the publication of my book, *Fifth Chinese Daughter*, in 1950. That book's rapid initial sales amazed us. It had been dedicated to my mother and father, and when the first royalty check came six months after publication, my reaction to its amount was to want to share it with my parents. Though my ways were different from those of their other children, I was no less filial and grateful. First, I asked my husband for permission. His reply was, "You don't have to ask me about anything which is right." He, too, is a Chinese son in a big family.

I telephoned my father to say we would come home to him for

dinner. He wondered why. I replied, "I have something for you."

He was suspicious, "What is the something?"

I was secretive, "A surprise—you must wait."

Daddy and Mama were both in the kitchen, preparing the dinner. My gifts had been properly wrapped in red paper, as at New Year's, for presentation. My father opened his envelope at once, beamed in excitement, and gave his hundred-dollar bill an American kiss. My mother continued to cook, and ignoring her envelope on the stove top, murmured a rare "Thank you." Later, she left the kitchen with it, but made no additional comment.

Sometimes my father's grace was routine, sometimes it was a silent moment, sometimes it was to ask forgiveness for our sins. But tonight, it had a different tone. As my younger sister and two younger brothers, my husband, my mother, and I bowed together with him, he said, "We are gathered here because of a book about which fellow villagers, merchants, and friends on the street have been congratulating me. For this book was written in America by a Chinese, not only a Chinese, but a Chinese from San Francisco, not only a Chinese from San Francisco, but a Wong, not only a Wong, but a Wong from this house, not only a Wong from this house, but a daughter, Jade Snow. Heavenly Father, this accomplishment was not mine but yours. From your many blessings this girl, raised according to your commandments, was able to do this work."

My father, mentioning me in a prayer for the first time, had accepted me, and a part of him had accepted America. At the age of seventy plus, after years of attending night classes in citizenship, he became naturalized. He embraced this status wholeheartedly. One day when we were discussing plans for his birthday celebration, which was usually observed the tenth day of the fifth lunar month by the Chinese calendar, he announced, "Now that I have become a United States citizen, I am going to change my birthday. Henceforth, it will be on the Fourth of July."

My father's realistic adjustment was the more unusual because I knew that his emotional orientation was to China. As long as I could remember, I had seen hanging above his bed a pair of portraits of his mother and father, with photographs of their funeral processions and other pictures of their tombs. Annually, he sent to his village a generous amount to pay for grave pilgrimages and the necessary offerings. He had shown me the family manual, which carried maps of the sites and stipulated the quantity of food to be borne there, all by foot.

A few years later, he was increasingly weakened by the infirmities of old age and various physical problems and was bedridden for many months at home, with my mother nursing him. Finally, he asked me to arrange for an ambulance to take him to the Chinese hospital. I longed to spend more time with him, for I knew it was a terminal illness, but a four-year-old, a one-year-old, and another baby on the way prevented much absence from home. He died twelve days before my second daughter's birth. My father had chosen Chinese names for my two oldest children. For this second daughter I chose alone, Beautiful Wisdom.

Even though a daughter, I make the pilgrimage to his south San Francisco grave, for my oldest brother died and is buried not far from him. Can we be sorry that Daddy's bones do not rest near his adored mother? For he has given his own loved ones expectations of life which could not have been theirs in Fragrant Mountains.

6
Time and Tide

ROOTS OF BLACK AWARENESS
John A. Williams

Of all the immigrant Americans, the blacks represent the only ethnic group still migrating in large numbers, and what they are leaving when they can, as other immigrants left, is oppression and economic and spiritual poverty. Their movements from South to North, from farms to city, express the unfaltering hope of all men that a better life exists in regions where they did not grow up.

As with most American Negroes of my age, my roots lie in the Deep South. My mother's family lived for generations in that most obscene, most vicious, most ridiculous and murderous state in the Union, Mississippi. When you are oppressed, as any immigrant can tell you, you fight back if you can or dare; if you cannot and you have the means, you leave. If that is impossible, you stay and accommodate yourself to it and hope for a break in the near future.

My mother was the eldest girl in a family of three boys and five girls. Her name is Ola, a name found also in West Africa. She went from Mississippi to Syracuse, New York, joining after World War I that restless wave of humanity shuffling from old home to new. Descended from a family five generations in America, she traveled within the boundaries of her country and was untouched by the immigration laws of 1882, 1917, and 1924. But she was a stranger who was quickly recognized by and restricted because of her color.

She met my father in Syracuse, a city that counted blacks among its residents in 1769. My father's family had lived in the city for many generations. They married, these two, and as my birth neared, they journeyed to Mississippi for the event. It was some kind of custom.

That journey to Mississippi in 1925 and the return to Syracuse still represent the longest trip my father has ever made. That trip, plus the memory of the trains that rolled down the street near our house, must have triggered something in me; I've crossed America five times and visited twenty-eight countries, some of them two or three times. The lust for travel could have started in the womb.

Blacks existed in the backwashes of the Syracuse community. The war had raised the economic level of the city. In fact, my mother had come north to work for a white family. She thought the North was salvation; while the streets were not paved with gold, she sensed opportunity. In Syracuse white people did not ride down upon you at night, and they did not lynch you. But she did not know that in Syracuse the white population simply left the black population to moulder in the narrow alleys along E. Washington Street, where the Negro section was.

There were few complaints of segregation or discrimination; the immigrant population the world over expects to start at the bottom and work to the top. I sometimes think that the blacks of my parents' generation were the last to believe, at least partially, that hard and honest work brought good reward. We moved about the city, within well-defined areas, most of them close to the New York Central rails that went through the heart of the city. Our moves, of course, were made hand in hand with our fortunes, and these were tied to my father's work. He was a day laborer; the label "non-skilled," bears a stigma today, but it didn't then. I live in New York City now and I don't often see men dressed in the clothes of a laborer—gray trousers, bulky, colorless sweaters, dust-lined faces, and crumpled caps or felt hats bent out of shape; nor do I smell honest sweat anymore, strong and acrid, as I used to smell it on my father and later on myself. I remember him—a chunky little man a bit over five feet tall, all muscle, and with the sharp face, high cheekbones, and prominent nose of an Indian—walking briskly down the street in the mornings, trailing his hand-truck behind him. He supported us on his back and muscle, his sheer strength, which was considerable.

Death visited our home twice, taking two girls in infancy. Not satisfied, it hovered about. My mother suffered a severe case of spinal meningitis, but recovered completely. My younger brother, Joe, fell ill with pneumonia, but my grandfather, Joseph Will Jones, visiting us from Mississippi, rushed to the hospital and gave Joe some of his blood and Joe pulled through. We like to remember that story; it somehow adds strength to the family.

Besides Joe, I had two sisters, Ruth and Helen. We had a host of minor illnesses: earaches, sore throats, and toothaches. We learned very early that one of the side effects of being poor is that you become used to pain. Medicine and doctors cost money. There were free clinics, to be sure, vast halls smelling mysteriously of medicines, nurses in starched dresses rustling by, and from some faraway room sometimes you could hear a scream or a groan. But to go to the clinic could cost a parent a half-day away from work and this in turn, would cost in food and rent. Therefore, if you woke up ill, you concealed it as long as you could for fear that the moment when you revealed the illness, the light of accusation would spring to your parents' eyes. We tried not to get sick.

I should not have survived childhood. Once I electrocuted myself (at least, that's what the folks said) by pounding a nail through the cord of a radio that was plugged in. Once I set fire to some flypaper and it fell flaming to the dining room table, which caught fire. Once I stumbled into a deep shaft and was just barely caught by the wrist by a stranger with red hair. Twice I almost drowned. When I was not in that kind of trouble, it was something else. I swiped the grape juice used in the church communion; I darted between the legs of passing women and looked upward; I snarled at strangers, was rude to elderly people, and regularly played house with the neighbors' daughters.

Then, peace, I discovered books.

The Syracuse Public Library on the corner of Montgomery and Jefferson streets, a gray limestone building of some mongrel design, smelled of books from downstairs and clay from the craft rooms upstairs. I was allowed to take out four books a week instead of two; the only kid in my class. I began to change, I think, when I discovered books and began to devour them. My chores seldom got done. The books were always being confiscated. "Those damned books," was a phrase I heard for a long, long time.

Of course, if I had read the Bible with as much diligence, it would have been all right. My mother was a Methodist. My father wasn't much of anything, as far as religion went. I did not like church, perhaps because we had too much of it. We went to Sunday School, stayed for church, and then either returned in the early afternoon or went to a local mission. I was usually given the longest speech to learn and recite for Christmas, Easter, Mother's Day, and so on. I did these in a secondhand black Buster Brown suit with a celluloid collar and tie which someone had given to me. The suit was the most durable piece of cloth goods I've ever worn; I spent the better part of my childhood Sundays in it.

The first Sunday of every month was Communion. I don't remember at what age I stopped taking it, but it was early. I recall deciding that I was no angel and I wasn't going to pretend I was, or would be, so I didn't go up to the altar and kneel for my grape juice and matzoth. The church was already filled with people who raised hell all week and became Christians on Sunday; I was not going to be one of them. I did not know then that that was the way things were; that that was the way they had to be if you were a black adult living in Syracuse. For if you thought honestly about your life there and did not bring in a deity to help see you through, you'd have to kill yourself. Church helped.

In the worst way my mother wanted me to stand, as is the habit in the African Methodist Episcopal Zion Church, and acknowledge God. The occasion for this opportunity was every Sunday when a part of the services were dedicated to saving sinners. I was not aware that I was a sinner. I had some knowledge that I wasn't a good boy at all times, but I was damned if I was a sinner. "Won't you come to God?" the pastor would intone, holding out his arms while the women wailed and men closed their eyes so they could not see which one of them would this time be the victim. The choir would sing chorus after chorus of its most gently menacing hymn; tears would flow and from time to time a muffled voice would cry out in a mixture of joy and anguish, "Oh, Lord God Jesus!" My father, who, at my mother's behest, had joined the choir, would sit up there looking straight ahead, seeing nothing. My mother would look at me, her eyes filled with tears.

My first Sunday in church after three years away in the navy during World War II, my mother and I sat in a front pew. I was in uniform. The pastor looked down at me during the "save the sinner" portion of the services and held out his arm. *He* cried, my mother cried, everybody cried, and the choir sang like it was really out to get me this time. My mother was pinching me and pleading with her eyes. "Go to Jesus, Johnny." I had to refuse her because I didn't have it in me. She gave up that day. It had been a long struggle; the clash of our wills had exhausted her. I don't think she thought that her God had brought me back from the war, and therefore, in her eyes I shouldn't have needed saving anymore.

But the church was more than a worshiping place; it was the place where the immigrant renewed himself as a member of the group, where the traditions of the group were reinforced, where shelter was found from the storm. The person who veered away from church was liable to get hurt. More important, by his acts, he could bring hurt to the group.

I had no clash of will with my father, for he left the running of the house and the disciplining to my mother. He was a soft-hearted man; not a coward, just soft. The world was running right up his back with all those mouths to feed, and he discovered he could not fill them. For a man who thought of himself as a man, he realized that he was failing in that most basic of manly tasks, to provide for his family. He was not privy to all the sociological and psychological information about why he could not; he might have blamed it on being black, and that was indeed correct. But there was also the Depression and he could not handle both. And so he left, repeating an old, old immigrant pattern. He didn't leave because he wanted to; he left because, being a man who for some reason was not able to perform as one, he was too filled with shame to remain with us.

Long before he left, however, my father and I had good times. He was a sports fan from his chitlins out; they don't put them together that way anymore. I don't know how many Sundays we spent walking or riding the streetcar to some far section of the city to watch a baseball or football game. Even today my father will not tolerate being disturbed on Saturday or Sunday afternoons when the football games are on television.

It took me some time to realize it, but both my parents were strong people; they had no choice, they had to be. But then, most blacks have had to be strong and were. Oh, they worked the most menial jobs, performed the toughest labor, but I remember laughter and parties and singing and dancing; remember picnics and loud voices; suits and dresses carrying the odor of just coming out of the cleaners that afternoon. All was not totally grim; life bubbled, or forever sought to, beneath the hard grind of everyday life. However, for me something of a pall settled when my father left.

But there had always been school to keep a kid busy. Sometimes I enjoyed it. Washington Irving School was in a mixed but predominantly white neighborhood when I attended it. I got along well with most teachers, but there were some who did not like Negro children.

It now seems that my generation that lived in cities like Syracuse went through what the black kids are going through now by entering neighborhoods and schools where they are not totally accepted. A child feels, but does not always retain the feeling; life is too filled to bursting with new experiences, why cling to the bad ones? So, I'd almost forgotten about Miss Wooley, whose name and image now came raging back without hesitation. She taught arithmetic. If you *looked* like you were going to make an error, she'd let you have it with anything handy, fists, an eraser, a ruler. Because of Miss Wooley, I make my eights from the wrong side. I know that it's easy to place psychological blame on the past, but the truth of the matter is that Miss Wooley scared me and ruined my capacity forever to deal effectively with numbers. That I *do* remember her and have written about her speaks for itself; Miss Wooley was one of those experiences I could not outgrow.

I can recall reading *Little Black Sambo* and feeling warm because the eyes of the white pupils were on me and the two or three other black kids in class. He was black, we were black, and black back then was neither an adjective or noun that Negroes spoke with pride. Little Black Sambo was grotesque looking; we were grotesque looking. *Little Black Sambo* hurt; it hurt very much. The story made me aware that I was different from the white kids I played with, and from *Little Black Sambo* on, I was likely to be more evil than pleasant or merely competitive when we played our games in the schoolyard. I had to prove, man, that *I* was not like that little clown in the book.

As a child I was more readily accepted in the homes of poor whites than in those on a somewhat better economic level. I can recall waiting on more than one porch or in more than one hallway while white friends ran into their homes for a moment, their parents standing guard across the door or watching me on the porch through curtains.

This was in the Fifteenth Ward, the nicest section we'd ever lived in. It was heavily populated with Jews, mostly from Russia or Poland, and a scattering of Poles and Irish. I did most of my growing up in the Fifteenth Ward and had as many white friends as black for a time. I didn't have any feeling one way or another when, upon reaching the sixth grade, the Jewish kids began to draw together, walked home in clots, and after school went to the YMHA; nor did I feel anything when the Italian and Irish kids began going to the Catholic Youth Organization. We went to Dunbar Center. Of course, we had our little battles with the Irish and Jewish guys; our snowball fights on the way home from school, which were continued after dinner and on into the night, degenerating into free-for-alls. We had our thing, they had theirs. Wasn't that the way it was supposed to be?

The center, named for the black poet Paul Lawrence Dunbar, was our home away from home. It was located on South McBride Street across the street from the building that served as the Syracuse University Medical School at that time. I was a bugler in the center's Drum and Bugle Corps. We were good enough to be asked to parade several times a year, and on one of those occasions a group of white businessmen gave us a plaque. It read: "*Dunbar Center* Fife *and Drum Corps.*" For years that plaque hung on a wall of the center and no one spoke of the error. I don't think anyone dared. That plaque always signified to me the futility of black existence in Syracuse.

After my father had gone, to be seen no more on Sunday afternoons dressed in a suit, vest, spats, and cocked felt hat, set off with a brilliant tie, my mother worked every day. Sometimes I went with her to take care of the heavy work. I came to hate the back doors of white people's homes, hate the sight of my mother laboring in kitchens—eyes sparkling, however, because she had a job. At home she was the figure of authority, but in someone else's house, she might just as well have been as young as me and without any authority at all. How white society undermined the relationships between blacks, even blacks in the same family.

My father was in the city, but we didn't see too much of him following a rather stupid agreement made by the children's court where we lived with my mother for one month and with my father the next. Finally, we settled with my mother and had to listen to her unending commentary on my father's "shiftlessness."

But he had not been a lazy man. Work as he knew it, as he had always known it, had run out for him. Poles and Italians who could not even speak English were given the few jobs available. There had been times when I went with my father in search of a job to those public places where jobs were sometimes available. The faces of the applicants were crushed, beaten; the men wore dirty, crumpled caps and the stink of poverty, black and white, hung thickly in the air. I remember the embarrassed greetings, the reek of stale cigarette smoke, the spittoon disinfectant. My father was not lazy.

At home we went on the dole. A great amount of illogical thinking went on in the public assistance programs. If you were on the dole you weren't supposed to work, even if you wanted to, or your dole would be cut down. Many people desperately wanted to keep their self-respect and would work at anything. Recipients cheated, but the cheating had little to do with money. It had everything to do with self-respect. My mother lied to the inspectors and told them she wasn't working when she was; she told us how to lie to them. A matter of self-esteem and survival. We survived and the wounds healed; a sleeve could be pulled down over the scars.

I could not, of course, depend on my folks for pin money. Sometimes I went out on Tuesday nights alone or with some kids from the neighborhood and collected magazines, newspapers, and metals and sold them to the junk man. If I knew of an empty house, I would strip it of its lead and brass plumbing to sell. When there was nothing else, I climbed over the fence of the junkyard at night, stole a bag of rags, put them into another bag and sold them right back the next day. During the high Jewish holidays, I'd linger in the street and wait for the Orthodox Jews to call me in to light the gas on their stoves or turn the lights on for them. I became, at a very early age, self-sufficient.

Long, long before my father left home I had become a runner-away. If I'd had a whipping coming, a real bad one, I simply cut out. If I believed the whipping unjust, I also ran, but for a kid who had wings on his feet, I only ran so far because I didn't even know the roads out of the city and I didn't know which relative to run to. I usually spent my nights in a pine grove on the Syracuse University campus. I swiped Christmas trees from this same grove whenever it began to look like a sorry Christmas was coming on, which meant no tree and no gifts. I'd take my sled and pull it to that grove planted by the College of Forestry, select a tree, whip out a saw, and cut it down. Things always looked better to my brother and sisters when I came home with the old Yule tree. We never had a Christmas without gifts, though. Never. As for the whippings, whenever I returned from one of my little trips, the whipping was ten times worse than it would have been had I stayed. It took me a long time to learn that by my behavior I was threatening the black immigrant group. Had I not returned, the police would have had to be called; there would have been notoriety. Mrs. Williams can't handle her son; he's a terrible boy. There was a tremendous amount of pride in that poor, black, pathetic in some ways, society, and there were values of the highest humanistic quality. Crime was not tolerated; neither was disobedience. One way or another the kids had to measure up, and those who couldn't or wouldn't placed their parents in awkward positions. And there was sympathy for the parents.

The immigrant poor are always torn between two poles: the immediate needs and the long-range satisfactions. For many the immediate needs were money, and money could only be obtained by working. Thus, parents watched their children grow and considered that at sixteen they could, according to law, drop out of school and take jobs to help support the family. On the other hand, the parents also realized that only with education could the vicious circle of poverty handed down through the generations be broken. In my family we, too, had to face these considerations.

I don't really know how I viewed school at that point. I was just starting to get into literature, and I liked sports. I ran track, played football, baseball, and basketball. I never realized until I was an adult that I was just a bit undersized for some of these things, which was a blessing; I grew an ego more than twice my size.

At first, staving off the inevitable, I worked mornings before school in a pet shop, and afternoons when classes were over as a delivery boy. It seemed then that just about every other elevator operator in Syracuse was queer. They came at you with jowly smiles and stiff forefingers; you were forever forced to keep your back to the wall on deliveries. Later I worked the four to twelve shift in a factory that made rifle stocks, for World War II was already on. Eventually, I started to work full time, and as a result, I didn't graduate from high school until after I was discharged from the navy, at the age of twenty-one.

If I had thought that discrimination affected my life before the navy, I was overwhelmed by it after I was in. From start to finish it was segregated. The navy was one great club for southern bigots and I hear it still is. Strange when you consider that once the American navy was heavily black. From Great Lakes, Illinois, to the Solomon Islands, the Marshall Islands, the Palau Islands to the Marianas Islands, Jim Crow walked the planks of the navy, on ship and shore. I had a little trouble with it.

And I had that trouble alone. No fellow marchers, no reluctant police protection, no newsmen to report the black side of it. My letters went Stateside with only the salutation and closing surviving the scissors, and many a censor ordered me to his tent, gave me beer, and explained why I shouldn't write what I was writing. But my personal war had to go on.

While I know that much of the popularity of writing by Negroes today rests on what we black writers call the "black crucifixion syndrome" (Look what you done to me, Charlie!), I don't set down the following for any other reason than to chart, to some degree, what goes into the makeup of a black immigrant.

It was inevitable that I would get into "trouble" in the navy, and I did. On Guam I was brigged within sight of Admiral Nimitz's headquarters for "disobeying an order"—one of those racial orders which I did not obey. My sentence was five days bread and water and hard labor. It was a marine brig and therefore considered to be much tougher than a navy brig. I had to walk two miles for the half loaf of bread and pitcher of water that I got three times a day. I was lucky. Four other black sailors had to go it in chains. They had killed a white officer who deserted during an action down in New Guinea. The trusty for my barracks was a cracker who'd put his .45 at the head of a Negro and made him go down on him. Most of the people in the brig were black.

On the way home I was brigged in the fire control room of an LST for washing my socks in fresh water, like the white sailors did. As I was led into the small room, two white marines tossed in packs of cigarettes and matches. There is no place to lie down in the fire control room of an LST. It's used only for the fire control officer to press the buttons that permit the guns on the ship to fire. I did three days there, bread and water and utter darkness. The marines dry-shave you when you become a guest in their brig. I was shaved often.

Once while *not* in a brig, I walked shaking into the mouth of a cracker's .45 and walked away without holes in me. Of course, I'd never do that now; I'd have me a .45, too.

In short, I was glad to get out of the navy, where I had started to write what I considered poetry. I don't really remember how or why I started. But I was drawing more and more within myself.

When I was discharged I returned to high school and finished the semester. I met my first wife during that time and we married the next year when I entered Syracuse University. I applied to Howard University, but they turned me down, so it was Syracuse, and like generations of black young men before me, I wondered how I would do in competition against white students. Of course, in the public schools I had met this challenge, and in athletic events as well. The navy, too, had prepared me for this. Still, to a small extent, I was apprehensive. I need not have been.

No one can point to my breaking any scholastic records while a student, because I certainly didn't. I was working part-time and raising a family as well. It did seem to me that the white students were a great deal more casual about the college experience than I was, and this went for the ex-GIs as well. Perhaps they understood that, being white, a college education was merely frosting on the cake they already had. I looked at college as though it were the hand-truck with which to secure work. My father had to take his with him when he was looking for jobs; a man who didn't own his own hand-truck was seldom hired. College, I thought, was to be my tool. There was a big difference between its being the frosting and the hand-truck.

I was writing poetry now, still not convinced that I would become a writer, and publishing some as well. I went through the regular and summer sessions and the summer I graduated, my second son was born; the first had come three years before.

To be married is strain enough, for there are always two urges, one male, one female. Infinitely more so than white females, the black female cries for security because it has been so lacking in black marriages for external reasons. The Negro wife directly or indirectly makes it known to her mate that she doesn't appreciate any divergence from the normal; security is the goal and all else—until very recent times—is virtually unimportant. (Much of this has changed, at least on the surface, with the advent of black awareness. Black women are just as outspoken, if not more so, than black men.) It is all right to want to be secure, to raise children in security; it is a fair and an utterly human desire. What is more fair, and we have now come to that time, is for the black woman to be able to share the dangers, with her mate, that lie outside what has been normal in past black existence. My wife and I simply grew apart. Once she had not the slightest desire to meet white classmates or coworkers. I thought this was a fear of competition, and if it was, she later overcame it and, indeed, far outstripped her white contemporaries in her career.

As for my sons, their lives will be vastly different from what mine was. The world may be the same rotten place, but their approaches to it are more deliberate; they are vastly more sure of themselves than I was. They are far less intense about how and where they will fit in. Gregory graduated from Syracuse in 1969. He is now teaching and pursuing a master's degree in education. Dennis entered Cornell in 1968 and shows considerable talent as a writer. Adam, from the second marriage, is only three. Greg has married and his mother's house seems empty with both boys away. There they had their own rooms; they drove their mother's car. They moved then and now, at ages twenty-two and nineteen, with a sureness I envy with all my heart, but I am grateful and proud that they are better able to handle the problems of today than I was when I had them yesterday.

But I often sense that they must prove themselves to be at least equal to, if not better than, me in all things, and I fear they may have built a trap for themselves. It is a human trap, but for black families where fathers traditionally have rammed the wall of failure (and I have not, just yet), the drives to outdo Dad can become all consuming, excluding goals that are more important to them. We have discussed this and we're all aware of the risks, and of the reasons why this feeling exists at all. This, of course, was something my parents never could have done with me because the situation was never present.

To speak of failure is to recall my own as a writer; I had just about failed on my terms. My first book was written when I was thirty and published when I was thirty-five. I came by writing accidentally; if there had been opportunities with white companies in a number of fields in which I trained, I'd have wound up in the nine to five routine, gladly. But I've found discrimination and prejudice in publishing and writing. I've not been freed from these things because I'm a writer, but, indeed, have just come in touch with an entirely new facet of race relations. I think I've grown accustomed to the fact that in America a black man, wherever he is and whatever he is, cannot escape racial considerations, an experience untrue with other immigrants. In publishing I've found just an extension of the old life, whether conscious or unconscious. The end is the same.

My family now has accepted my being a writer; it did not at first; they seemed to feel that writing was like a bad cold and soon would pass. In a family where everyone for generations had earned their bread with muscle and sweat, as I once earned mine, I felt I had become a freak. I was like a brain-damaged child born into the bosom of a hearty, muscular clan, and I felt guilty for a long time.

Young black writers will go through the same thing until we have established as a race here in America a tradition of books, literature, and writing. Once in this nation, it meant death for a black man to even learn to read; but we are freeing ourselves of this fear.

Like most American blacks, with the coming of what has been

called the "black revolution" I thought more and more about where my family came from. Other immigrants had roots in Europe or Asia; they could return to those homes and feel a sense of continuity. Not so with the Negro immigrant.

My father's family was a mess. There was an Uncle Bernie in the family, as white as this page, with blue eyes. A couple of cousins have freckles, and in the correct sunlight, red hair. Still, my father's name was John Henry and some part of the pure black South must have touched his ancestors at one time.

Ola, my mother's name, always struck me as odd, and Mississippi was a great state in numbers of slaves. It happened then that I went to Africa twice and in Nigeria found my mother's name. It has two meanings: in the eastern region, the land of the Ibo who make up the dominant tribe, it means "courageous one" and "keeper of the beautiful house." In the western region where the Yoruba live, it means "he who wants to be chief." All three fit very well.

I told this to my mother and showed her slides of buses with her name on them, but she remained unimpressed. She has always been concerned with the here and now; the problem of finding roots was an intellectual one for which she had little time in her life. She only knew that her parents had given her the name; she did not recall any grandparents or great aunts having it, and yet through the curious routes of the mind she was given it, an African name.

Because Negroes were excluded from American society, many of us turned with a vengeance to Africa and African "culture" with the coming of the "revolution" in the late fifties and early sixties.

We didn't seem to feel or notice that the independence sweeping Africa was at best tenuous, filled with economic considerations that were still very much tied to Europe; nor did we pay attention to the sudden rising of the "black elite" on that continent who were just as officious and just as cruel and greedy as the Europeans had been. We were so eager for a small sign of black self-assertion in this great white-dominated world that we accepted African independence without reservation.

I had met a number of African students and they always seemed to me somewhat distant; and I had worked for a time with an organization concerned with the politics of the African countries. Like many organizations with like interests in this country, we were always backing the wrong man to become premier. So it happened that I became one of the few, very few American Negroes, compared to the black population in the United States, to visit Africa, and I went twice, in 1964 and in 1965.

I met American blacks who had fled the United States and its segregated social systems who were anxious to return to New York, Chicago, Detroit—wherever they came from, for they had discovered that Africa, after all, was not a place of refuge for them. Many African communities in the western part of the continent set aside a small portion of their villages for people who did not have family or tribal ties; in Nigeria this part of the village is called the Sabongari, and a man may live in it all his life and not ever really belong to the community. The American blacks did not live in these areas, but they were just as effectively cut off. As a result, American blacks and whites in Africa tended to be closer there than at home. Single Negro women from the States tended to fare better; these usually were with the foreign service or the Peace Corps.

One of the saddest cases involved a young Negro man who had worked at the U.S. satellite tracking center in Kano, Nigeria. He resigned from what obviously was a challenging and lucrative position as an engineer to help the Nigerians; he planned to teach electrical engineering. The Nigerians did not accept his offer and he had to move into the Sabongari, where he did odd jobs in order to survive. I hear that he finally left the north and went down to Lagos to sell American-bred chickens in a supermarket.

I traveled through ten countries trying to see reflections of my family, but what was most obvious was that the white man had done as effective a job on the Africans in their own land as he had done with blacks in America, for everywhere those Africans who could appeared to be living by or trying to live by the standards of the European. In the Congo and in Nigeria many of the young women wore wigs; I even saw a couple of young men with the processed hair one used to see occasionally on young "hip" Negroes here.

Much of this piece has been given over to reviewing the past, but a black immigrant must also look to the future. It is a future in which all the other immigrant groups have been absorbed into the

American system; so absorbed, in fact, that Afro-Americans stand
alone as an outgroup, with those who came long after him barring
his entrance to the supermarket of the nation.

I see this as a most dangerous time for the black immigrant.
After eight generations his patience has run out. What nonsense is
it that he cannot have as much as those who have been here but
one generation and contributed far, far less? It is dangerous because
the black man can no longer be turned away with faulty education,
the dregs of a technological system already outmoded, and the
clichés of the past. But the system is not now geared to even care
more than adequately for the white population, which in any case
regards what it has as being too much for the Negro. The clash
appears to be inevitable, which is fitting because the system was
established on nearly free black labor in the first place.

Negroes held in slavery, in fact, could be said, as Ralph Elli-
son has said, to have subsidized immigration. They were the back-
bone of an agricultural society, providing the wealth therefrom to
kick off the industrial revolutions, which in turn required more
labor, cheap, of course, from Europe.

The most unlikely white coalitions have been formed; white
immigrant neighborhoods have spawned the likes of Daley of
Chicago and Louise Day Hicks of Boston and Spiro Agnew of
Maryland.

Disaster can only be deflected by the back-to-the-ghetto movements by educated blacks who are taking the time to help train
Negroes who haven't had their opportunities. And what we say
at the conclusion of meetings or seminars with the man in the street
is that when we do come out, we're coming out bad. That means
with all the skills, education, and tools this society demands—plus
whatever else is necessary to secure a place and function in it as a
black human being.

In America the black immigrant looks around the world and
sees that it is the nonwhites who have the poorest educations, and
he asks, "Is that an accident?" He sees that it is the nonwhites who
are always starving, and he asks, "Is that an accident?" He sees
that it is the nonwhites who have the highest death rates, and he
asks, "Is that an accident?" More and more by circumstances, by
awareness, he is being drawn outside his nation to other nonwhites

because he is weary of the global "accidents." He is coming to know that his salvation lies with these liaisons because white America has demonstrated time and again that it doesn't mean what it says.

The black immigrant has settled, I think, into a pattern of cynicism out of which he has begun desperately to cope with his problems. He can't count on anyone else. Not anymore. I share this view; in fact, I help to promulgate it.

In that respect my views and the views of some children of other immigrants are the same. The lid has been lifted off the can; America, man, do you stink.

But in my time I've also been a garbage man and as such I handled the stinking cans, turned them up and emptied them, banged their edges on curbstones until the last white maggot fell out to cook on the hot asphalt roadway; and sometimes with lye and brush and steel wool and boiling hot water, scrubbed those garbage cans until they glistened, could never stink again as before, and maybe, never stink at all.

7
America, the Thief

A JEWISH SEARCH FOR FREEDOM
Harry Roskolenko

It was another time and another place, then, on Cherry Street. It was the lowest part of the East Side amid crowded-together, five-story, wash-hung tenements. Everything was immigrant laden, a bazaar of colors and bizarre languages. It was 1907 and a year of panic.

I was born into a self-contained Yiddish ghetto. Though we were the majority, the ghetto also housed Poles, Russians, Irish, and Italians. All of us had our special places, dictated to us by our faces, our speech, our jobs, our music, dances, and books—and, of course, our religion and country of origin. Each one lived in a ghetto within a ghetto. Did we mind it? We wanted to be among our own people, our own language, our own religion, and to be ourselves down to our last Jewish roots.

Home came equipped with a fire escape for summer sleeping— an iron porch open to the world. Every floor had four railroad flats. On our floor, the one toilet in the hall served the four families— two Jewish, one Russian, and one Polish. There was a yard in back and a house in the rear, two stories high. Here, in their own selectivity, lived the poorer of the poor—in back, unable to see what went on in the tumbling, fierce activity and continuous gabble of the strident streets.

The architecture was created some time before 1870 by the Tenement Houses Building Company, by variously borrowed English conceptions for mass housing for the poor—and by the Tenement House Law enacted in 1901 to safeguard the poverty of the poor from the hazards of the planners, the builders, and the city's early breed of real-estate profiteers.

But whether you lived in the front house or in the rear house, it was a home if your parents made it a home. We had a Russian-Jewish home that included three beds in tiers, warmed by a Russian stove; a samovar; huge, downy comforters; great, soft pillows; Jewish charity boxes; no pictures; mirrors that faced the wall—to offset vanity, my mother said, though this was traditionally done for mourning. The stove, a mammoth iron and brick affair, had been built by my father and took care of all heating and cooking needs. We had towel racks, boxes and bottles for cereals, tea, and vegetables, ice in the icebox—and six children warmed by my two God-graced parents.

We wore what my father could buy for us. It meant old clothes, bought secondhand, for school and for play, and new clothes, first-hand, for the Sabbath. My father, skilled and unskilled, had no trade worth much when I was a child. He was, at times, a cloak presser, which paid little in wages and took its sad toll of his health. I used to see him sweating in a Greene Street factory during the summer, steam rising from the heavy pressing iron and enshrouding his thin body. Scars across his naked back recalled the lashes of the czarist *nagaika* from his soldiering days. Another trade, earlier, had taken him to the slaughterhouse of Wilson & Company on First Avenue, on the site where the UN keeps the peace of the world today.

Before coming to America he had been a Jewish peasant in the Ukraine. He had run a mill, as well. A man of the land, he was to spend most of his life in sweatshops after he arrived, in 1895, at the age of thirty-five. And he was never to know anything good no matter where he worked in New York. For it was the wrong time for a man of half skills who preferred God to the making of money to be in the United States of America. My mother, who was not financially illiterate, was soon calling America "America, *Gonef*" (America, the thief).

My father, named Barnett, was called Berel by all—and no one understood how he had gotten that English name. He was five feet five inches tall, slender, brown-eyed, half bald, whimsical, hardly a great scholar, but sufficiently learned in the endless concerns of Judaism. His small black-gray beard, which he trimmed for the Sabbath, made him look like a doctor who had too many patients without money. To see him walking in the street, most professorial and dignified, was hardly to recall that he was a cloak presser, a leader of a Judas goat, a man with half skills who looked too neat for the slaughtering century that had just begun.

My mother, Chai-Sura (Sarah), lived for God's graces even more than my father did. Short, a peasant by her way of talking and walking, she was blond, blue-eyed, and high-cheeked. She had a rosy glow and God figured endlessly in her conversation. She could neither read nor write, but she memorized every prayer and ritual and knew as much as the old rabbi did at the *shul* on Madison Street off Montgomery.

God was in every mystery for my mother. *Gehenna* (hell) was there as well. And *Gan Eden* (heaven) would assuredly come the "day after the day after." *Gan Eden* was a mystery she was always trying to unravel for me, and when I told her that Catholics and Muslims also believed in the hereafter, I would get a small lecture about the impossibility of God's existing for anybody but us—the chosen of the chosen. When I said that there were Negro Jews in Harlem, she was astonished at first and later insisted that I had invented them. When I was ten years old and I asked her, "What if your daughter Edna wanted to marry a Negro Jew—what would you do?" she slapped my face and that ended my sociological explorations. For my mother there was only God, *Gehenna,* and *Gan Eden*—the hereafter for all good Jews on Cherry Street.

Cherry Street had great traditions, we knew. It had once been most important. Even George Washington had had his official home there in the early days of the republic. As kids we reenacted this bit of history and selected sides. One side became the British redcoats, the other the Colonials, and the leader took over as George Washington himself. We battled by land and by sea. It was our way of acting out American history in fact and in legend—as new Americans.

Three blocks south of Cherry Street ran the East River to the Lower Bay and out to the Atlantic Ocean, with ships going to every port in the world. It was later to become the liquid route that I took to leave the ghetto's circumscribed interior life, the squat-smelly streets—and my parents' Judaism. The East River was my Jordan River, crossing into the unknown Gentile world of other woes, fears, and disguises.

I had almost drowned in that river when I went sailing to the Statue of Liberty on a raft. The river was my refuge when I needed to escape from fatherly rebukes, minor beatings, garbaged streets, dead horses, shrill laments—and the rabbi. Then I would sit on a decaying pier under the Manhattan Bridge or the Brooklyn Bridge and watch freighters slide through the scummy river; or old schooners that still had golden figureheads under the foresail; or the hustling ferries going to Brooklyn, passing the fishing boats that put in at Fulton Street with a load of fish just caught in the Atlantic. The piers were my second home—before and after the synagogue's spiritual ravishment.

I was part of a once-large family, but only six of us were left —four boys, and two girls, all born on the Lower East Side. In the Ukraine, before the turn of the industrializing and ravaging century, eight others had been borne by my stolid mother. They had died in infancy in those times of easy dying. But we, Americans all, were tougher, burlier, hardier, and better fed. We were another set of health statistics. We had more possibilities, if less of God; though my father tried to give us both with the bread my mother baked, the wine he made, and the guided spiritualism of a man who was as Old Testament as Moses with his stern, fatherly hand.

The vast migrations from Eastern Europe created the Jewish ghettos on the Lower East Side. What cities and villages did the new arrivals not come from? The place-names, like the burial societies and other *vereins,* have their own sociological myths today. When you talked Yiddish, you did it with a special accent, as you did English. We were either Litvaks or Galicians, and soon somebody was laughing at the heavy accents with which we pronounced words like "bread" and "butter." But we laughed loudest at the Hungarian Jews, for they had the funniest and broadest accents on the block. And, occasionally, the teasing about accents would start a fistfight. Over bread? Over butter? It was insane in a happy Jewish kind of way.

But whoever our neighbors were and no matter from where

they came, they had, like my parents, come with bundles, bags, old books, downy pillows, feather comforters in red-pink coverings, copper pots, samovars, candlesticks for the Sabbath, and menorahs for lighting up a golden holiday.

All of them were seeking the *Goldeneh Medina*—the Golden Land—within a few square miles of the Lower East Side. But what they found became New York's triumphs and tragedies of reckless architecture, sudden slums, terrible factories—and the high-rises that still signify rush, hurry, ghetto gutting, and today's city living and dying from every pore. They had come in a hurry in the holds of ships, to build the *Medina* in the New World. They had come from something much worse, but between 1900 and 1970 they and their sons contributed much of what we have today, including the garment industry, the jewelry trades, the retail shops, the current medical and dental professions, and some of New York's searing landscape.

It was a long haul for all. It was a time for speed, not for permanent values. It was the time for mass living, mass production, mass consumption—and the massing city was unable to plan for anything but immediate living space.

The Jewish immigrants, from my parents' total view, had enough sustenance in their vision of God; though God was hardly enough in tough New York's mammoth encampment. But if God was enough for men like my father, their sons, in time, changed the tokens of value. God became success. Success became money. The rigid rituals and values of Judaism were changed by default. Their sons, of course, joined the temples of worship. But going there on the High Holy Days did not make them *frume Yidn*—religious Jews. In my time we had called the temples *shuls*. They were simple buildings, primitive, hardly worth an architect's time. We went there to pray, not to play bingo and run raffles. We had one purpose—to go to God. All our words were God-graced, and we were humble as we prayed and sang about the glories of the Lord on Cherry Street.

That has changed, of course. America, as an image, has changed the edifice, the manner, if not all the tokens of faith. The American way, for all of us, from Jews to Gentiles, has given us the vulgar interludes of added attractions to a fading faith. The dollar's green sign hangs seen and unseen from churches and synagogues. Faith is not enough today. The dollar and doubt are more inspirational, at times. The "big giver" and the sociological lecturer have replaced the moral and spiritual leader who guided my father in his time.

When I was a child, New York was the natural Mecca for the immigrants coming to the New World. And every letter to my father, written in Russian, Polish, or Hebrew, from some relative in our Ukrainian town, Zareby Koscielne, usually ended with the question. "When will you send money for a *shifskart?*"

The ship's ticket was a passport to Cherry Street, East Broadway, Delancey Street, night school—to all of the United States taking in the huddled masses. It was a ticket to family honor— redeemed at Ellis Island by brothers, sisters, cousins, uncles, and friends. It was money given like a grant-in-aid, rather than as a returnable loan. It was blood money in its most honorable sense— money given so that others of one's clan could get to Ellis Island, and, soon enough, to the Orchard Streets all over the hustling, emerging United States of America.

When the newest arrival was picked up at the huge immigration terminus, he or she was soon bedded down in my father's house. Cots were pulled out. Children's sleeping arrangements were doubled up. The kitchen became a bedroom. The living room was a room for everything, especially for mass meetings of relatives.

How was everybody in Zareby Koscielne? Who was the rabbi? Had the *shul* gone under? Was Uncle David still on his farm? How many cows did he have? What, a new wife? His fifth? Such strength! How many children does he have now? An army full!

"God should forbid such things," said my mother.

"Why?" asked my father. "Uncle David is built like a bull— and what should a bull do?"

Within a month the new arrivals had jobs, a flat, and they were saving money for other members of the Roskolenko tribe left over in Zareby Koscielne. And that was the way a minor portion of a street in New York City was settled, the unions built, the sweatshops worked in, new trades learned, new children born, new *shuls* attended. The studious traveled even farther. Those who could afford to study and manage to work their way into the professions left the pushcarts and the sweatshops to their fathers—for American-made professional bargains. For all of us soon learned that the green dollar did not grow on green trees. It came via Ellis Island, heartbreak, bad health, and pain.

The search for an easier life made some members of my father's large family go off to Chicago, into the heartland of the Middle West. Before them there had been other Jews taking this same route, with wagons, horses, and their huddled energies, spreading their arts and crafts toward the West. But we remained on Cherry Street, content with having a great river as our neighbor. On Cherry Street everybody knew everybody. There were no strangers, Gentile or Jewish. And my mother could talk Russian to Russians, Polish to Poles, and Yiddish to our own. But whatever Cherry Street was, it was no bargain for anybody on the block. If you worked twice as hard as the next man you would soon transform yourself into a normal American immigrant on your way to everywhere and nowhere.

What had brought them all to Cherry Street and the other ghettos? Czarist persecution, anti-Semitism, impossible old worlds, conceits about the New World—as well as a mishmash of feeling and relationships. My father had never seen a pogrom, though after he left Russia, a relative was killed in the Kishinev pogrom of 1903. My father had left because he got tired of being a conscript soldier and of being beaten, scarred, and humiliated. Russia had lost a war to Japan; a revolution had taken place in 1905; and, as usual, the Jews became the scapegoats of the *pogromchiks*—the czarist-inspired hordes who murdered the Jews. Eight hundred and ten Jews were killed and 1,770 were wounded. After that, the Jewish immigrants arrived at Ellis Island in droves. In 1906, 150,000 Jews migrated to New York.

The Jews, believing that God's ways, though mysterious, would nevertheless protect them—fled from Russia, and Cherry Street, one of a hundred blocks to receive these new hordes of immigrants, was fully and finally settled as a ghetto within a cosmic, freewheeling nation. In fifteen years, between 1899 and 1914, more than a million and a half immigrants came to Ellis Island—and most remained in New York.

Our home was a little bit of Russia made by my father as a self-taught carpenter. The beds, for the children, formerly triple-tiered, gave way to American bedding, especially to the iron folding cots and beds that every Jewish household hid behind doors or in corners. In the center of the living room was a huge table with the breathing, bubbly samovar. A gas mantle, the white webbing encasing the gas jet, burned above it. In the kitchen, which consisted mostly of a tub, a huge stove, a round table, and us, was a gas meter. Over the stove was a water boiler. The tub, which had been built for washing clothes, was used for our weekly bath before the Sabbath or when we were not being rushed down to Rutgers Street Public Bath with towels and soap. We lived between bits and pieces of two countries, the mixture serving to fuse and confuse us all the more.

As children, we were American-grained from the start. But to our parents we were always Jews, never Americans, though we lived within a perplexing set of physical and spiritual nuances. Our Jewishness came with the preparation for the Sabbath. It meant going to the bakery with a ten-pound iron pot filled with meat and vegetables, the *tsholnt*. The pot cover was tightly sealed to keep all the odors in the pot, and I was usually the one in our family who carried it to the bakery on Monroe Street—a sweaty, flour-laden place operated by a family of four. They baked and they shouted. They were down to their underwear at the back of the bakery, shoving the pots into the huge hot recesses of the baking oven. There the pots remained for twenty-four hours, baking slowly; and there I would go back after Saturday's morning service, to take the hot pot back home for the best meal of the week. My mother blessed the *khale*—the Sabbath bread—over the candles still burning from Friday; my father blessed the wine, and all of us turned to the *tsholnt,* awaiting the pot's exotic revelations. The slow cooking of the *tsholnt* was always done at the bakeries—we could not do it at home, and nobody ever did.

All these acts were ritualistic. Like the coming of the *shabes goy* to turn off the gas mantel on Saturday or to light the stove and heat something for our big feast. On the Sabbath only a Gentile boy or man, the *shabes goy,* was allowed to do that.

The drinks, too, were ritualistic. My father, an old Russian hand at religious-type bootlegging, made kvass, a scarcely alcoholic beverage made from stale bread, as well as schnapps, mead, and beer. During the week, since he worked twelve hours a day, he had his schnapps on coming home. We watched him sip it, turn red in the face, cough, roll a cigarette, ask what damage I had done that day—and then sink into dinner. It might be fish, borscht with meat and potatoes, or a stew, always with black bread, tea. Then he turned to his Jewish newspapers.

During the week he was worn out. On the Sabbath he glowed. During the week he was the presser of cloaks, standing on his badly varicosed legs, pushing a ten-pound pressing iron. It was piece-work from factory to factory; from Greene Street up to Seventh Avenue. The factories made religious Jews turn to socialism, anarchism, and unionism in those harrowing, deadly days before World War I. And on the seventh day, as he filled a thimble full of schnapps for all the children and my mother, he rested. . . .

He was to vote Socialist often, though occasionally for a Democrat, depending on whether the candidate was Jewish. He voted racially, as did most Jews on the Lower East Side; and, good union member that he was, he went to meetings regularly on East Broadway, or to his Bialystoker Sick and Death Benefit Society, named after his native province of Bialystok and meeting over the burlesque show on East Houston Street. He read all the newspapers, mostly Hebrew and Yiddish, that my mother sold from her newsstand at the synagogue on Madison Street . . . and he would, on occasion, grin while reading.

My mother would ask, "What is so funny, Berel?"

"Nothing is funny, Chai-Sura. Everything is tragic everywhere . . ." yet he was smiling, hiding some private joke, turning pages of *The Forward, The Journal, The Tageblatt, The Stick*—papers that had a variety of political outlooks and, one of them, *The Forward*, later reached a peak of 220,000 readers. Today, with only three of them remaining, *The Forward* has seventy-five thousand readers. My father is no longer one of them.

"You can vote," I said one day, forcing him into embarrassment. "A big letter came today. You are a citizen, Father."

"I am a citizen?" He smiled whimsically. "After all these years? I must vote?"

"Got zol ophitn—a citizen *nokh* (God forbid—a citizen yet)!"

went my mother. "How much money did that cost you that you don't have? Is God a citizen?"

"Money like that cannot be counted, Chai-Sura. I must vote, of course. God does not vote in America. . . ."

"For whom will you vote?"

"For Meyer London, of course. . . ."

"Not for Dickstein?" said my mother. "He wears glasses too, Berel."

My father voted for a man he believed looked even more distinguished, Meyer London, a Socialist with glasses, who ran for various offices. I had taught him enough English to enable him to pass the literacy test. I had taught him how to sign his name—but in the area of politics he was so knowledgeable that there was nothing that I could tell him about Socialist and Democratic politics on the East Side.

"Did God tell you how to vote? Did the rabbi?" asked my mother. "If you're looking for yesterday—you won't find it today."

"Voting is not one of God's problems. As for the rabbi, let him be the good Jew and teach us God's ways and not democracy," answered my father, rolling another cigarette.

My mother never voted. She had piety, not literacy—she believed in more God, more faith, more charity. These were enough, then, to give her immortality and to make a family grow up on Cherry Street.

Our folkways were based on daily verbal festivals. We talked a blue streak in Yiddish about everything. The radio had not reached us, though some neighbors had a crystal set, with earphones —and they would occasionally call us in to listen to strange voices crystallizing from a black box made of Bakelite or some tubes burning brightly. My mother listened and said that it was God, of course. The telephone was also God's work. So was seltzer water, for getting the gas out of your stomach. So was the schnapps, that made some men *shiker* down in the saloons—the Irish and the Poles, but not the Jews, who never went into the cellar saloons off the corner of Gouverneur Slip. And despite all the festivals we had on holidays or when relatives and friends visited, no one ever got *shikered* (drunk) in my father's flowing house. There tea took the place of too much schnapps; and *lekakhs,* a brown honeycake, went with the fruit and the diverse talk.

Our folkways also included a warning song, *"Shikker iz a goy vayl er iz a goy."* (As long as a man is a non-Jew, he's a drunk.) It was a song from Russia and Poland used against the *pogrom-chiks,* and it had a mocking racial air. You laughed, felt superior —being nonalcoholic—and you went on to other rational matters.

Goy, then, was as much a word denoting a possible Christian drinker who might drink too much as it was a word merely denoting a Christian. Today, in retrospect, with many cheap ironies being used for galling twists in linguistic humor, I am hardly able to appreciate racial jokes, or Jewish comics, or rabbis turned professional comedians. But in those days we were just Galicians and Litvaks—able to laugh at each other. You laughed and you laughed! In England it must be the same between a Yorkshireman and a man from Lancashire.

For reasons that were as much physical as psychological, sickness among Jews had a high ratio then. They were strangers, aliens, Jews—who'd always been preyed on. In those days, the small fat man or the tall thin man with the goatee and the black bag who walked up to the fifth floors of our tenements must have taken the Hippocratic Oath seriously. The doctor came. He had his basic equipment. Your lungs, your heart, your fever, your sores, your eyes, your throat—whatever your trouble, the visits all cost a dollar or less, with the medicine. If you did not have the dollar you owed him a dollar. The doctor, too, came from the same *gegent,* or district. He was a *landsman.* He had been a neighbor in another country. He knew the history of your kith and kin. He was an honored man, then. He healed. We believed in doctors, for they were like the rabbis. They smoked. They smelled of tobacco. They were tired all the time—and when they visited, they were soon drinking a glass of tea and eating some Sabbath cake.

The visit of the doctor was as social as it was medical. We usually got better and without psychological overtones. Up at three and four and off to work, we were too harried to conceive of anything psychiatric in our myth-laden midst. We had God, we knew. After God, or before, there was no one with whom one could talk anything over except the dollar doctor, a man related in a thousand ways to our past, especially on the strident, hectic Lower East Side.

Accidents were always with us. When I was six my mother was run over by an ice truck. She had crawled beneath it to pick up some fallen pieces of ice—a habit of poverty to keep the food we had from spoiling. The truck ran over her right shoulder. Her right arm was amputated . . . and we were amputated, with permanent grief. She was fifty-one then, and went on selling newspapers and taking care of us.

Horses kicked you as you patted them. We were clumsy with horses, though they were then on the way out, as electric cars purred with increasing frequency along the dirty streets. Horses, dirt, mobs of kids—everything and everybody took to the middle of the street, and accidents were the natural result. The sidewalks were for stands selling fruit, newspapers, shirts, and old clothes. The gutters, where dead horses lay for days or until a special truck came along to haul them off, were most of our playgrounds.

"Horses have nothing to do with God," said my wisdom-laden mother. "Nor do dogs, cats, and rats. They *peyger* (perish like dogs, without an afterlife). . . ."

I used to insist that horses and animals were like human beings, but somewhat dumb. Many of my friends were just as dumb though they talked forever about everything and nothing. A cat was a cat. A dog was a dog. An animal *peygered*. Did animals suffer? My mother doubted that animals suffered. Jews suffered, she was certain. There was sickness. There was sin. There was death . . . and in our home there were no animals—not even cockroaches, we were so clean.

Animals suffered. I knew. There was that cat that I had thrown into the East River off Corlears Hook Park, to teach the cat how to swim. It swam, but back to me. Did I want to drown the little cat? I wanted the cat to do what I could not do—to swim to the Brooklyn Navy Yard, just across the river. Instead, the cat drowned —and I suffered for years after that. Today, when most of my friends are cat lovers, cat dander plays havoc with my nose, and, without doubt, my floating subconscious.

Half heathen that I was in my mother's eyes, I cried over the drowned cat. It meowed into my dreams, and the Brooklyn Navy Yard howled in my dreams. That cat, a stray without a tag, with no special color, just pure cat, turned me into an amateur lover of animals. It made me take to nature and eventually to the wilderness, all over the world.

We knew about death as children learn about death. Death came to sick people. Death came from accidents, horses, trucks, broken heads, cops' clubs, gang fights—and sickness. But only the old died, we thought. Death was for the aged, a phantom without a calling card. When one of our young died, we thought it strange, hardly in keeping with God's design and will.

My sister Esther was killed by a truck at the age of fifteen. Elsewhere I have written about the accident but not much about Esther. She was the oldest of the then six children. She was all glow, most beautiful—on her way to becoming a *femme fatale*. She worked as a salesgirl at Hearns on Fourteenth Street. She walked the two miles to the store in the morning, a book and some sandwiches in her arms, and she would read her book in Union Square during her lunch. She had no particular gifts except her beauty— dark, Russian, and Semitic. She was all smiles, warmly affectionate with my one-year-old brother Bill, called Velvel; always hugging the pink baby, talking about making a middy blouse, helping my one-armed mother get the house in order—and she was killed by a truck that belonged to Hearns as she was walking down Lafayette Street on her way home.

Who knew about lawyers? What we knew, we got—a shyster, called so by all of us Jews and for basic reasons. In those days some lawyers had just begun to chase ambulances—to gear up their law practices. My mother found one without much of a practice. Some years later, five hundred dollars was given to her for my sister's death. What the lawyer got—the lawyer knew. We never found out.

"What is there to find out? The ways of the law outside of the synagogue?" asked my mother.

All those accidents! I often wonder how any of us, though agile enough to escape getting our heads broken daily, managed to live through our growing-up days. Gas explosions occurred regularly in the tenements. People fell down open elevator shafts. The wooden floors of the tenements fell in. Fire escapes broke, flinging sleepers into the streets. There were terrible fires.

I was the permanent witness to pain at home. My father was locked into a freezer at Wilson & Company. My father was hit by bricks—almost losing an eye. On the outside, the fights between the gangs were routine—and often they occurred on the quiet Sabbath. Then Jews were attacked because they were Jews. A bearded man, or one with a yarmulke, would not dare walk down certain streets. A democratic civil war went on continually all over the Lower East Side.

Gangs and politicians went together. Tammany Hall had its gangs—for Election Day routines. Each block had its fighting gang, taking in everybody. It was pure block kinship—disregarding origin, speech patterns, and religion. The gangs were nations unto themselves . . . and when we fought each other, we acted as early heralds of darkness on the American soil. Years later, in Spanish Harlem, the gangs were to fight over their turf, over their girls, over their alleged cultural differences, including the color of their skin.

In our day the fighting was seldom about religion, except when it came to the Jews. Then we were suddenly Jews—they, Christians. The saloons, always open, and too many to a block, brought out the drunken fighters. Who did not get a beating in those primitive days after the turn of the century? Women, children, strangers —and even cops.

Occasionally I would go to meet my father up at Wilson & Company, the slaughterhouse. It was a long walk to First Avenue and Thirty-eighth Street. But I did not walk. I hitched rides on the trolleys—for no kid ever paid his way when he could hitch it. Once at Wilson & Company, I would find my father deep in blood and slaughtered sheep. I was there to see him because I had a letter from Russia that looked as if it needed an immediate reply.

I saw the sheep and I saw the endless rivers of blood. Behind a gate was the ram, the Judas goat. Behind other gates were the sheep. Down a dirty track he led all of them . . . and I would say,

"Papa, how can you do this? Does God know what happens at the end of the track?"

"He knows, son. There is no other job here or over in New Jersey for a Jew. . . ."

Poles, Swedes, and the Irish worked there at Wilson & Company. They slaughtered for the Gentiles, not for Jewish rituals. What was my father doing there among all the Gentiles? They thought he was a whole Russian, not a Jew.

"What does the letter say?" I asked.

"It's from Gidalya—Mama's half brother. He wants to come to America. He has four sons and a wife and they are hungry, he says. I will call a family meeting for Sunday. . . ."

On Sunday, they came—a mob, all of them relatives. My mother would tell me who they were—for the tenth time. When they left, I forgot them again. Who was the fat woman with the skinny husband? Who was the man with the bulging gold teeth? Who was the short woman with the gold watch on a chain over her big bosom? Who was the one with the gray wig? Who was everybody and anybody? They were uncles, cousins, and aunts in a glorified Gilbert and Sullivan opera, Russian-Jewish style.

They crowded into the living room. They stood. They sat on the floor and window sills. They ate herring and black bread. They drank up all the homemade schnapps, kvass, and mead. Nothing was left but words, promises, some torn dollars that were pushed over to my father—all entered into a ledger.

Somehow, within a year, Gidalya arrived. Later his wife and their four sons came. It was all very simple from the herring and the schnapps to bring a new greenhorn, often called, when angry, a *maki,* a *griner,* or a *griner tukes* (a green ass), to Cherry Street. When Gidalya came, my father told me to take him to the baths on Rutgers Street for two hours, "So he does not bring Russian lice and the ship's lice into the house."

We knew the seasons the way we knew God in the synagogue, for the holidays denoted the weather in our souls. Spring meant joy. Summer's heat meant fire-escape sleeping, flies, bugs, the praying mantis, butterflies—and swimming bare-assed in the East River. Fall meant the harvest festival of Succoth, with a beautiful little grass hut, in the back yard, that my father built to honor the gathering in of the crops. Around the little hut we ate and danced. There we sang Hebrew songs. There we left Cherry Street and went back thousands of grassy years. We thought of Moses in Egypt—and all the prophecies that my mother insisted would soon be fulfilled.

The seasons, too, had their patriotic holidays, with July 4th as the hottest and holiest of them all. Bonfires—great conflagrations. Speeches, along with rotten eggs. Stink bombs, along with patriotism. Brass bands. Noise. Cops acting kind on that day. But, when Columbus Day came, there was always an argument. Somebody said that Columbus was a Jew, wandering about like one. My mother merely said, "A curse to Columbus," with the traditional Yiddish *"A klug tsu Columbus!"* He had discovered America. But so had my father, born in 1860, coming four hundred years after Columbus. And all my father could say, when asked about Columbus Day, was, "I will not get paid for this *yontev* (holiday). A double *klug tsu Columbus!"*

Schooling in my time, at PS 31, was very stern. The teacher, though not a cop, was nevertheless a ruler-wielding teacher. We knew the ruler because it was often applied to our asses by both teacher and principal. We would get slapped, and they were right. I was never right at any time—said my parents, who were immediately told of each incident by a note from the teachers or the principal. They sided with the teachers, and my report card proved that I was sleeping when I should have been studying. I was *left back*—a phrase that became quite familiar around our house.

Besides going to the bakery and carrying important letters to my father, I had other chores, like getting up at three in the morning to help my mother at her newsstand. This chore did me no good at school; I slept and was slapped. I answered questions wrongly and was slapped. For every error, from spilling ink on girls' dresses to feeling their bottoms—I was slapped. Schooling, oddly, was very stern even when I was not getting slapped.

Nevertheless, all of us learned quickly. There was no easy route to high school and college. We did not smoke or take dope, though opium was not exactly illegal. We saw the smokers in Chinatown or up on Sixth Avenue under the El and they were strange people. They had glassy eyes. They shook with palsy.

None of us wanted drugs, nothing but ice cream sodas and swimming at Coney Island.

When I asked my mother about opium, she shook her head.

"What is opium?" she asked.

"They put it into a pipe and smoke it in a hurry. . . ."

"I'll ask the rabbi about opium," was her next statement. "Do Jews smoke it?"

"Only the Chinese in Chinatown," I said.

"Then it's not God's or the rabbi's problem."

"Whose problem is it, Mother?"

"The Chinese, son."

Election time came with bands and orators without loudspeakers. The orators stood on hurriedly made platforms and shouted to us from cupped hands about poverty, working conditions, sweatshops, and child labor. For the Socialist-minded Jews, there was always Meyer London, who lived on Grand Street and wore those fancy glasses my mother had mentioned. Obviously, his glasses made him a great man in our eyes. He had some special vision, we thought, as we listened to his Socialist explanations regarding our human situation.

Who was not a Socialist then in our midst? It was hard to conceive of a Jew who was a Republican, yet there were men like Dickstein, a Democrat, who always managed to get elected to Congress. After Meyer London there was Judge Jacob Panken, who, to my mind, merely had a first name called Judge. He was always being elected. As a Socialist with a heart, he gave out lighter sentences than many other judges. And there was the really great Socialist leader, Morris Hillquit, our Marx and Engels by Jewish fiat. We had not yet heard of Norman Thomas, although we knew of Eugene V. Debs.

The Socialists would do their best talking in Yiddish in front of *The Forward* building on East Broadway, up against Seward Park. It had to be Yiddish to get any sort of sympathetic listeners. Women in babushkas, just as they wore them in Russia and Poland, listened and cried. Men, who from their appearance might just have come over from Warsaw and Lodz, looked stern, shaking their heads at what was happening to them. Twelve and fourteen hours a day. Lunch, about twenty minutes. Piecework, which meant self-slavery. Strikes. Cold factories. Hot factories. Airless traps. Fires, always fires. The 1911 fire at the Triangle Waist Factory, that killed 146 girls and women, was constantly referred to by organizers from the Amalgamated Clothing Workers Union and the International Ladies' Garment Workers Union. The Socialism of panic was all over East Broadway.

Socialism, with its idealistic language, had special appeals for us Jews. After all, had it not come from Europe? But this was New York, corrupt and democratic, but with amazing energy. We could vote—and they could not vote in another country. There were no cossacks on horses whirling the *nagaika*. No Siberia, either. But it was capitalism terrorizing the working class, said Morris Hillquit, our leader—"so vote for Meyer London and Jacob Panken. . . ."

When we talked about Socialism at home, it was more through the use of symbols than from actual knowledge. Had my father read Marx? He'd heard of him. Had he known any Socialists in Russia? A few. Would he vote for a Socialist who was not Jewish? He looked puzzled—then said no. It was Yiddish Socialism with East Broadway, his sick and death benefit society, his membership in the union. It was Socialism over a glass of tea with lemon on a side dish.

Who wasn't poor in those days? When poverty included 80 per cent of the people on the Lower East Side, it lost its private meaning. It was there for all. Of course, we had charities for the really poor and the sick. Children without fathers or sad-looking orphans received special attention. Jewish orphans? That was too much for my mother, who immediately started collecting for them. She had dozens of *pushkes* in the kitchen closet. The *pushkes* were the little boxes made of tin, with openings small enough for nickels and pennies. They were charity boxes—emptied every week by a little old man with a black bag—and many an orphan who became a doctor is indebted to my mother for at least one month of his medical education. But it was the Jewish Socialists, who were not the most religious of men, who rallied us instead to the then pink Red Flag of municipal Socialism in the making.

By 1904, the Socialist party had twenty thousand members.

It was, then, municipal Socialism, gradualism, and talk about the eventual disappearance of capitalism. There was, of course, the IWW, the Wobblies, which numbered few Jews among its members—and was named Wobblies by a Chinese cook who could not make his way through so tough a name as the Industrial Workers of the World.

In my father's time, from stories he told me later, he had not heard of the 1903 split in the Russian Socialist movement. As for the word "Bolshevik," it was first heard by him in 1917, when all of us heard of it on Cherry Street. It was a frightening word—with exploding bombs attached to it by most Socialists who opposed it. By 1918, when the Bolsheviks took over Russia, the revolution split the Socialist party in the United States, and many friends and families also split over the issue.

By 1908, when my father had been in New York for thirteen years and was attending Socialist mass meetings, the Socialist party in the United States had doubled its membership. It had twenty-five hundred locals in the country. It flooded through the East Side, from synagogues to unions. It had its great proselytizers, men like Abraham Cahan, the novelist-editor of *The Forward*. My father liked the gradualism of Abraham Cahan and the social ideas of Morris Hillquit, the party's theoretician, who said in 1910, when my father walked the picket line during the great Cloakmakers' Strike, "Our principal efforts must be directed towards the propaganda of Socialism among the workers. But they should by no means be limited to that class alone. . . . The ultimate aims of the movement far transcend the interests of any one class in society, and its social ideal is so lofty that it may well attract large numbers of men and women from other classes. . . . [The workers] are by no means the only class which has a direct economic motive for favoring a change of the existing order. . . ."

Under these all-inclusive words, my father, good Jew that he was, hard working every day, was a Socialist.

I remember my father's telling me, a few years later, on a Sunday, of a meeting he had gone to in 1910 to hear Debs at the Hippodrome.

"Debs spoke. What did I understand in English? Almost *gornisht* (nothing). But there must have been ten thousand people there. It smelled like my old barn used to smell—from animal *drek*."

Socialism, Judaism, concerned parents, and the local boys' clubs, kept the errant among us somewhat straight. Since Cherry Street, where a half-dozen model tenements were put up in 1887, did not have a settlement house, we went to Madison House and the Henry Street Settlement for games of play that kept us from mass mayhem in the streets.

The Neighborhood Playhouse on Grand Street was then about to start its exercises in dramaturgy and make some of us actors, poets, playwrights, and spectators, as we saw the great English classics for the first time in our culture-hungry lives. But it was the Educational Alliance, a massive building on East Broadway, four blocks from my home, that was to have the major portion of our youthful allegiance. There we became gymnasts—to tumble our way onwards. We became Boy Scouts, to camp overnight in the Palisades, quite a frontier of rocks in 1916 when I was nine, with a Hudson River you could swim in, and with rattlesnakes that you impaled with a stick. When you got your first snake, you were definitely an all-around American Boy Scout ready to tame the rest of the nearby American wilderness.

The Educational Alliance gave us what we could not learn at school, in a setting created for energetic scholarship. The alliance, formerly known as the Hebrew Institute, supported by wealthy American Jews, set up the huge building at Jefferson Street and East Broadway in 1893. It was the intellectual heart of the Jewish ghetto. And there I could write my early poetry, have it read, then laughed at by my friends all the way home through the dark, dirty streets. The Alliance Art School was founded by the painter Henry McBride. There, earlier and later, men like Jacob Epstein had come to sculpt; and the members of the eventual school of realism-cum-proletarianism had their basic education there with live models. There, too, some ranking artists of the modern era studied— Leonard Baskin, Peter Blume, Adolph Gottlieb, Chaim Gross, Ben Shahn, and William Zorach. For the Education Alliance was an intellectual and moral testing ground for those not about to become antisocial gangsters and killers. Years later, students of mayhem and murder were to enroll in other alliances like Murder Incorporated.

The Educational Alliance made some of us boxers, as well. There were Benny Leonard, Sammy Sieger, Sid Terris, Ruby Goldstein, Charley Rosen, Barney Ross, Terry Roth, Lou Kersch, Johnny Clinton—who always carried a Yiddish newspaper in his pocket. Boxing, then, was the way to the top, American style. It was, then, as Jewish as it was Italian and Irish, with few Negroes able to get past the managerial edifice, to slash their way upward.

But most of us worked after school at diverse jobs for a nickel an hour. I rolled empty milk cans for Breakstone & Levine, then starting out in business across from my house, at 365 Cherry Street. There was Breakstone, in a white coat, and Levine, in a dirty coat, checking fifty-pound tubs of butter; sour milk cans, pure cream cans, pot cheese pots—and for a nickel an hour we got the containers into the freezers in the back, taking a little cheese away with us for home use to help fill out the black bread, the herring and potatoes, and the thick meat borscht that was always on tap.

My two older brothers, Mike and Herschel, were a different sort; for my mother soon taught them the value of a trade to make real money. By the time they were fourteen and sixteen they had learned all there was to a new American trade—soda jerking, which they picked up after school at Marchiony's Italian ice cream parlor on Grand Street.

My mother had a passion about success, American style. It was in the streets, easy to find. All that a boy or a man had to do was to seize the opportunity. It was not garbage, if you worked it over. It was for the sons of immigrants who were willing to apply themselves to stuff the American dream with the dollars of success . . . and with my mother as a suddenly inspired banker, my two older brothers by the time they were, respectively, eighteen and sixteen, already had a future.

She had saved fifteen hundred dollars for them from their earnings. She gave them fifty cents a week to spend recklessly; the rest of their earnings she used to buy a partnership in a luncheonette on Duane Street and Broadway. Soon they bought out their Greek partner and he went off to Lesbos to retire among the olive groves.

The cash logic of the purchase was all very simple for my mother, who told us: "Don't work for others. Work for yourself. Don't be like your father, a wage slave. . . ."

They became millionaires. They bought restaurants, developed them, sold them. Herschel, the oldest, became the *gevir*—rich enough by all the values crowding us off the American earth. It was to be a traditional success story—a *mayse*, told over and over again on the Lower East Side.

Who was not a wage slave on the East Side? But with World War I everything changed in value, price, and wages. My brother, Herschel, even before the luncheonette, had gone off to the Hog Island Shipyards, to become a riveter and hold the Hog Islanders together. Later, as a sailor, I was to live on these ships for seven years. Herschel, liberated at age thirteen, was making three times as much as my father was, still sweating over a pressing iron, unable to rivet, too old to change his trade, too tired to transform himself into any sort of storekeeper, entrepreneur, war profiteer, rag merchant, or shortage specialist.

There was money in the streets, at last. America was at war and President Wilson said it was "to make the world safe for democracy." America was no longer a thief. But among the cynical Socialists and anarchists, many of them in jail, it was a war "to save the capitalistic Democratic party. . . ."

My mother lamented for my future. I was warned too late. I had read the English classics. Byron decided my destiny along with a Russian named Pushkin. Further, I had the wrong sort of friends to think of working in an ice cream parlor. I had also been liberated, at ten, by the war and its outcome. My official Judaism ended with my bar mitzvah, a last concession to my family. I was hardly the Jew my father was. I was hardly my father's son, as well, in my interests. My friends, in their fashion, were breaking all their own ties with rigorous Judaism. A few were reading German philosophy, especially Schopenhauer. Poetry went with pessimism, I was soon to find out. It did not go with joy, I was to learn forever. My four good friends, who made up a circle of boy writers, thinkers, adventurers —as strong in body as they were then, muscular with grand thoughts—were all to go on from Cherry Street.

The synagogue meant nothing to me after thirteen, though

Judaism is still my private world. Long fascinated with rivers, at thirteen I ran away to sea, after an argument with my father, following with my whole self the eye that had gazed across the Hudson. I never went back to school for long, but remained a reader of books, because I had to read to know. Pagan almost; then Marxist. Marxism replaced the phylacteries that I left one day in a barn. And, some years later, Marxism was to go as well—along with other self-delusions about the social nature of man.

As I was growing up, my mother in anger would say to me after some errant adventure, "You act like a *goy*. You will *peyger* like a *goy*. That *meshugene* (crazy) river! Where does it flow? Through your *narisha kop* (foolish head)? Through your books? *A po-et vilstu zayn? Mit vos—mit narishkayt?*" (A poet you want to be? With what—your foolishness?)

My friends did not become boxers, businessmen, or gangsters, but that other thing—the *narishkayt mentshen* (foolish people). One foolish friend became a professor of English literature and a specialist on Henry James; a second became a scientist, specializing in mathematical values; a third, a social historian; a fourth, once a famous editor, soon became a Soviet spy, to specialize in another form of *narishkayt*. I became, in time, a poet for seven books, as well as the revolutionary organizer, a prophet for the new order. By the time I was sixteen, I was a Marxist-cum-Trotskyite when I sailed in the black gang and on deck through the political and physical seas around the world.

In an earlier book, *When I was Last on Cherry Street*, much of my family's history appears. In poems written years after, I am still the kid running away. I am within the structures of my Judaic upbringing. I am dreaming of sexual adventures. I am, endlessly, the sentimental boy and man, afraid of the lyricism we have lost and frightened by what we have gained in our American growth—a megalopolis, in stone and people.

I left the East Side and came back a yearly visitor, to note all the changes—the high-rises making a more anonymous world of the new tenements. The East River still flows by. The Brooklyn Bridge, with its skeletal, Hart Cranean mystique, is still there—to numb us with its frames of meaningful creation. One world has gone. Another, less giving, all concrete, flows up yearly. I have a major

lament for the death of my father's world and his time. The death
of that world is permanent and will never be reborn in our massive
rush to Nothingness. Death is a tombstone that is often not en-
graved . . . but I write my own signature to our 1971 preview of
hell. . . .

When I was a Trotskyite from 1927 to 1938, I could hardly believe that Trotsky was a poor sort of Jew, and, much worse, was a
former commissar. What Stalin did Trotsky would have done, had
he remained in power. The theoretical differences did not really
change their basic philosophy of how to keep Russia under a Communist dictatorship.

A man changes all the time. It is like his body. How does one
grow up? What does one give up? You drop your romantic views, in
time. You take up things that are easier on your spirit, your dreams,
your future. Is there one? There was one—when I was much
younger. There is still the city that houses me—the poured concrete
that God did not create for us. The green things of my youth are
gone . . . and we live within a contemporary vacuum.

I preferred to escape our *growth*—and I long ago gave up this
concrete world. My resignation included many things that are materialistic but few things of the spirit. It included organized Judaism.
I am not organized for anything now. Poverty will always be here—
and I have accepted it for myself. My few ambitions mostly deal
with writing, with going to desolate places, with waters—alone. God
is there for me. I do not need choruses on the Sabbath; nor *Yisker*
(prayer for the dead), to lament for my parents; nor Yom Kippur
to lament for what we were and what we have become. I lament
alone.

I was, even in my Marxist days, the odd man—a Trotskyite,
when almost everybody was a Stalinist. I was a Jew who went to sea,
when others went to factories, shops, and Madison Avenue. I was
the muscular poet of the revolution among thin poets. I was the
wanderer, looking for desolate places to take me away from the original images of Cherry Street, East Broadway, Delancey Street—
and Judaism. I had, I learned, become the Marxist so as not to be
the Jew—the permanent scapegoat I thought that my father was. I

did not have side curls. Today, when Judaism is often a sentimental awareness of differences and the memory of pain and the past, I am the Jew all the time. But then I hated the symbolical uniform that the *frume Yid* (the ultrareligious) adopted. "God is in your heart, not in a uniform," I used to tell my mother.

"Is God in a long black satin coat?" I would ask my mother. "Is God in a wide fur hat?" Is God within a woman shaving off her hair as the good religious Jewish woman did? Why all this stupid separation? We were in America, free, with jobs. The Jews had broken out of their mental and physical ghettos—almost at will. We were not Negroes—and they were the saddest-happiest people—for they had a permanent identity as very old Americans. Did I like them? Yes —why not? They laughed. They cried. They sang. They came from Africa—and we were almost neighbors thousands of years ago. They were separated by their color—and we by our pretensions toward a vague spiritual purity.

"Who chose us for what, Mother?" I would ask. "Why this ridiculous separation in clothes, customs, and habits of another time? Did God create these habiliments and give them to Moses too?"

"If the Jews do not separate themselves, they will be lost forever—intermarried," my mother would say. "They cannot merge their hearts, my son. They cannot fuse Judaism with *goyishe* paganism. . . ." and paganism, to her mind, soon became the word *peyger* when she was critical of my ideas.

"We were chosen by Abraham, Jacob, and Isaac—and by Moses. For what? To go back to *Eretz Yisroel*—for our purity, my son. . . ."

Our purity consisted of many things. One day, the land of Israel —*Eretz Yisroel*. It was an illusion, we knew. Who believed? Zionists and Orthodox Jews believed. Did I then? Hardly. It was a needed myth, an essential myth for Zionists, I thought—then. Socialism was easier to believe in. There were hundreds of thousands of American workers voting Socialist. The Balfour Declaration had not yet been "declared." My father, voting Socialist, believed, however, in the myth of *Eretz Yisroel*. I believed in myself—young, indestructible, combative, verging on atheism, suspecting all the appeals of Judaism, especially of *Gan Eden*. There was no heaven on Cherry

Street, but lots of hell, and I was getting it in heavy doses, daily, as I matured by the minute.

I remember, when I was ten, stealing an apple from a fruit-stand. We had bushels of apples at home sent to us by Uncle David from his farm at Accord, New York. Uncle David had remained the farmer, moving from the Ukraine to New York City. Using the money he got from the sale of his farm in the Ukraine, he returned to the soil in Accord, where land, then, was cheap—and possessed what most immigrants, including my father, dreamt of but never attained. In Accord, David had horses, chickens—and apples. He died at the age of ninety-seven, an oak of a Jew. But despite David's apples, I had stolen an apple from an old woman at the fruitstand. I confessed to my father.

"How much can I, now a *goy*, confess?" I finally managed to ask, dodging a third slap. "It was just an apple, Papa."

"A thief is a thief!"

"They are God's apples," I said, turning everything around.

"They were God's apples until they reached the tree. Do you understand, *meshumed?*" *Meshumed* meant a convert to Christianity. I was hardly a convert to anything but my inner Judaic self.

"It is Socialism on the tree," I answered, baffling myself and my father by this strange conceit.

"Nar! Meshumed! Peyger!"

Called a fool, a Christian convert, and told to die like a dog, was now part of my father's permanent rebuke . . . and it was to grow worse within three years, soon after I was thirteen, when I had my head literally opened up by my father's strange anger at my questing inquiries.

I struck back and I ran, making the irreparable break, to the sea that was then the focus of all my imagination. It was my last defeat, and my first, if final, victory over my father. I had struck back—and I was no longer his Jewish son. I was a radical. All the signs were there. I was the poet using my own fists to defend the boy becoming the man—but I was running, leaving God behind along with my family; leaving a home to become the traveler to other worlds. My broken skull made me the total atheist as God leaked out of my bleeding head.

My father died at seventy-seven, in 1937—just before another war broke up the world. Before his death he was to move from Cherry Street to the Bronx and then to Brooklyn. He went to *shul* every day after he retired. He stayed longer. He prayed more. He wondered more. And he was to say to me one day in 1937, "Son, I am dying. My left arm . . . my chest . . . my head . . . my feet." He was as thin and pale as the death now feathering his mind. He would still roll a Russian cigarette, smoke it slowly, tears coming, then talk about old dead friends. Socialism meant nothing but a name to him anymore. He had stopped voting at seventy, saying, "Enough! Enough! Does it matter who is elected? They are all thieves, Jewish and Gentiles alike. Please, son, roll me another cigarette. Please find the cognac. It helps a little bit. Please stay for supper. I never see you, son . . . you are always running to those crazy political meetings. Are you writing something that I would like to hear—something about the *alte gegent* (the old neighborhood) or about God?"

He had died, actually, years before 1937, over a pressing iron, in his unions, meeting halls, Second Avenue benefits societies, his *vereins*—and in his Zareby Koscielne memories. He was hardly an American by his habits. He had elected a few Socialists—and he was never to know that Israel was to become a state.

My mother died during the Christmas of 1949 while I was in London. A cable from my religious young brother, Bill, said: "Mother died yesterday. . . ." I had seen her a month before. She was eighty-seven, blind, and in a nursing home. The wealth of my brothers kept her there with other old Jewish women. Someone fed her. Other old women talked with her. She smiled, stroked my face, cried a little bit, called on God for the end. She remembered little then of Cherry Street, of Zareby Koscielne and the blond woman who had come from there in 1895, at twenty-five; who had known every tragedy and nothing of sin; who was always with God, charity, good deeds, unable to ever learn to read or write; too simple yet very skillful; who made my brothers do the things they did to become rich; who had called me a *goy*, but had taught me so many universal values—from charity to my own conception of faith in myself. But *Eretz Yisroel*, one of her prophecies, was, to her, now a reality.

The Lower East Side still has its vestiges, old tenements about to be bulldozed into high-rise city projects. The hundreds of thousands of immigrants who came there have scattered into American statistics. Between 1950 and 1960, two hundred thousand left those streets. They are now in the middle class in other parts of New York, Queens, New Jersey, and Westchester. They are in the working class as well. It is another racial vista, with some exceptions on East Broadway, on streets that cannot hold out . . . an area of cultural ghosts.

Like Second Avenue, which bloomed on every corner with a Yiddish theater, a café, a cuisine that was as intellectual as *tsimes,* that old life is dead. Where the great Café Royale once was, there is a cleaning store, symbolic of the dry cleaning and the vacuum that has replaced Yiddish theaters, Yiddish characters, Yiddish poets and playwrights—and the language itself. For the Café Royale, an establishment with a past as rich as Café Le Dome or Le Select on Montparnasse, was where all of us went to during the twenties, thirties, and forties. Instead of a *Yidishe* culture we have the illusion of values in cultural concrete pouring over people and places.

Yiddish culture is a ghost, the sentimentality to recall it is awe inspiring the more it disappears. It is like the Socialist party and the men who built it—gone. It is like my relatives, evaporating into the vacuum that New York has become. Only yesterday I went to the funeral of Gidalya, my mother's half brother, whom my father brought over fifty years ago. He had lived in two houses—and he died at 300 Cherry Street, a city housing project. Three of his four children became in time what many of the sons of immigrants became—American businessmen. And one became a professor of sociology—to haunt his own immigrant past in Zareby Koscielne.

8

The Center of Impermanence

NEW YORK IN THE EYES OF AN ENGLISHMAN
Alan Pryce-Jones

"There are, I suppose, two kinds of imaginative writers: those who need the presence of their own home in order to write; and those who, like the tortoise, carry their own home with them wherever they go."

With these words I began an address to the Grolier Club in New York. That was in 1966—in other words, in a different age. Different, because time has been undergoing one of its periods of acceleration. From dividing it into centuries, men came to tailor it into generations, then into decades. Now, each year involves a fresh break with the past. And so one is compelled to rethink one's attitude to the world at ever more rapid intervals.

The subject of my address—those four long years ago—was summed up in its title, "Exiles and Expatriates." I was trying to make a valid distinction between the two: between those who chose to live and work away from home and those who have been forced, willy-nilly, to do so; between, say, a Vladimir Nabokov, forced into international fame by the Russian revolution, and a Henry James.

Being myself an Englishman who chooses to live in the United States, I have an interest in making the best of my condition. I had no reason to leave England at the age of fifty, beyond inclination. Yet I very well remember the day when I was accepted as a foreign resident. I remember walking along Madison Avenue—not the most romantic of thoroughfares—with a sense of sharp exhilaration, coupled with useless regret that I had not taken my step towards expatriation thirty years earlier.

That was more than ten years ago. During those ten years I have changed, and so has my world. And without in any way regretting my action, I have been trying to make a fresh assessment of what it means to the kind of man I am to have chosen so radical a departure.

I begin by roughing out a background. It is a background which has no parallel in American experience, simply because it was appropriate to a small, centralized, hierarchical kingdom, rather than to a vast, loose-limbed republic.

In my parents' world everybody knew everybody, and most people were, if not cousins, connected. There were, of course, supporting groups: employers and employees, people you bought things from, people who served you, whether as bankers or cooks. But these were only by courtesy "people"; they were not "people" in the same sense as Aunt Louisa and Cousin Granville.

You could count on the reactions of the people who were truly people. They were almost surely conservatives. They deeply disapproved of Winston Churchill until the day in 1940 when he was elevated to the role of savior of his country, all in a night. Their educational backgrounds were much the same. The men had been to Eton—though Winchester or Harrow was a possibility. The girls had not been anywhere beyond the schoolroom and the presence of a French or German governess.

Is was assumed that the men, having finished Eton, would wish to join either the Brigade of Guards or one of a handful of cavalry regiments. I very well remember, at the time when I was first invited to dances, my mother's saying sadly how brave she thought me to accept the invitations, "because, darling, as you're not in the brigade none of the girls will care to dance with you." This may have been true in 1905, but I soon noticed that the contrary was the case between the wars, by which time guards officers were thought, anyway in *my* world, amiable figures of fun. Still, among my elders, who resisted change, the norms of 1905 were still very much alive.

This resistance was still a part of the conservative ethic—in the days before conservatives, like orthodox Catholics, decided that it was best to be "with it." My grandfather, for instance, was per-turbed when his elder son married into a great liberal family. "There are," he is recorded as saying, "only two kinds of people I detest: Buxtons and clergymen. And dammit if my son doesn't marry the one and my daughter the other."

I did my duty. I attended Eton—without enthusiasm. I went on to Oxford, which I enjoyed to the point of getting myself into early disgrace. Removed by my father as a hopeless case, I was given a talking-to. The Coldstream Guards would not have me—that I had no remote wish to join their company was irrelevant. I could not marry because my future in-laws would discover how wretched was my record. I could not go to the colonies because the colonies did not welcome wasters, and I was unemployable at home. Furthermore, it was no use my hoping for an allowance. My friends, for instance . . . and here my father's tone rose steeply. My friends were pulling me down. They wore wristwatches—a sign to my father of dubious morality—and even suede shoes. They persuaded me to take taxis when the bus would do. They read books rather than shot grouse. They drank cocktails and smoked Amer-ican cigarettes; "gaspers," my father called them, since he himself forbade any cigarette in the house which was not vaguely connected with the Turkish Empire.

My spirits sank. I went for a walk to revive them, and almost at once ran into an old friend, who asked me what was the matter. I told him. Life, it seemed, ended at nineteen. The old friend denied this. If all I wanted was a future, he said, why did I not go into the National Liberal Club where, at that very moment, the poet J. C. Squire was having his hair cut. He needed an assistant editor for *The London Mercury,* at that time a literary monthly of conse-quence.

I took the advice I was given and got the job. Unpaid, but still a job. The hoodoo was broken.

For the next twenty-five years I was very much a European. To my father's intense satisfaction, the machinations of Hitler—which he took in a purely personal spirit as directed to himself—put my brother and myself into the army after all. Mellowing with time, my father also became rather proud of having a literary son. He recalled that two of my uncles, both generals, had published verse, thus underlining a dictum of Squire's that all senior officers in the Brigade of Guards, whatever their devotion to the hunting field, had at some time written a sonnet.

I remained, I repeat, a European. Americans came to London, certainly; but I saw them on my own ground. In these last days of empire, America appeared remote. One read Thornton Wilder and Edna Ferber, Willa Cather, Thomas Wolfe, Vachel Lindsay. But one thought confusedly of America as a kind of arsenal or storehouse, from which right-thinking Americans came to Europe in search of themselves. We approved T. S. Eliot, Hemingway, Edith Wharton, Louis Bromfield, Ezra Pound, because—or partly because—they came to us and saved us the trouble of going to learn about America for ourselves. Our reactions were remarkably ignorant: we tumbled names together pell-mell.

At the same time I was not very content with England. I had married a French wife, and we spent as much time as we could on the continent, pursuing that ancient highbrow's dream of living quietly in a beautiful place and writing the book of one's choice, not, oh certainly not, so much for profit as for the glory of art.

Then the war was over, I decided that the times were unpropitious for art. Settled again in London, I took a fresh job, and for twelve years I edited the *Times Literary Supplement,* in connection with which I made my first extended trip to the United States.

That was in 1951, and the knowledge it brought me, if superficial, was a revelation. My wife felt the same. We were not very enterprising—there was too little time—but we went from New York to Chicago, to Boston, to North Carolina, to Washington; we stayed in country houses on Long Island and visited universities here and there. This, we said, when the plane at last took us back to Europe, is where we shall end our days.

Why? It was, I think, chiefly because Europe, and England especially, struck me as dangerously overripe. The European wars, which had abolished the civilization into which I was born, were proofs of overripeness; not unlike the fate which destroys a Camembert cheese left too long in a warm kitchen. It cracks its rind, it runs, it stinks, then goes dry and angrily brown.

Europe, furthermore, seemed to me like an overfilled attic.

Nothing was thrown away; the junk of years weighed down the inhabited rooms below. Words like democracy, liberalism, liberty even, had evaporated. What remained was an ossified social system, not fundamentally changed since 1900, however great the superficial adjustments.

Twenty years ago, the United States looked like the Promised Land. It was the land of generosity, of unlimited possibility, the land of welcome and peace. It was also becoming the land of pilgrimage. The Huxleys and the Audens were reversing the trend of the past, and, a little late in the day, I was happy to be of their company.

Perhaps we, the latterday immigrants, asked too much; perhaps we went beyond what human nature is capable of offering. Or perhaps it is only that the seesaw of history has now again tipped the other way, so that once again the traffic goes more smoothly from West to East than from East to West. Not because of Vietnam, campus unrest, crime in the streets, and pot in the home. These are only symptoms of what must be called a failure of nerve. It is not clear to me that any nation in history could have picked up the threads strewn about the world in 1945 and woven them into a sound fabric. The marvel is that America tried, not that she failed.

The England I had known as a young man—the writer's England above all—had changed enormously by the end of the war. In the heyday of English writing there had been two main divisions among writers, as among cricketers. There were the professionals and the amateurs, most of whom rejected the title. Which was Shelley? Which were the Sitwells? Maurice Baring? Virginia Woolf?

Certainly they were distinct from Dickens, Trollope, Arnold Bennett. But distinct not from lack of professional skill but because they reasserted an amateur status whenever it was convenient.

Suddenly there emerged a new generation of professionals pure and simple. The kind of writer who owned a library and had what used to be called "good connections" came to seem out of date, if not positively venal. The young provincials were the rage, the angries, the disestablished. No such invasion of literature could have occurred in the United States, because the social context, outside the Boston of the mid-nineteenth century, made no allowance for groupings of this order. And it is not really relevant that fifteen years later these invaders from the provinces have turned, as often as not, into prosperous Londoners—John Osborne and Kingsley Amis are obvious examples—veering increasingly rightward as their incomes rise.

What is relevant, however, is the attitude of the British writer to the income which keeps him alive. Traditionally, he has needed very little. In the latter days of Cyril Connolly's monthly, *Horizon,* the editors organized a questionnaire among writers as to what money they needed in order to live. Elizabeth Bowen was the most extravagant. She topped five thousand dollars a year. The others, many of them already well known, asked for very little indeed; which was just as well, for a generation ago, as now, the average earnings of the writer in England bore no comparison with those of his American contemporaries—not to speak of the occasional jackpot, peculiar to the United States, which falls to the writer of *In Cold Blood, Myra Breckinridge,* or *The Love Machine.*

But then, in England the rich writer, from Thackeray to Somerset Maugham, was traditionally the exception. Writing as a business brought its rewards, but seldom very large ones.

The intangible rewards of writing were very different. They were bound up with a sense of belonging to a small and special world. There were many such worlds: Bloomsbury, for one; and the more fashionable world of the Sitwells; a Catholic world which included Hilaire Belloc and G. K. Chesterton; a political world headed by philosopher prime ministers such as Balfour and Asquith. The young writer who scored a success was usually caught into one of these worlds. One year it would be Evelyn Waugh, another Stephen Spender; there was room for everyone of talent. Somebody or other had enough money to pay the bills; and nobody expected millions where thousands would do.

Such worlds still exist. They are one of the things which make London a pleasant city to live in. But a penalty of living on a small island is that there is no room for other cities. Oxford, Cambridge, Edinburgh do very well. From time to time a city like Nottingham or Swansea briefly becomes a home for the muses. But in the end there is only London.

I do not look on myself as a representative British writer of my time. I was never either rich or poor, never a spectacular success or a resounding failure. I did much what I wanted in agreeable circumstances. I had, and keep, the suspicious-seeming qualities of tending to enjoy myself, of liking people more often than not.

But I found that I was not alone in feeling mildly suffocated by the atmosphere of Great Britain after the war. It was a kindly atmosphere, a genial one even. The talk was good, the bores were under control for the most part. But it was with an uprush of relief that I and others like me saw the towers of Manhattan outlined against the sky as our plane glided down to what was still Idlewild, if not LaGuardia.

The relief is not easy to define with precision. It was a little like getting out of the schoolroom into real life. That life might be harsh, without the protection of home, but it was at least a heady affair. There was also, of course, the universal American kindness to newcomers to bewitch us.

Later, much later, I found it possible to make some estimate of loss and gain. But even now I have only to see the towers again, to recapture that first euphoria at being able to claim that New York is now *my* city—a fact which in middle age represents some kind of conquest, since one never loses one's native land except by an act of will, and therefore any second home is something which has to be won before it can take its natural place. Like a wife.

There is one great disadvantage in living as a foreign writer in New York: it is too hard a city to write about unless one has grown up in it, or at least in its shadow. A foreign ear does not catch New York speech—as any novel will show, set in the city and written by a nonnative from abroad.

For some time now I have given a monthly broadcast talk to the British radio, a relaxed talk in which I can pick up whatever catches my fancy, from politics to theater, from local color to bicycling in the park.

Naturally I want to say something pleasant about my new home. And yet month after month I find myself struggling with more bad news—more smog, more crime, more police corruption,

worse prisons, worse-mannered audiences at the Met, more un-
collected garbage, sillier pronouncements from those who should
know better.

The city I describe might be an inferno, rather than an earthly
paradise. Yet I go on living there, though I have no reason whatever
to do so except my own wish.

One reason is that it is possible to look out on the rest of
the world from New York, as though one were on another planet.
It is possible to live in New York with the minimum of human
contacts and yet not to feel lonely. In a way, there is no such
place as New York, so provisional, so haphazard are its appoint-
ments; and yet the show it puts on is unequaled. And this is good
for writers.

What is less good is that the show lacks quality. It is the British notion, by contrast, that quality is an outcrop of tradition.
This makes for a certain dullness, but it also assures the maintenance of a standard. When it rains in New York the gutters at
once overflow; when it blows, the streetcorners are stacked with
umbrellas standing inside out. Small things, you may say; but
symbolic. London gutters are built to drain, and London umbrellas
to outlast a hurricane.

In New York things are cobbled together, whether they be big
things like political parties or small things like an umbrella. We
have our traditions in New York, but they exist in order to be overturned, or at least superseded. And because New York sets a pattern for the Western world, this habit is growing elsewhere. The
British notion of quality is dwindling fast, but while it lasts it is
impossible for one brought up to it not to be impressed by the ease
with which New Yorkers accept the second-rate.

On the other hand, is it possible for a city temperament so
quick, so volatile as that of New York to achieve the first-rate in
its workings? Is it even desirable? Many years ago, in Peru, I was
talking to an engineer on the railway. He told me that the rolling
stock was British built and then went on to complain that it was
much too lasting. Year followed year and the trains never wore out;
therefore they were never replaced, therefore they became increasingly out of date.

There is a parable in this. Englishmen like myself were likely

to live in old houses, surrounded by the evidences of craftsmanship. Things did not totally stand still, but changes were seldom
decisive. Fashion might reject, say, eighteenth-century furniture,
but the furniture was only stored away until fashion changed.
Fashion might order hideous color schemes in a good room; but it
was always possible to strip off the gravy-painted paneling and
reveal the natural pine below. And, among those who rose above
fashion, it was reasonable to preserve rooms exactly as they had
been a century or two back.

I was once taken by the owner round a Jacobean house near
Oxford. As we walked through the rooms, I said to her that it was
a lucky chance that no forbear had ever ruined them by redecora-
tion. "That is because," she said, "we have never had any money
in the family since the war." She meant the Civil War which cost
Charles I his head three centuries ago.

While I lived in this atmosphere I found it oppressive. How
much better, I thought, to adopt American procedures: to keep
continually on the move; to throw out whatever has ceased to
please, and always to keep in mind, when buying a piece of furniture, that its eventual destination may well be the Salvation Army.

Today I am not so sure. I regret the American reverence for
the old and bad, the determination to see in any old piece of junk
a memorable antique. If the standards of Mies van der Rohe,
Philip Johnson, and their kin were upheld as a matter of course,
I should not mourn the craftsmanship of the past. But I suspect that
too many of my new fellow citizens really prefer Grand Rapids
furniture supporting a plastic gloxinia.

These questions concerning tradition and taste are fundamental to the work of a writer. Not that writers live in beautiful
surroundings—witness the home of Bernard Shaw, possibly the
ugliest house of its time and place. But if they are not at least aware
of the first-rate in their society, they will also fail to be aware of
it in their writings. So that, though I respond with warm affection
to the vitality, the recklessness, the spendthrift generosity of
American living, I also see its disadvantages compared to the so-
berer society of Great Britain.

For one thing, it slows life down. Try to buy a pair of shoes,
a railway ticket, an orchestra seat, in New York and compare the

operation with what it would be in London. New York is trepidant, vigorous, on the run. New York gives you a mass of unnecessary information, like the name of the man in the thruway booth who is about to change your dollar or of the lady in Penn Station who would be selling you your seat on the train were she not constantly absent on the telephone.

In London such operations are carried through quickly and easily. You can cut corners in London, but you do so in orderly fashion. People both think and act with refreshing speed. In New York—perhaps in part because of a half-forgotten tradition of German thoroughness—action is slowed down to a snail's pace, whatever the fuss which accompanies it.

Take a New York committee—especially a committee of intellectuals. Over and over again the members fill in a background perfectly familiar to one and all; the matter under discussion peters away in an avalanche of slow talk. When a foregone conclusion is reached after what seems like hours of debate, fortified by a tuna salad sandwich and a carton of milk, it is hard not to make a cruel comparison with the brisker, if more slapdash, procedures of London.

This shows in American writing. I have sometimes wondered if the undue care expended by Henry James on his syntax and vocabulary were not a symptom of his rejection of America. With a convert's zeal he took on the colors of British prose at its most elaborate and surpassed them. Whereas it is rare, nowadays, for the texture of American writing to satisfy the reader. When a book like *Mr. Sammler's Planet* appears, it stands out as an extraordinary event, simply because Saul Bellow has taken the trouble to *write* it rather than wrap a typewriter round it.

Because of this lack of affection for prose, workaday writing, such as you may find in a magazine, often has no exact meaning at all. It is not hard to discern what the writer is trying to say, but, in terms of precise words, he has not in fact said it. Again, the provisional has taken over. The sentences destroy themselves, like the autodestructive sculptures of Jean Tinguely.

And then I begin to wonder. How much do the virtues of durability, craft, precision, really matter in the world of today? Is it not these virtues which discouraged me when I lived in Europe?

Seen from New York they are tinted by nostalgia. I am regretting, if I regret them, a past which gains in fulfillment as it recedes—after the usual manner of the past.

The whole tenor of the times is against the durable, the first-rate. Moreover, it is against words, except in unconsidered handfuls. Since people no longer write letters, very little of our intimate contemporary life will survive the living of it. If, therefore, anybody is enough of an anachronism to be a writer at all, why not live at the center of impermanence, New York?

The London writer always has his eye on the past. He feels the noble dead breathing over his shoulder, from Chaucer to Dickens, according to his bent. He wishes, like them, to build a monument; he sees the whole pantheon of literature as though it were an extension of Westminster Abbey—filled with exhortation and statuary and memorial tablets to one of which he must claim a right.

He probably does not think this with his conscious mind. But inevitably his view is steeped in the past, for the past is still more alive than the present. It is there before him, in buildings, in objects, in the straightness of Roman roads, and the twistiness of farmyard lanes, in turns of speech and oddities of survival, like the Welsh language and the tiny religious sects which have outlasted the eighteenth century.

Not so the New York writer. The past for him is no more remote than the bound numbers of *Vanity Fair* or the echoes of old jokes at the Algonquin. Everything has to be thought anew every month of the year; the words fly up like a firework and drop right back like the dead stick of a rocket.

He also, at least in theory, has more to write about than his London counterpart. It is one of the weaknesses of the British character that it takes refuge in what looks like sagacity but is as often as not lack of interest. The British have been interested in many things for a long time: in fighting for survival against their kings and their barons; in plunging into religious controversy; in building a world of commerce which turned, half by accident, into an empire; in worrying (and with good reason) about the balance of power in Europe; in trying first to create and then to maintain a viable political system without becoming laced into a straitjacket of rules; in wars, just and unjust; in the horrid consequences of wars. And, above all, they have had to try their hands at the hardest of all maneuvers—that of climbing down from an imperial stance without falling to pieces in the process.

It is not entirely surprising that, after five hundred years of expressing and acting on these diverse interests, they have become tired. They have reached the stage, in writing, where form seems more important than content, where it is more satisfying to act with grace than with energy. The British have, in parallel, always had a derisive streak in their character. They perceive the ridiculous side of things and they perceive it clearly. So that, while the main line of British writing has become increasingly sober—no contemporary novelist would dare adopt the bravado of Dickens in dealing with the life of his own times—there persists a sharp satiric comment, day in day out, on the ways of the Establishment.

The New York writer ought to have a much wider field of action. But in practice he does not. This is chiefly because he has not so very much past against which to measure his own efforts. And, into the bargain, his efforts are seldom designed to last. You might think, at the moment of writing, that there are only half a dozen subjects of any general interest. The books enlarge on what has been published in the magazines, the magazines expand what has appeared in the few surviving newspapers. And in the process of homogenization there comes to be less and less to write about. Moreover, what really touches the heart and mind of the New Yorker is overlooked; he is reduced to a kind of zombie, one eye over his shoulder, sharing the elementary hopes and worries of all the other zombies on the block.

A reader with any sense of history, any concern with human personality, or awareness of what in fact engages the attention of society as distinct from what publicists impose on their fellow citizens, must flinch from the picture offered to the world of what Americans do and of how they think.

Campus unrest, hippiedom, the Black Panthers, the dim politicking of public men each enclosed in a private capsule cut off from the real world—can these exhausted themes represent the true limit of interest for writer and reader? I suspect that the great success of a book like Erich Segal's *Love Story* has less to do with its literary merit than with the fact that it avoids the trampled wasteland of ideas in short-term circulation and tackles the problem of living at a point of universal concern.

It would be asking too much of a writer who is trying to conform to the mode of the moment to stop and think about the fine detail of writing, from the organization of a paragraph to the exact meaning of a word. There may even be some merit in the approximations which often have to make do for prose in what the New Yorker reads. Somewhere, in the heap of words before him, there is a seed of life, and that life is preferable to the quiet gentility of much British writing.

All the same, it is hard to live in New York without feeling that its size, variety, changeableness, excesses of wealth and poverty, racial complexities, its sheer rascality, too, are wasted on those who do not trouble to record them. There is no New York Steele, Lichtenberg, Gissing, Wells; no vision of New York to be compared with that of London in *Bleak House*. To look at a Hogarth is an act of recognition. We can understand Hogarth's London because we can read about it in a score of books; from Boswell alone we can see why Johnson said that "when a man is tired of London he is tired of life." It may even be significant that Hawthorne, in his *English Notebooks,* wrote more perceptively of England than of his own land.

Whereas of New York we have no comparable vision. The steamy wonders of the streets go by default, and the recorded New York past is far too single-mindedly directed to nineteenth-century Washington Square or to the vagaries of the Village—while beyond Manhattan Island there might be a desert unless a Jewish highbrow inclines to recall his difficult childhood.

This may sound like the voice of a disappointed lover, as if, having come all this way and survived a decade of adaptation, I were concluding that I am unadaptable after all.

I do not see it like that. True, one cannot avoid being a child of one's place and time. By learning an Arkansas accent I should be no more a true American than by sticking to what I have. By tying my hair Navajo fashion and wearing a necklace or two I should achieve nothing except the ridicule of being an elderly Britisher in fancy dress.

But I can see, perhaps better than native New Yorkers, the

vast possibility of the city. I can respond to the kindness of its people, once their attention is caught and held. I can relish the electricity behind the smog. To be a foreigner in Manhattan, a willing foreigner, is to keep the best of two worlds. My country of origin looks the more delightful because it is far off; when I criticize it, it is like criticizing my own family, with the additional fact that as I no longer live there I must be aware of falling behind the times.

New York, on the other hand, will always be slightly out of reach and the more exciting for that. When I was a child there was a race game called "The Prince's Quest." It was played with dice and counters. If your counter fell on a certain square you jumped six places; on another you fell back three. And New York, not least for a writer, is like that. The fall of the dice determines the speed of your advance. It keeps one young.

Nothing is out of reach; nothing is stable or dull—nothing, I must add in justice, except conversation, which is often dull to a degree, because of an odd reluctance among respectable citizens to speak out. And there is always the chance when something needs to be done of doing it. The inertia of Europe has not crossed the Atlantic along with vodka, the Mercedes Benz and Pucci prints.

I began with a quotation and I shall end with one. In a magazine article now three or four years old, I summed up my situation thus:

"Having chosen a new pattern for myself I am content with it. Naturally, when the taxi driver is rude, when the subway refuses to change a $5 bill, when it takes ten minutes to buy a railway ticket and twenty to find a New York post office, I curse my choice. I long for an older, smoother civilization where the streets are not hacked up by Con Edison and the buildings seldom or never burst into flames; where theaters have seats for sale and cathedrals wear a proper patina. But the mood passes. I would (and do) go back, yes. But never willingly for good."

9
Biblical Heirs and Modern Evils

A POLISH POET IN CALIFORNIA
Czeslaw Milosz

For many years I have had the same dream with a number of variations. Uniformed men have blocked the only way out of a tall building and are making arrests, beginning with the lower floors, gradually working their way to my place. Their uniforms are German, or sometimes Russian. Yet even though the dream is usually composed of recollected fragments of streets and houses, I do not consider myself a man haunted by nightmares. A recurrent dream is like drawing a bird or a tree after your hand has got the feel of it—its realistic features soon vanish, what remains is a sign, a hieroglyph. I participate in that dream with only a part of myself. Another part of myself knows I am just dreaming—that, in a moment, I will wake up.

People who have preserved the capacity for awe are rare—awe, for instance, for the first and basic human discoveries like the striking of fire and the shaping of the wheel. No less amazing is the idea that the power of the state should have limits prescribed by law and that nobody should be thrown in prison on the whim of uniformed men. All the more so since, while the wheel is here to stay, the protection of law secured by the independence of the judiciary is constantly being threatened by the ambition to rule others without any obstacles or checks. Yet only the experience of living in systems where the individual is at the mercy of the rulers enables one truly to prize democracy, which submits to the control of the citizenry, albeit incompletely and with reluctance. That is why I have always observed American rebels with a bit of irony. For them the rule of law is either a cliché, something obvious, a bore, or deserving of hatred and scorn, because the Establishment invokes law to mask existing injustices. And I concede, law, if one has never had to live without it, does not stir our imagination and is much less attractive than slogans calling for a perfect society.

I did not, however, migrate directly to America (in 1960) from a totalitarian country, but from France, where, after leaving Poland, I had lived for ten years. With France I had many ties and in the details of its landscape, in the little old streets, in wooded dales (like the banks of the rivers L'Isle and Vézère in Dordogne) I often found reminders of my native Lithuania. Unfortunately, France could not be my home for reasons which were not only personal but indicate as well what seems to be typical of a new migration, the "migration of talents." Therefore, my views on America are colored not only by my memory of the eastern parts of Europe but also by my long stay in its western half.

A certain permanent feature can be observed in the historical existence of particular countries—we might call it the principle of continuity through change, change through continuity. Continuity is so strong in Western Europe that the structures of the nineteenth century seem to persist there unchanged. As far as the brutality of the struggle for survival is concerned, those writers who chose it as their main theme—Balzac, Dickens, Zola—are perhaps less old-fashioned today than they appear. The America of Mark Twain or of Upton Sinclair no longer exists, but France, to a considerable extent, is still the France of Balzac; yet, even in the nineteenth century, European and American capitalism were different. The violence in Europe was becoming formalized, coalescing with class divisions hallowed by centuries; it was interiorized, ingrained, or baked in, if one may use such an expression. American capitalism was founded on daring, resourcefulness, largesse, waste; European capitalism was founded on one powerful passion, miserliness. These patterns, enduring up to the present, explain why America succeeded in creating a vast, new sector of the economy adapted to needs which become increasingly evident the closer we come to the twenty-first century: the sector of universities, research institutes, laboratories, with billions of dollars invested in them. Western Europe, where education has always been the preserve of a narrow elite, did not manage to produce anything similar. The prodigality of private capital in America made the beginnings possible; money from taxes joined in at the next stage. The miserliness of capital in Europe effectively prevented the laying of foundations for this new sector and it is doubtful whether the government treasuries will ever be able to overcome the ever-widening gap.

During all the years I lived in Western Europe I did not have even one offer from institutions concerned with propagating knowledge. It is true that my field, Slavic literatures, is slightly exotic. Yet one can draw all sorts of conclusions from the fact that it is considered so on a continent at least half of which is occupied by Slavic peoples. All the truly intelligent persons I met in my French period were European federalists. They were convinced that only the political and economic unification of the lesser powers could offer any sort of counterbalance to both the U.S.A. and Russia. The obstacles they encountered, which allowed their plans to be realized very slowly and halfheartedly, were to my mind caused by the same parochial spirit which rejected my qualifications as superfluous, just because I was a newcomer from the other side of the fence. After all, if the Slavic domain was beyond the pale of the projected federation, any far-reaching thought would still not write off its closest neighbors. It looked like a weakening of the European will to live—to live as a subject of history. Instead, there was a tacit acquiescence to the role of an object protected by the might of America. I could not help thinking about my being superfluous when Charles de Gaulle proclaimed: "Europe to the Urals"; I simply could not take him seriously.

Besides, it is not Slavic studies that matters here. Many educated people who could not find any employment for their skills were in the same position as I was in the postwar years. Knowledge as a totality of mutually connected and mutually determined parts is based, to a considerable degree, upon apparently esoteric disciplines; if it is also considered economically important to increase knowledge, then ichthyologists, historians of Byzantium, and specialists in Urdu will find a place. The unemployment of the educated stagnating in miserable jobs, working in underequipped labs, was accepted around me with humility, as some-

thing normal. It is quite possible that my observations are somewhat narrow because they are limited to Paris, an exceptionally
hard city, but their application is probably larger than this.

It is not the bitterness of defeat that speaks in me. If one lives
by his pen for ten years and his books, translated into several
foreign languages, have relatively high sales, it is difficult to speak
of defeat. The trouble is that I didn't like my profession of European litterateur. The translation of my books from Polish caused
immense difficulties, but I could have taken that. The literary
profession, however, is not only paper and pen. It also requires
abilities like those most likely possessed by courtiers who maintained themselves near the throne of a king or prince through
carefully thought-out tactics, the play of alliances, and through
constant reminders of their presence. Now I can smile at my gaffes
of that time and could without any hostility draw a portrait of the
European publisher upon whose signature so much once depended.
It would be, no doubt, a composite portrait, unjust toward some of
my well-intentioned employers but nevertheless depicting some of
their traits. This sort of book-world potentate is a living contradiction of the maxim "business is business." His decisions cannot
be boiled down to calculation, since he publishes what he wants,
often exclusively for the honor of the house; his behavior makes
you understand that the royalties he pays his authors are not
something he owes them, but rather are an act of his favor. Everything hinges on how near you are to his person, in the noise and
warmth of the beehive over which he rules. If you are close to him,
he is capable of opening his purse and giving you the considerable
sum you need to buy an apartment, to undergo a cure, or to finance
your daughter's wedding. He is also capable of treating his authors
to culinary debauchs, picking up checks equal to their yearly
budgets. But when it comes to normal payments, it's another story;
even modest sums must be laboriously squeezed out of him. Besides this, his bookkeeping is often submitted to mysterious machinations aimed at lowering his taxes. I simply cannot understand
how this type of feudal lord has survived in capitalistic enterprises.

It was not only the obvious motives which forced so many
Western European scholars and scientists to emigrate to America
in the last two decades that determined my farewell to Europe.

Ours is a century of mass migration set in motion by political up-heavals and this, on such a scale, is new; a formula of adaptation had to be invented, the past being unable to provide cues sufficient-ly valid for living today. No matter how strong the attachment to one's native land, one cannot live away from it very long and still resist what is seen every day—cannot go on complaining of the strangeness of the new language, mores, and institutions, straining sight and sound toward one's lost country. We are nourished by our senses and whether we are aware of it or not, we work constant-ly at ordering our chaotic perceptions and composing them into harmonious units. Total uprootedness is contrary to our nature, and the human plant once plucked from the ground tries to send its roots into the ground onto which it is thrown. This is so because we are physical beings; the place we occupy, bounded by the surface of our skin, must be located in space, not in a "nowhere." Just as our hand reaches out and takes a pencil lying on a table, thus estab-lishing a relationship between our body and what is outside it, our imagination extends us, establishing a sensory-visual relationship between us and a street, a town, a district, and a country. In exiles from the eastern part of Europe one often notices a desperate refusal to accept that fact. They try to preserve their homeland as an ideal space in which they move, yet since it exists only in memory, not strengthened by everyday impressions, it stiffens and is trans-formed into words that grow more obstinate the more their tangible contents fade away.

That I grew into France with my five senses was understand-able, since, in spite of all the differences between its various prov-inces, Europe is a whole shaped by a common past. Nevertheless the choice confronting one in France was not to my liking—you can be either a Frenchman or a foreigner. Actually there is no choice at all, since Frenchness has a nearly metaphysical character in no way connected with residence or passport. My accent marked me with the stigma of a foreigner, in the same manner as some old Parisian taxi drivers were marked, eternal emigrés—I have almost never been mistaken when, after a few words, I addressed them in Russian. That accent, however, was mine, my property, and I did not attempt to get rid of it, just as I didn't attempt to get rid of my old attachments and loyalties. This was not frowned upon, but only because foreigners were forgiven all eccentricities. It is even hard to grasp how much such exclusion interferes with the ordering activity of the imagination—that activity through which we strive to assimilate, for example, the province Dordogne so that it is "mine" and not external, the temporary property of the tourist. In America the impulse to be at home, most likely an ordinary and healthy one, did not encounter any such obstacles because here everything was just the reverse; my Slavic accent, my coming from a distant country, the indestructible habits and reflexes which excluded me permanently in France here contributed to my normalcy so that I am one of many in a crowd composed of newcomers, "American" precisely because I did not have to renounce anything.

Our thinking is always imprisoned by notions which once corresponded to a reality but which later lead an autonomous and unseasonable life. Immigration to America in the second half of our century is not the same as it was in the nineteenth century, not even what it was a few decades ago. The spiritual remnants of the epoch of the steam engine are already disintegrating and disappearing. Man has found himself before something still unnamed and though his consciousness lags behind general transformations, he does perceive what is happening to our entire species as enormous, ominous, perhaps ultimate. This is not the first time in the history of civilization that men have lived with a sense of crisis, disintegration, finale. Many generations lived with it in Imperial Rome, probably something similar oppressed the medieval millenarians, and the Renaissance was lucid and transparent in appearance only; in fact, it took great pains to preserve classical order while darkly contemplating the loss of the traditional certainties, hierarchies, virtues. When the suffering of America, the violence of its nearly insoluble conflicts, the uncertainty of America, are seen against the background of this new large crisis, they lose that peculiarity which its spontaneous development in colonizing the continent once possessed in the eyes of Europe. The destructive influence of technology on the popular religious imagination, automation, the spread of education, man's fear in the face of self-destruction through gradual or sudden poisoning of nature, show the universal features of the American adventure—it condenses and exemplifies what has overtaken or is now overtaking people all over the world. There is no returning from the discovery of fire and the discovery of the wheel. Similarly, there is no turning back the chain-reaction consequences of modern knowledge, though here and there, for very local reasons, they are slowed down. Sometimes, too, a whole complex of nonideological factors—the spiritual and social reactions of the people to the unforeseen development of a particular industry or technological innovation, for example—necessitates a reaction, in turn, from an ideologically oriented ruling group that is unprepared for it. Since self-accusation and the feeling of being lost are more out in the open in America than anywhere else, America is the testing ground for all mankind. It is also possible that the corrosive tone and the alliances between revolutionaries and bohemians are the price a materially powerful country must pay in the process of transforming itself into a country of poetic and philosophic enterprises.

As to my homelessness, my integration into America is made easier because its inhabitants have always suffered from homelessness and uprootedness, later called alienation. No wonder that the very core of American literature has always been the question "Who am I?" The individual establishes his identity physically, relating himself to objects within the reach of his hands and eyes. Through his expanding perception he extends his own identity, first spatially, including a village, a district, a country, then temporally, extending himself into the past and creating relationships with its details, lest it remain for him a "nowhere." Where such steps are impossible, one looks for substitutes, as did Walt Whitman when he borrowed from the French the expression *"en-masse,"* and applied it to the American scene. If I am *en-masse,* I do not, as in the stratified life of Europe, set out to define myself in terms of my knight's castle, my peasant's hut, my burgher's store. I am everyman and I must define myself in a universal fluidity, in a human collective in motion, composed of everymen. This is superhumanly difficult, because the distinctive features supporting and aiding my individuality disappear or are rendered universal and therefore neutral; for instance what is closest to my body, my clothes, no longer functions as a sign of one group as different from another. The "I" is then seen by itself from outside, like an item in a store window; and this contradicts its uniqueness. I am not speaking here about dissolving into the mass, nor about communion through temperature and rhythm (it is characteristic that in Europe Whitman was read as the bard of mass meetings and marches), but rather about relating oneself to other separate people thrown in the same geographically shaky position. As far back as one hundred years ago that *"masse"* was a "lonely crowd."

Human particles were torn from their ground earlier and on a larger scale in America than anywhere else and this made America the unintentional precursor of modern life. This was to be generalized due to the late arrival of the industrial revolution in many countries as well as to wars and political upheavals. This land of the uprooted became almost a paradigm of every exile and also of the exile from a mental space made hierarchic by the Throne of God. European civilization was founded on certain spatial equivalents of religious truths. These were vertical patterns—Heaven, Earth, Hell—as well as horizontal—the perilous travels of knights in search of the Grail, the legend of the Crusades and their struggle for the tomb of Christ, or journeys on treacherous roads illustrating the soul's slow advance towards salvation in spite of devilish temptations. The spiritual space of this linear universe was kept taut by its unmoving poles; men knew what directions were open to them. Even a sixteenth-century Polish treatise in verse on the carrying of wheat by river barges is, at times, an allegory of the temporal pilgrimage of a Christian to the desired harbor. Quite different images appear when people try to express their disorientation in a space made limp and amorphous by the weakening of religious faith. This is a space not subjectable to the will, useless, senseless; so there are, above all, images of the wastelands of huge cities, dumps, vacant lots covered with scrap metal and overgrown with nettles, a kind of limbo once supposedly inhabited by souls without knowledge of Good or Evil. In the two perhaps most representative plays of the theater of the absurd, Becket's *Waiting for Godot* and *Beautiful Days,* the action takes place "nowhere," material shapes are only symbols of aimless time closing circularly upon itself. But because of its spontaneous and yet antiorganic growth, America created landscapes of refuse, dumps, slums, neon wildernesses earlier than the artistic imagination concerned itself with them, so that without exaggeration one can say that an unstable space contradicting our desire for order serves here as scenery for a play not performed on stage, a play whose characters are everyman and everyman. Perhaps inhabitants of other continents assimilate the products of American culture with ease because the reality which those products represent is in itself already a metaphor, revealing man's disinheritance.

One of our civilization's constant ingredients is a complaint of loss, a nostalgic dream turned toward the past, a dream idealizing the ancient harmony with nature, primeval innocence, the full integration into a tribal community, a hieratic space spread between a rural district and Heaven. It goes hand in hand with a rage against the world to which we were born, growing imperceptibly into a rage against existence in general. The contrast between the historically unique achievements of technology and medicine, basically favorable to the human milieu, and such gloomy states of mind is quite enigmatic, all the more so since the fear of a final catastrophe (atomic war, pollution of nature), which may or may not occur, seems to be only a mask for a malaise more profound and more difficult to name. "The impossibility of living" so oppressing young Americans probably testifies, as has previously been the case, to the exhaustion of some spiritual resources and to a feeling of hanging between something which is ending and something which has not yet begun. An American philosopher, José Ferrater Mora, writes about the Roman schools of Stoics, Cynics, and Platonists practically as if they were our contemporaries because they all searched for salvation, trying to stay sane in a society they saw as chaotic and on which an individual could have little influence. It was probably their works which, much later, when the medieval order was "out of joint," Hamlet studied at Wittenberg—though he, in his moment of truth, did not limit himself to withdrawal but decided to his grief to cure the evil in Elsinore.

America was first Europeanized technologically, but in that respect soon outdistanced Europe. We are now witnessing another Europeanization of America. The spread of education and the respect for literature and art inculcated by legions of the intelligentsia employed by colleges, universities, and research institutes can only mean that various European ideas together with their internal logic of development are being grafted onto the native tree. Similarly, when Greece was being grafted onto a not particularly sophisticated Rome, this was not limited to Homer or Pindar; Roman minds also absorbed all of decadent Hellenistic thought and art.

The commercial efficiency of the mass media which favors garishness, brutality, sex, the nearly suicidal freedom of expression under the pretext of art, and the peculiar traits of American schools provide the young generation with something that can only be called nihilism. The raising of the young without indoctrination is something new—until now there have always been attempts to indoctrinate them with a religion or a socialistic or nationalistic creed, yet American educators themselves have no fundamental creeds from which they could operate. According to Herbert Marcuse, it is exactly this lack of any direction which constitutes the insidious preparation for a bestial existence reduced to earning and spending. Yet Marcuse represents the European postnihilist phase; i.e., he speaks for men who have attempted to go beyond utter disillusionment. Finding themselves without metaphysically grounded images and values which could order and structure space, they then decided to turn to society and to postulate values themselves, on the premise that social space could be rational and transparent only if political terror is applied. Thus the quarrel of Marcuse with America is a quarrel with an indefinite opening up to what is called culture, something in which bourgeois Europe specialized on a less gigantic scale. That opening up usually resulted in the equal importance and relativity of all ideas, while in practice sonority and range were granted only to ideas shaping attitudes of bitterness, despair, and the sense of man's superfluousness in the universe. The fruit of all this was either the acceptance of earning and spending, or, among bohemians, the worship of Art as the only absolute. Also, in the next phase, a longing for political terror.

The lack of indoctrination today is not only equivalent to an opening up but also to a submission to certain kinds of unplanned propaganda. The mass media are like a magic ring which, when you put it on your finger, enables you to see in a moment all the suffering, all the oppression, all the injustice in America and the whole world. The good, the triumph of the human will, and persistence are excluded as insufficiently exciting and not salable. Scientific discoveries, the construction of gigantic dams, bridges, freeways, those achievements which, in totalitarian countries, would have been trumpeted as historic events, are put in small print or get half a minute on television—who cares about such ordinary, boring things? Of course in America there is the monstrosity of the Negro ghettos, there is much injustice and poverty, but there was more a half-century ago—then, however, our consciousness did not have to deal with them every day. The earth has always been full of human sufferings, but the inhabitants of closed-in communities and regions had no way of embracing them all simultaneously. Today the anger of moralists who rebel against evil provides justification for masochistic orgies. Blind, emotional protest blurs the distinction between lesser and greater evils. A tender-hearted president of a college who opposes senseless demands of students is publicly denounced as a Hitler or an Eichmann; the president of the country is depicted in a play as a Macbeth with bloody hands and his wife as a Lady Macbeth. In such a state of mind it is hardly surprising that political terror ranks as a plus and that it is considered inappropriate to reflect upon how much one gains or loses by using it.

The contradiction that exists between our desire to have a human world, which would be transparent and rational, and the rule of law which invalidates or postpones reasonable plans is real and not illusory. That contradiction becomes particularly acute when we confront great changes demanding quick and radical remedies—for example, the destruction of the natural surroundings turning whole regions of America into wastelands and dumps, and the struggle, rarely won, for laws which threaten private interests. If an individual sees what would be rational and yet is powerless, a feeling of the general opaqueness and absurdity of existence arises, which in turn leads to dreams of political terror, for the most part finding substitute expression, among the intellectuals, in the violent tone of poems, novels, and paintings. Though the progressive intelligentsia had other reasons to worry in czarist Russia, their pattern of thought was not so very different from that of their American cousins of today. Nonsense had to be changed into sense, corruption had to be cured by force. Unfortunately, that intelli-

gentsia was to learn that the victory of political terror drove out
one absurdity only to replace it with another, and that the bureau-
cratic jungle is far from transparent.

How the American system works, I do not understand; neither
do I understand how the pragmatic mind works. It's quite possible
that it has a particular loathing for logical sequences such as, if
a, then *b*, if *b*, then *c*, as well as for any planning in advance; it
always begins dealing with urgent problems at the last possible
moment (if not five minutes too late) under utmost constraint.
Often it seems to me that the vocation of America consists in a
duality not met anywhere else—the duality of desperation and
success. A distant predecessor of mine in migration to this continent
was Julian Ursyn Niemcewicz, who came to these shores in 1796.
He was a man of the Enlightenment, an enemy of autocratic mon-
archies and an enthusiast of the American republic. He took a
moderate position in the great quarrel of that time about the French
Revolution—he sympathized with it in its beginnings, then, in the
period of the Terror, cooled considerably. In his *Travels in America* [1] he records his visit with a well-to-do farmer; that hardy citizen irritated him by complaining of general stagnation and apathy.
As was to happen often with refugees from Europe in their conversations with desperate American moralists, Niemcewicz fell silent
and noted for himself:

> "We must have a revolution," says Mr. Logan. "That alone
> can save us: but would you believe it, our people do not want
> to hear talk of it. They are already corrupted. Ah! if I were
> now in France, if I might see all that goes on there, how I
> would rejoice." Madman, I said to myself, you do not know
> what you want; you have a large and comfortable house,
> fields which give you four times your need. You live under
> wise and free laws and pine after upheaval and blood. You are
> a fanatic, my friend, your brain is sick. The tranquillity, the
> abundance with which you live weighs you down; you feel the
> need of being aroused and shaken up, even if it means the

[1] Published recently in English translation as *Under Their Vine and
Fig Tree*, The Grossman Publishing Co., 1965.

ruin of your house or of your country. But go to France, go
to Europe, see what goes on there and you will return cured
of your madness."

When I was a student in Wilno, then in Poland, sobriety of
thought or scepticism about the magnificent slogans promising
total solutions made us angry and ashamed; those feelings had to be
stifled in us as a weakness. Undoubtedly when I now look back
with some perspective, I must concede that reason was always the
loser, as if confirming that its advice is valid for the individual and
not for human collectives. Yet it was the loser only in the short
run, for it turned out that in fact only the individual is real, not
the mass movements in which he voluntarily loses himself in order
to flee himself. I have never considered myself a political writer and
have no ambition to save America or the world. I am only asking
myself what I have learned in America, and what I value in that
experience. I will summarize my answers in three pros and cons:
for the so-called average man, against the arrogance of intellectuals;
for the Biblical tradition, against the search for individual or collective nirvana; for science and technology, against dreams of
primeval innocence.

My self-education has profited, I hope, from living in avant-
garde California. Here one must come to terms with one's own
pride. In his most optimistic moments every writer considers himself a genius, and if he lives in his own small country, different
in language from the neighboring countries, there will be no lack
of support for his favorite self-image. Writing in America in Polish
(for the poet can use only the language of his childhood) I deprive
myself of that comfort. But, to tell the truth, it is not the language,
or, as in France, being an alien that is important. As a result of
America's vastness and human mass, the bonds between a poet
and his audience are weaker than those that exist where I come
from; indeed they have always been very strong in Slavic countries. So I must simply state that I am one of many poets in the
San Francisco Bay area. Most of them write in English, but there
are those who write in Spanish, Greek, German, Russian. Even if
one of them may have some renown he is, in his everyday dealings
with people, anonymous, and so again, one among many—but in

another, larger, sense. Whatever satisfies our vanity is a very effective divertissement, one of those which, according to Pascal, men constantly clutch at, precisely to veil the futility of our scurryings and the fear of death. At least one divertissement, perhaps the most effective, that of loving recognition, is in America, where we are particles of a lonely crowd, rarely attainable. Probably the inhabitants of cosmopolitan Greek-Jewish-Latin Rome felt something similar. I don't mean to say that I am above wanting such trifles as fame and recognition, but America forces one to the wall and compels one to a kind of Stoic virtue: to do what one is doing in the best way possible and at the same time to preserve a certain detachment that comes from the awareness of the ignorance, the childishness, and the incompleteness of all people and of oneself.

"Of all people." I am fed up with dividing people into those few who know and the dull masses who don't realize what is useful for them. I have no desire to be one of the elect dragging the masses by force to Utopia. Youth brought up in affluence, masquerading in beggars' clothing and revolutionary ideas, commands less of my respect than hard-working lumberjacks, miners, bus drivers, bricklayers, whose mentality is an object of scorn for the young. Perhaps that mentality, so often ridiculed, is that of the Bible-reading American entrenched in self-righteousness; and yet the fact that America is still the country of the Bible cannot but have lasting consequences. No matter how deeply religious beliefs have been eroded, the King James version is still the very core of the language and a determinant factor in its literary development. The work of Whitman and Melville and their successors always takes us back to it, the Scripture is the common property of believers, agnostics, atheists. Whoever has verified empirically, as I have, how much depends on hidden human qualities will not frivolously call a certain heavy decency and disinterestedness just plain stupidity, even if they go together with mental limitations. Nor will he shrug off the contrast of goodness and wickedness originating in the Bible. In spite of arguments to the contrary, in spite of the paradox of brutal and cruel deeds with unwilled effects to the good, or perhaps just because of that paradox, America is the legitimate heir to Judaeo-Christian civilization summoned to technical works made possible by that civilization and no other. Therefore it was just and beautiful that the American astronauts flying over the surface of the moon addressed the inhabitants of Earth with an old message, reading the beginning of the Book of Genesis.

The blurring of the hierarchy between various domains of our activity is one of the causes of the present chaos in thought. The human labyrinth grows more and more complex, and language changes from connective tissue into a superior power, whether it is a language composed of words or of images transmitted electronically. Considering the autonomous, crazy proliferation of language, we don't even know whether we should use the notions "literature" and "art," which may be obsolete; but since they got into the habit in the nineteenth century, people have expected revelations from language. Yet our own fate no longer depends on what was once called *humaniora,* but on religion and science. Fortunately both the Bible-reading past and the technology of America remind me of this, despite my professional humanistic bent. The tomorrow we would like for planet Earth—justice, peace, elimination of hunger and poverty—is not very likely unless a fundamental conversion occurs. There have always been preachers calling for the inner rebirth of the heart and this has not helped matters very much. My friends would think I had lost my mind if I put my confidence in sermonizing. I do not count, however, on an effort of the will, rather on something independent of the will: on data which would again order our spatial imagination.

There is no halting the imagination which, aided by symbols, always tends to compose everything we learn about the cosmos and man into harmonious wholes, i.e., into a unified image of the world. If one of those wholes is lost, the imagination either moves in a void, creating images of depressing senselessness (which is itself a kind of sense, but a negative one) or proceeds to introduce order according to the materials at its disposal. Without feeling ashamed of it, let us admit we are children before a pile of blocks; no child can resist the desire of his hand to express the need of his mind. Political and social ideas cannot be treated as things apart, because they are linked to a few basic images. The ideas which are today an active force arose out of the disintegration of the pre-Copernican design. That was a static design in which Heaven pulled up, Hell pulled down, and evil was, in a sense, tamed, since its dosage did not vary. This was supplanted by a dynamic design in which the "withdrawal" of God did not necessarily mean the renunciation of Heaven: space became the movement of providential, redeeming time, Hell was the present, Heaven the future. Before anyone writes all this off as only my obsessions, let him consider for a moment what Catholic theologians are currently concerned with. They noticed, belatedly, that religious truths adapted to the pre-Copernican design encounter the unconscious resistance of even the most zealous Christians, so they began to dynamize them, introducing images of humanity's march through time, of diminishing evil, of history as a Christological process, to such an extent that some Catholic catechisms open with chapters that seem right out of a textbook on material and moral evolution. This is legitimate since "divine pedagogy" which regulates movement is at the very heart of Judaeo-Christianity, in contrast to the cyclical vision of the Greeks. It is not hard, however, to see that this sudden zeal is an attempt on the part of the theologians to adapt themselves to shifts in the collective imagination which occurred outside the church, without its participation and against its intent. Competing with lay progressives in providing people with solace, they sometimes go as far as considering it improper to mention the devil. Many pronouncements of high-ranking Catholic figures sound as if they came from socialists of a hundred years ago, i.e., noble-minded dreamers who were then treated by the church with disapproval at the very least. It looks as if there was no other way out of nihilistic inertia except by a leap into the future, a denial of the evil present. An American hippie switching to political action and a clergyman who wants to win him over proclaiming to all and sundry his social fervor travel the same road.

The dynamic design is with us and here to stay. The old argument of the conservatives that since man is perverted, the earth is and will be a vale of tears, that *"plus ça change plus c'est la même chose,"* does not entirely convince us. Yet it is difficult to rid oneself of the suspicion that the imagination, if it is able to maintain a kind of equilibrium only as long as it rushes forward outdistancing time, has recourse to surrogates; it is moved not so much by a belief in some better humanity as by a loathing for the nothingness and chaos in which it must remain unless it leaps across the distance between today and a hypothetical tomorrow. That hidden motivation may encourage grasping at anything, even the most stupid and inhuman ideologies. Instances of self-deceit, skillfully maintained, are in our epoch so numerous that it is not even worthwhile to cite examples. So the question is whether even modest wisdom does not depend primarily upon our finding a spiritual home in the here and now. If any hope is possible, it is only because those images of the universe and of our fate in it, which are simply unbearable for man, seem to be the belated heritage of Newton's concept of the great mechanism, while the new elements are still scattered and haven't been integrated.

In spite of an internal erosion of the creeds, religion may be in a better situation today than it was a hundred years ago. From thousands of works in anthropology and psychology, from thousands of studies of myths and symbols in literature, what penetrates the collective consciousness is a sort of humble amazement at the archetypes which take their shape in religion and at the vague outlines of something that can only be called an unchangeable human nature.

As to the influence of science, it is felt with a considerable lag; it spreads slowly like a drop of water on a blotter. Science acts upon the imagination either directly, or indirectly through technology, and yet at least half of ourselves inhabits the space of the eighteenth and nineteenth centuries. We cannot even try to guess how that other space of our descendants will look; at best we can collect signs, announcements, veiled and uncertain, because gradual transformations are so devious. Somehow this is like looking at the Earth from the moon. From Jules Verne on, authors of science fiction familiarized us with this view; but in fact to see, as we now have seen, our huge, blue, round homeland, we sense to be an experience of a different sort, though we can't say why. Perhaps it's a throb of the heart, a premonition that the Earth was really destined to be the center as it was before Copernicus and that a geocentric and an anthropocentric vision is nothing to scoff at. Perhaps instead of anger at existence, for a moment we feel love for good water, good trees, and good plants. Or the morality play of the absurd, which supposedly shows the human condition faithfully, all of a sudden seems shameful because, juxtaposed to the cosmic ballet, it reveals its dependence on one transient variety of sensibility, like the fashions of 1880. Besides, it is not only interplanetary voyages that imperceptibly reconstruct the imagination but also time which has lost its homogeneity; the multiplicity of possible spaces; the incredible complexity of the mind of so-called primitive man; everything science reveals, changing reality from a mechanism into a crystal cabinet of wonders, with reflections flashing from mirror to mirror. Not long ago science was still inclined to reduction; it used to explain away the miraculous and the splendid as "only" the simple consequences of certain causes. Today, instead of reductions, there is multiplication, and the laboratory makes space as sublime and magical as a tale about elves.

So much is happening all at once that to guess what is repetition and what is augury is practically impossible. The complexity and chameleonlike mutability beneath seemingly simple, well-known forms spreads all over the earth, and to write about the present is to act like the blind man who, touching the elephant's trunk, proclaimed that the elephant is long and snakelike. The only thing of which I am certain is my amazement. Amazement that there is something like America and that humanity still exists though it should have exterminated itself long ago or perished from starvation, from epidemics, or from the poisons it excretes. But amazement belongs to silent contemplation and whenever I take up my pen which itself pretends to knowledge, since language is composed of affirmations and negations, I consider this only as an exorcism of the evil spirits of the present time.

Translated from the Polish by Richard Lourie.

The Contributors

Jack Agueros was born in East Harlem and has been active in anti-poverty work in New York City and Cleveland. He is now Executive Director of Mobilization for Youth in the Lower East Side of New York. He is also a writer; the selection in this volume is his first published work.

William Alfred, raised in Brooklyn, is a poet and a Professor of English at Harvard. He is the author of the memorable play, *Hogan's Goat,* also about Irish immigrant life.

Eugene Boe, raised in Minnesota, came East as a young man and is an entertainment critic and social commentator in New York City and the author of many magazine articles.

Czeslaw Milosz, born in Lithuania and raised in Poland, was a writer and editor for Resistance publications in Warsaw during World War II. He lived in France for ten years before coming permanently to the United States in 1961. A poet, he has published extensively in Polish and is a Professor of Slavic Languages and Literatures at Berkeley. His books in English are *The Captive Mind, Native Realm* and *The History of Polish Literature.*

Alan Pryce-Jones, English born and one-time editor of the *Times Literary Supplement* in London, has chosen the United States as his residence. A widely published literary critic, he lives in New York.

Mario Puzo, now living on Long Island, grew up in Hell's Kitchen. He is the author of three novels, *The Fortunate Pilgrim,* an evocation of Italian immigrant life, *The Dark Arena,* and the recent bestseller, *The Godfather.*

Harry Roskolenko, poet and narrator of his times, left New York's Lower East Side as a boy for the world. Among his many books are *When I Was Last on Cherry Street,* an autobiographical exploration of the early ghetto and his later travels, and the recently published *The Time That Was Then,* a recollection of life on the Lower East Side in the early 1900s. New York remains his home base.

John A. Williams has published a number of books including *The King God Didn't Save,* an evaluation of Martin Luther King, and the novels *Sons of Darkness, Sons of Light,* and *The Man Who Cried I Am.* Raised in Syracuse, he lives in New York and is editor of the new periodical of black writing, *Amistad.*

Jade Snow Wong grew up in San Francisco, where she is now a professional ceramist. She has published *Fifth Chinese Daughter,* an autobiography of her Chinese-American experience, as well as magazine articles.

Some other books published by Penguin
are described on the following pages.

Edited by Edward W. Ludwig and James Santibanez

THE CHICANOS
Mexican American Voices

An anthology of writings by and about Mexican Americans. The editors have chosen fiction, poems, and articles. Together, their selections form a realistic picture of Chicano life in the United States today. Included are reminiscences—pleasant and unpleasant —of Mexican American childhood; accounts of Chicanos in the American school system; reports on strikes by Chicano workers . . . and poems and stories that reflect the hard realities of poverty and alienation. Among the contributors: Cesar Chavez on the California grape strike; Joan Baez on her experiences as a Mexican American; and José Alvarez on the Chicano and the law. Edward W. Ludwig and James Santibánez are both at San José State College, San José, California.

Arthur Asa Berger

THE COMIC-STRIPPED AMERICAN
What Dick Tracy, Blondie, Daddy Warbucks,
and Charlie Brown Tell Us about Ourselves

Comics are the collective daydream of the American imagination, says Arthur Asa Berger, and they reveal a great deal about our national character. For example: *Little Orphan Annie* is a morality play dealing with the preservation of innocence and democracy and based on the myth of the chosen few. Dagwood Bumstead represents an important archetype in the national psyche—the irrelevant male. The schizoid split within Superman symbolizes a basic split in the American mentality. This unique volume ranges from *The Katzenjammer Kids* at the turn of the century to *Barbarella* in today's age of eroticism as it uncovers what the comic strips are really saying. Arthur Asa Berger is Professor of Popular Culture at San Francisco State College.

Allen Wheelis

THE MORALIST

The Moralist is Allen Wheelis's most powerful book,
and its subject is nothing less than the survival of
morals in a universe seemingly empty of everything
but ignorance and maliciousness. In spite of this
moral vacuum, Wheelis formulates a credo for
modern man: "There is a path to follow, the course
of which we cannot foresee, a plan of which we may
have intimation but can never master. Whirl need
not be king. Something draws us as by an invisible
hand—not God, but the advancing edge of our being
which goes before awareness." *The Moralist* is a
meditation upon this "advancing edge," a confident
yet illusionless look at the progress of man's awareness of others—a progress that is now humanity's
only hope. Author of *The End of the Modern Age,
The Desert,* and other books, Allen Wheelis is also a
practicing psychoanalyst.